ENGLISH GRAMMAR
Volume II

D0465834

ENGLISH GRAMMAR

A FUNCTION-BASED INTRODUCTION

Volume II

T. GIVÓN
Linguistics Department
University of Oregon

JOHN BENJAMINS PUBLISHING COMPANY
AMSTERDAM/PHILADELPHIA

1993

TM The paper used in this publication meets the minimum requirements of American National Standard for Information Sciences — Permanence of Paper for Printed Library Materials, ANSI Z39.48-1984.

Library of Congress Cataloging-in-Publication Data

Givón, Talmy, 1936-
    English grammar : a function-based introduction / T. Givón.
    p.   cm.
    Includes bibliographical references and indexes.
    1. English language--Grammar. I. Title.
PE1106.G57   1993
428.2--dc20   93-18295
ISBN 1-55619-459-5 (set hb)/1-55619-466-8 (set pb) (US alk. paper)   CIP
1-55619-457-9 (hb vol.1)/1-55619-464-1 (pb vol.1) (US alk. paper)
1-55619-458-7 (hb vol.2)/1-55619-465-X (pb vol.2) (US) alk. paper)
ISBN 90 272 2100 6 (set hb)/90 272 2117 0 (set pb) (Eur alk. paper)
90 272 2098 0 (hb vol.1)/90 272 2115 4 (pb vol.1) (Eur alk. paper)
90 272 2099 9 (hb vol.2)/90 272 2116 2 (pb vol.2) (Eur alk. paper)

John Benjamins Publishing Co. · P.O. Box 75577 · 1070 AN Amsterdam · The Netherlands
John Benjamins North America · 821 Bethlehem Pike · Philadelphia, PA 19118 · USA

CONTENTS

7 | VERBAL COMPLEMENTS

7.1. INTRODUCTION

Verbal ('sentential', 'clausal') **complements** are one type of **subordinate ('dependent') clauses**. Semantically, a verbal complement is a full-fledged proposition with its own predicate and arguments. Syntactically, however, it is an **embedded clause** placed inside the verb phrase of another — a **main clause**. Superficially, a clause embedded inside the verb phrase of another clause occupies an *object* position. In English, however, there are clear syntactic and semantic differences between complement clauses and **nominalized clausal objects**. To illustrate the distinction briefly, consider:

(1) a. **Nominal object**:
         She's expecting **a baby**.
     b. **Nominalized clausal object**:
         She expected **his resignation from the committee**.
     c. **Verbal complement**:
         She expected **to resign from the committee.**
     d. **Verbal complement**:
         She expected him **to resign from the committee**.
     e. **Verbal complement**:
         She expected **that he would resign from the committee.**
     f. **Finite main clause**:
         She would resign from the committee.

Prototypical objects are nominal, i.e. noun phrases, as in (1a). A fully nominalized clausal object is maximally non-finite, as in (1b). Such a clausal object resembles the fully nominalized **clausal subjects** discussed in chapter 6. Of the three verbal complements in (1), two — (1c) and (1d) — are *less finite* than a finite main clause (1f), but *more finite* than a fully-nominalized clause (1b). The third type of verb complement (1e) is the most finite of the three, syntactically closest to the prototypical finite main clause (1f).

In this chapter we deal mainly with three types of verbal complements, defined by the type of main verb that precedes them. The three classes of main verbs involved have already been noted, albeit briefly, in chapter 3.[1] Syntactically, complement clauses reveal some degree of adjustment toward the nominal prototype. So that they are always less finite than the prototypical main clause, but more finite than the fully nominalized clause (see chapter 6).

The main theme of this chapter is the isomorphic relation that exists between the meaning of a main verb and the syntax of its complement clause. This isomorphism is one of the best examples of a correlation between form and function in grammar. We will first outline the semantic dimensions that underlie the grammar of complementation. Taken together, these dimensions involve the **semantic bond** — or **semantic integration** — between two events, one coded in the main clause, the other in the complement clause, to yield a **complex event**. Not surprisingly, the complex event is in turn coded by a complex syntactic structure. The isomorphism between the semantic and syntactic dimensions of complementation may be given as the following overall prediction:

(2)   "The stronger the **semantic bond** is between the two events, the more extensive will be the **syntactic integration** of the two propositions into a single clause".

7.2.   THE SEMANTICS OF EVENT INTEGRATION

7.2.1.   Preamble

In this section we outline the semantic — thus also cognitive — dimensions of complementation. These dimensions may be expressed, up to a point, in terms of the semantic properties of the **main verb**, thus the **main clause**. We will be dealing here with further refinements of the semantic classification of complement-taking verbs given in chapter 3.[2] As noted there, the syntactic properties of the simple clause depend on the **semantic frame** of the verb. When a complement clause is integrated into the semantic frame of the main verb, the main verb exercises a controlling role on the syntax of the combined complex clause, including the complement clause. Much like the way a main verb *selects* it subject or object arguments, it also selects the type of its complement clause.

Complement-taking verbs fall into three major classes:

(i) **Modality verbs** ('want', 'begin', 'finish', 'try' etc.)
(ii) **Manipulation verbs** ('make', 'tell', 'order', 'ask' etc.)
(iii) **Perception-cognition-utterance verbs** (P-C-U verbs; 'see', 'know', 'think', 'say' etc.)

The scalar semantic dimensions that underlie the grammar of complementation may be demonstrated for each verb class independently. However, the scale is probably an overall single continuum, whereby classes (i) and (ii) run in parallel from the top toward the middle, displaying roughly the same semantic and syntactic transition. At a section around the middle of the scale, classes (i) and (ii) both shade into class (iii), which then covers the bottom section of the overall scale. The entire scale may be thus likened to a tuning-fork shape:[3]

(3) **Overview of the event-integration scale**:

P-C-U verbs   modality verbs

-----------------------------(
                              (--------------------------
                              manipulation verbs
weakest bond........................**strongest bond**

We will illustrate the overall scale first with examples from classes (ii) and (iii), then come back to class (i).

7.2.2. Sub-dimensions of event integration

7.2.2.1. Semantic and syntactic definitions: manipulation and P-C-U verbs

For **manipulation verbs**, the semantic and syntactic relations between the main and subordinate clause may be given as follows:

(4) **Definition of manipulation verbs**:
   a. The main clause codes an event of *manipulation* by one agent of the behavior of another agent.
   b. The *manipulator* is the subject-agent of the main clause; the *manipulee* is its dative-object.
   c. The complement clause codes the *target event* performed — or to be performed — by the manipulee.
   d. The manipulee is thus also the subject-agent of the complement clause.

Conditions (4a-d) above are represented syntactically in the tree diagram
(6) below, representing sentence (5):

>   (5)   Mary told John to leave

>   (6)   **Tree diagram for manipulation verbs**:

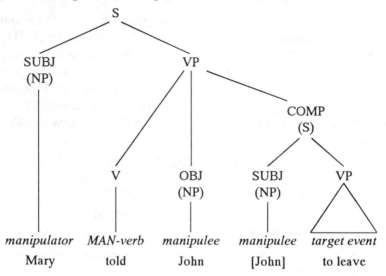

For **P-C-U verbs**, the semantic and syntactic relations between the
main and complement clause may be given as follows:

>   (7)   **Definition of P-C-U verbs**:
>
>   a. The main clause codes *mental* or *verbal activity*, with a
>   verb (or adjective) of perception, cognition, mental
>   attitude or verbal utterance.
>   b. The state or event coded in the complement clause is
>   the *object* of the mental or verbal activity coded by the
>   main verb.
>   c. No coreference restrictions hold between arguments of
>   the main clause and complement clause.

The definition in (7) may be summarized in the tree diagram (9) below,
representing sentence (8):

>   (8)   John knew that Mary had left

(9)   **Tree diagram for P-C-U verbs**:

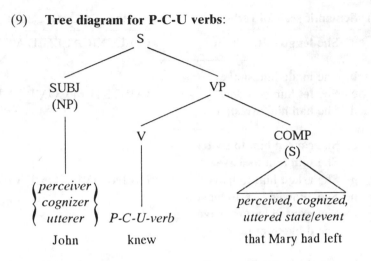

In table (10) below, a representative sample of manipulative and P-C-U verbs are ranked according to their position on the scale of **event integration**, on the left. On the right, the matching syntactic scale of **clause integration** is given.

(10) **Semantic scale of verbs**   **syntax of COMP-clause**

    a. She **let go** of the knife   CO-LEXICALIZED VERB

    b. She **made** him **shave**
    c. She **let** him **go** home   BARE-STEM COMP VERB
    d. She **had** him **arrested**

    e. She **caused** him **to switch** jobs
    f. She **told** him **to leave**
    g. She **asked** him **to leave**   INFINITIVE COMP VERB
    h. She **allowed** him **to leave**
    i. She **wanted** him **to leave**
    j. She**'d like** him **to leave**

    k. She**'d like for him to leave**   FOR-TO COMP

    l. She **suggested** that he **should leave**
    m. She **wished** that he **would leave**   MODAL-SUBJUNCTIVE
    n. She **agreed** that he **could leave**

    o. She **knew** that he **left**
    p. She **said** that he **might leave** later   INDIRECT QUOTE

    q. She **said**: "He **might leave** later"   DIRECT QUOTE

7.2.2.2. Implicativity, co-temporality and control

In our earlier description of the semantics of manipulative verbs (chapter 3), we divided their continuum into two segments only, **implicative** and **non-implicative** verbs. These traditional labels translate into, respectively, successful vs. unsuccessful manipulation. Thus, in (10) above, expressions (10a-e) code successful manipulations, ones that may be couched in logical terms as the implication:

(11) **Implicative verbs**:
    "If the main clause is true, then the complement clause
    is also true".

That is:

(12) She **made** him **shave** > He **shaved**

In contrast, expressions (10f-n) code manipulations that are not necessarily successful. That is, implication (11) does not hold true.

(13) She **asked** him to **shave** *> He **shaved**

The traditional logic-based division into only implicative and non-implicative verbs is useful but limited. To begin with, it cannot predict the variety of syntactic coding-points that cover the manipulative-verb range. Thus, for example, 'let' (10a), 'make' (10b) and 'cause' (10e) are all logically implicative; but the syntax of their complements is different. From a purely logical perspective that difference is arbitrary. Further, the emphasis on logical truth tends to mask the many semantic sub-dimensions of **event integration** that have little to do with truth. And those sub-dimensions turn out to predict the nuances of syntactic form.

Implicative verbs indeed occupy the top of scale (10). This is so because the implicational relation between the two events is not merely a matter of **logical dependence** — it is also a relation of **temporal dependence**. When the main verb is implicative, the two events — in main and subordinate clause — tend to be either **co-temporal** or **temporally contiguous**. Such co-temporality (or temporal contiguity) is indeed a necessary pre-condition for two events to become, cognitively, a single complex event. This pre-condition may be summarized as the following probabilistic inference:

(14) **Temporal contiguity and event integration**:
      "The more temporally contiguous two events are, the more likely they are to be represented cognitively as a single event, rather than as two independent events".

The second major semantic dimension relevant to the complementation scale is the degree of **control, freedom of choice** or **independent action** ceded to the subject-agent of the complement clause. In a successful manipulation, with an implicative main verb, the manipulator succeeds in imposing his/her intent on the manipulee. The manipulee thus displays less control, less freedom of choice, less independence of action. The manipulee is thus less like a prototypical agent, and more like a prototypical patient. In contrast, the manipulee of a non-implicative verb retains his/her control,

---

freedom of choice and independence of action. Such a manipulee thus resembles more closely the prototypical agent.

The relation between success of manipulation and controlling agent may be given as the probabilistic inference:

(15) **Successful manipulation and controlling agent**:
"The more successful a manipulation is, the less likely is the manipulee to retain control, choice and freedom of action. In a successful manipulation, the manipulee is thus less agent-like".

The dimension of control — or agentivity — may be further broken down into a cluster of sub-dimensions:

(a) The degree of **intent** or **authority** exerted by the manipulator
(b) The degree of **direct contact** (or conversely, of **spatial distance**) between the manipulator and the manipulee
(c) Degree of **resistance** by the manipulee, thus also the degree of **coercion** used by the manipulator

In the following sections we describe and illustrate the various semantic sub-dimensions that are relevant to the scale of event integration.

7.2.2.3. Intent, control and agentivity

Consider first the contrast between the two implicative (successful) manipulation verbs, 'make' and 'cause':

(16) a. John **made** Mary quit her job
     b. John **caused** Mary to quit her job

At first glance, these two successful manipulations seem rather alike. However, 'make' is a verb of **intended manipulation**, while 'cause' is much less so. This is suggested from the contrast between (17b,c) and (18b,c) below. Respectively:[4]

(17) a. She made him quit his job
     b. **?Without intending to**, she made him quit his job
     c. **?Inadvertently**, she made him quit his job

(18) a. She caused him to quit his job
     b. **Without intending to**, she caused him to quit his job
     c. **Inadvertently**, she caused him to quit his job

The more deliberate, controlling, agentive nature of the subject of 'make' is also evident in the reduced control ceded to the manipulee. Thus, the intentional, agentive adverb 'deliberately' is tolerated more in the complement of 'cause' but less in the complement of 'make':

(19) a. *She made him **deliberately** quit his job and leave
      b. She caused him to **deliberately** quit his job and leave

The more agentive nature of 'make' as compared to 'cause' is further illustrated by the fact that the subject of 'cause' can be a non-agent or a nominalized clause. In contrast, the subject of 'make' can only be an agent:

(20) a. ***John's behavior** made Mary quit her job
      b. ***The political situation** made Mary quit her job
      c. **John's behavior** caused Mary to quit her job
      d. **The political situation** caused Mary to quit her job

In spite of the fact that the manipulee-object of 'make' has less control, it must still retain *some* agentiveness. This is evident from the fact that only volitional-control verbs may appear in the complement of 'make'. To illustrate this compare the three verb-pairs below:

(21) a. Mary made John **quit** his job
      b. ?Mary made John **lose** his job
      c. Mary made John **drop** to the ground
      d. ?Mary made John **trip and fall** down
      e. Mary made John **climb** faster
      f. ?Mary made John **grow** faster

The verbs 'quit', 'drop' and 'climb' in (21a,c,e) are volitional; the verbs 'lose', 'trip & fall' and 'grow' in (21b,d,f) are not.

In contrast, 'cause' does not impose such restrictions, so that its complements can be either volitional or non-volitional. Thus compare:

(22) a. **Office politics** caused John to **quit** his job
      b. **Office politics** caused John to **lose** his job
      c. **The low visibility** caused John to **drop** to the ground
      d. **The low visibility** caused John to **trip and fall** down
      e. **Wanting to finish first** caused John to **climb** faster
      f. **High potency vitamins** caused John to **grow** faster

The verb 'let' fits into two distinct positions on the complementation scale (10). Its first variant occupies the very top of the scale (10a). Its other variant occupies a slightly lower position (10c). The manipulee of the top-of-the scale variant of 'let' (10a) is *not* an agent, even when it is human. The manipulee of the other variant (10c) must be human, and in fact must retain a degree of agentiveness. In this, as well as in syntactic form, this variant of 'let' resembles 'make'. The two variants can be seen in:

(23) a. She **let go** of him
      b. She **let go** of his arm
      c. She **let** him **go**
      d. ?She **let** his arm **go**

The two variants of 'let' differ predictably in their tolerance to adverbial expressions that highlight the manipulee's volition and agentivity. The top-of-the-scale variant (10a) is incompatible with such adverbs, while the other one is compatible:

(24) a. *She **let go** of him on his own
      b. She **let** him **go** on his own
      c. *She **let go** of him away
      d. She **let** him **go** away

Adverbs that highlight the patient-like status of the manipulee, on the other hand, are compatible with the top-of-the-scale variant of 'let' (10a) but not with the other (10c):

(25) a. She **let go** of him like a sack of potatoes
      b. *She **let** him **go** like a sack of potatoes

Finally, participial adverb clauses,[5] whose unexpressed subject is normally co-referential with the subject of the main clause, tend to allow co-reference only with the agent-subject (but not with the manipulee-object) of the top-of-the-scale variant of 'let' (10a). In the other variant (10c), on the other hand, either the agent-subject or the manipulee-object of 'let' can be co-referential with the subject of the adverb clause. Thus compare:

(26) a. She **let go** of him, breathing hard
          (> { **She** / ***He** } was breathing hard)

      b. She **let** him **go**, breathing hard
          (> { **She** / **He** } was breathing hard)

This difference underscores our suggestion (see 7.3.2. below) that the 'let-go' variant (10a) is a **co-lexicalized** expression, a fully merged single clause with a single lexical verb. The manipulee in such a construction retains few if any subject properties, as compared with the manipulee in the looser construction (10c).

7.2.2.4. Control and temporal contiguity

Both 'make' (10b) and 'cause' in (10e) are logically implicative verbs. They differ, however, along the dimension of **temporal contiguity**. The event in the complement of 'make' must be **co-temporal** — or **temporally contiguous** — with the manipulation coded by 'make'. In contrast, the event in the complement of 'cause' need not be co-temporal with its main-clause event. To illustrate this, compare:

(27) a. **Two years ago** John finally made Mary quit her job
      b. John made Mary finally quit her job **yesterday**
      c. *__Two years ago__ John made Mary finally quit her job **yesterday**
      d. John's behavior **two years ago** caused Mary to finally quit her job **yesterday**

The correlation between control and temporal contiguity (or its converse, temporal separation) may be given as the following probabilistic inference:

(28) **Control and temporal separation**:
      "If manipulees are acting under their own motivation and retain control, they can act **in their own good time**".

The subject of 'cause' is thus not the **causer** of the manipulee's behavior. Rather, it is the **reason** — chosen by the manipulee himself/herself — for his/her self-motivated behavior.

7.2.2.5. Direct contact and spatio-temporal contiguity

Both 'make' (10b) and 'have' (10d) are logically implicative verbs. They differ, however, along the dimension of **direct contact** during the manipulation. While 'make' tends to code **direct manipulations**, 'have' may also code **indirect** ones.

This is evident in the contrast:

(29) He wasn't in the room when she entered,
    a. *so she **made** him come in
    b. so she **had** him come in

The requirement for direct contact between manipulator and manipulee in 'make' but not in 'have' is further underscored by the compatibility of *passive* complements with 'have' but not with 'make':

(30) She $\left\{ \begin{array}{l} \textbf{had} \\ \text{*}\textbf{made} \end{array} \right\}$ him **brought** in (by two burly officers)

The manipulee of 'have' in (30) is not directly manipulated by the agent of 'have' in the main clause, but rather by the agent of the passive 'brought' in the complement clause. Since 'make' codes direct manipulation, indirect causation via the agent-of-passive in the complement is indeed odd.

A similar contrast may be seen further down the scale between 'want' (10i) and 'wish' (10m). Typically, 'want' as a manipulative verb denotes **directly communicated desire**, thus **direct manipulative contact** between the manipulator and manipulee. When the probability of such direct manipulative contact is lower, 'wish' is used instead. To illustrate this contrast, consider:

(31) They had an argument;
    a. he **wanted** her to quit smoking,
       but she said she wouldn't.
    b. ?he **wished** that she would quit smoking,
       but she said she wouldn't.

Direct manipulative contact necessarily implies **spatial contiguity**, i.e. co-presence at the same location. Under such conditions, 'want' is preferred over 'wish', as in (31) above. In contexts of **spatial separation** and no direct manipulative contact, 'wish' is preferred over 'want', as in:[6]

(32) He left a week earlier. Now, sitting there all alone,
    a. she **wished** that he **had** come back.
    b. she **wished** that he **would** come back.
    c. ?she **wanted** him to come back.

The contrast between 'tell' and 'insist', or 'allow' and 'agree', is broadly similar, along the same dimension of direct manipulative contact. Thus compare:

(33) a. She **told** him to leave
      b. She **insisted** that he must leave
      c. She **allowed** him to come in
      d. She **agreed** that he could come in

'Tell' in (33a) and 'allow' in (33c) are more likely to involve **direct contact** between the manipulator and the manipulee. And direct contact in turn involves spatio-temporal contiguity of the cause event and effect event. Consequently, the two events are more likely to be construed as a single complex event. 'Insist' in (33b) and 'agree' in (33d), on the other hand, are more likely to involve **indirect communication**. This in turn means a more likely spatio-temporal separation between the manipulator and the manipulee. Consequently, the cause event and the effect event are more likely to be construed as two independent events.

The relation between direct manipulation and spatio-temporal contiguity may be given as the following probabilistic inference:

(34) **Direct manipulative contact and spatio-temporal contiguity**:
      a. "The more direct the contact is between the manipulator and the manipulee, the higher is the likelihood that the two events are spatially and temporally contiguous".
      b. "When two events are spatially and temporally contiguous, they are more likely to be construed as a single event".

7.2.2.6. Resistance, coercive effort and independence

The verb 'force', just like 'make' in (10b), codes an intended, direct, successful manipulation. Nevertheless, 'force' is ranked below 'make' on the complementation scale (10), where it displays the same syntactic form as the non-implicative 'tell' (10f). At first glance, such ranking seems counter-intuitive, given that the agent of 'force' exerts more **coercive effort**, and thus presumably has more control, than the agent of 'make'. What is at issue here, however, is not the agentivity of the manipulator but the agentivity and independence of the manipulee. As noted earlier above, the lower a verb is on the complementation scale, the more control and independence are retained by the manipulee. And for the manipulee, independence implies the ability to mount **resistance**. The coercive meaning of 'force' thus suggests that it is used to describe contexts where the manipulation is meeting resistance.

The relation between coercion and resistance may be expressed in terms of the following probabilistic inferences:

(35) **Control, coercion and resistance**:
"If the manipulee is capable of mounting resistance, then
it is likely that
a. the manipulator has *not* established firm control;
b. the manipulator must use coercive effort to overcome
resistance; and
c. the probability of sucessful manipulation is lower".

7.2.2.7. Event integration vs. causation

Some of the discussions thus far may have raised the false impression
that **successful causation** — thus **logical implication** — is the central ingredient in the complementation scale. In this section we will note a number of
reasons why this assumption may require revision, and why **event integration** rather than successful causation remains the central feature.

Consider the use of the verb 'see' in three positions on our scale: first
with a complement form akin to 'make' (10b), second with an -*ing*-infinitive
complement form, and third with the syntactic form of a C-P-U verb much
lower on the scale:

(36)   a.   She **saw** him **come** out of the theater
       b.   She **saw** him **coming** out of the theater
       c.   She **saw** that **he came** out of the theater

No manipulation or causation, successful or otherwise, is involved in (36a)
or (36b). Nevertheless, 'see' in both is logically implicative in the conventional sense — if the main clause is true, the complement clause is also true.

The P-C-U variant of 'see' (36c) contrasts with variants (36a,b) in
another important respect. In both (36a) and (36b) the two events — 'see'
and 'come out' — are **co-temporal**. Such co-temporality is indeed a prerequisite for construing two events as an integrated single event (see (14)
above). In (36c), on the other hand, the two events need not be co-temporal. Further, 'see' in (36c) is not a **physical perception** verb anymore, but
rather a verb of **mental reflection**. When one perceives an event, the perception is co-temporal with the perceived event. On the other hand, when
one reflects upon an event, all manner of temporal gapping may exist
between the reflection and the reflected-upon event. To illustrate this, compare the reflection sense of 'see' in (37a,b,c) below with the perception
sense in (37d,e,f):

(37) a. She **saw** that he **had already** come out.
      b. She **saw** that it **would be a while before** he came out
      c. She **saw** that he **would never** come out
      d. *She **saw** him **having come** out
      e. *She **saw** him **being a while before coming** out
      f. *She **saw** him **never to come** out

There remains, finally, the feature of logical implication. This feature, so it seems, is inseparable from co-temporality. It is precisely when two events are co-temporal that the truth of one implies the truth of the other. Tentatively then,[7] one may suggest that the crucial feature that places a verb at a higher range on our complementation scale is neither successful causation nor logical implication *per se*. Rather, the dimension underlying our scale is that of **spatio-temporal integration** of two events into a cognitively unified single event-frame. The two events — one in the main clause, the other in the complement — *could have* been framed as separate. But the higher a main verb is on the scale, the more likely it is that the two events are framed as a single complex event.

7.2.2.8. Referential cohesion and event integration

Referential cohesion across contiguous clauses is the **sharing of referents** across those clauses, i.e. referential continuity. Let us consider again the contrast between the three variants of 'see':

(38) a. She **saw** him **come** out of the theater
           (> As *he* was coming out)
      b. She **saw** him **coming** out of the theater
           (> As either *he* or *she* was coming out)
      c. She **saw** that $\left\{ \begin{array}{l} \textbf{he} \\ \textbf{John} \\ \textbf{Mary} \end{array} \right\}$ came out of the theater

In (38a), the subject of the complement clause *must* be co-referential with the object of the main clause. In (38b), an option is available: The subject of the complement must be co-referential with an argument of the main clause, but that argument may be *either* the object or the subject. Finally, in (38c) the subject of the complement verb is unconstrained by co-reference with any argument of the main clause.

Referential integration is indeed an important sub-dimension of event integration. Thus, for example, both verb classes at the top of our event-integration scale, modality verbs and manipulation verbs, require co-refer-ence. The subject of the complement of a modality verb must be co-refer-ential with the *subject* of the main verb, and the subject of the complement of a manipulation verb must be co-referential with the *object* of the main verb. In contrast, P-C-U verbs occupy the bottom of our event-integration scale, and their complements require no co-reference with any argument of the main clause. That is:

(39) a. **Modality verb**:
          Mary wanted to leave
              (> Mary wanted, Mary leave)
      b. **Manipulation verb**:
          Mary told Joe to leave
              (> Mary told Joe, Joe leave)
      c. **P-C-U verb**:
          Mary saw that Joe left
              (> May saw, Joe left)

The relation between referential cohesion, the semantic integration of events and the syntactic integration of clauses may be given as the following probabilistic inference:

(40) **Referential cohesion, event integration and clause integration**:
      "The more the two events in the main and complement clauses share their referents, the more likely they are to be semantically integrated as a single event; and the more likely is the complement clause to be syntactically integrated with the main clause".

Finally, example (38) above also suggests that the scale of referential cohesion involves an implicational hierarchy of co-reference, from the high-est to the lowest:

(41) **Hierarchy of referential cohesion**:
      SUBJECT CO-REFERENCE >
      ANY CO-REFERENCE >
      NO CO-REFERENCE

The implicational hierarchy in (41) is indeed a widely-noted constraint that tags subject co-reference, thus **subject continuity**, across contiguous clauses in discourse as the highest degree of referential coherence.[8]

7.2.2.9. Authority and verbal manipulation

The manipulations discussed thus far here have all been reported manipulation. That is, they all involved manipulative verbs in a **declarative** main clause. But the very same constructions, with a first person subject, can also be used as actual, if 'indirect', manipulative **speech-acts**.[9]

There seems to be a consistent correlation between the ranking of manipulative verbs on scale (10) and their ranking as manipulative speech-acts. That is, manipulative verbs that are higher on our complementation scale (10) also tend to be used as more direct, authoritarian, coercive speech-acts. And manipulative verbs that are lower on the complementation scale tend to be used more as indirect, tentative, softer manipulative speech-acts. To illustrate this, consider the contrast between 'want' and 'wish' as manipulative speech-acts:

(42)   a. I **want** you **to stop** harassing her, immediately!
       b. ?I **wish** that **you'd stop** harassing her, immediately!

The adverb 'immediately', hinting at a stronger manipulation, is compatible with 'want' but less compatible with 'wish'.

The same contrast can be shown between the two versions of 'expect', one ranking higher on the scale (with the same complement form as 'want'), the other lower (with the same complement form as 'wish'):

(43)   I **expect** you **to be done** by noon,
       a. ...so get on with it!
       b. ...?if you don't mind.

(44)   I **expect** that **you should be done** by noon,
       a. ...?so get on with it!
       b. ...?if you don't mind.
       c. ...if everything goes on schedule.

While 'expect' in (43) may function as a manipulative speech-act, in (44) it is rather more like a *prediction*, so that neither ending (44a) nor ending (44b) are appropriate, only (44c).

Finally, a similar contrast in manipulative strength seems to exist between the simple infinitive complement form in (10f-j) and the *for-to* complement form in (10k). When such expressions are used in manipulative speech-acts, the simple infinitive complement form imparts stronger manipulative strength, the *for-to* form weaker. Thus compare:

(45) **Infinitive complement (stronger)**:
I'd like **you** to
a. ...leave right away.
b. ...?be able to leave when you're ready.

(46) **For-to complement**:
I'd like **for you to**
a. ...leave right away.
b. ...be able to leave when you're ready.

7.2.3. From manipulation to preference to epistemics

We turn now to discuss the middle-to-bottom portion of the complementation scale (10), the portion that is coded by P-C-U verbs. One of
the best arguments for the existence of a single scale across the two verb
types — manipulation and P-C-U verbs — involves the persistent overlap
found in the mid-section of the scale. In terms of the syntactic form of the
complement clause, this overlap spans two portions of our scale:
  (a)   infinitival complements; and
  (b)   modal-subjunctive complements.
The overlap is manifest by the presence of the same or similar lexical verbs
bridging the semantic scale — from stronger **manipulation** to weaker **preference**. Thus, the more direct-manipulative 'want' (10i) has its weaker
counterpart in 'wish' (10m). The more direct-permissive 'allow' (10h) has
its weaker counterpart in 'agree' (10n). And the more direct-manipulative
'tell' (10f) may itself appear at a lower portion of the scale, resembling
there its weaker relative 'suggest' (10l).

The graded transition between the **preference** range, coded with modal
complements (10l,m,n), and the **epistemic** range, coded with indirect-quote
complements (10o,p), is just as striking. The very same lexical verb may
take a subjunctive complement as a weak manipulation verb (47a,b), a
modal complement as a preference verb (47c), a modal complement as a
verb of epistemic uncertainty (47d), or an indicative complement as a verb
of epistemic certainty (47e):

(47) a. **Weak manipulation (subjunctive complement)**:
        She suggested that John **leave** right away.
     b. **Manipulative speech-act (subjunctive complement)**:
        I suggest that you **leave** right away.

    c. **Preference (modal complement)**:
      She suggested that John **should leave** right away.
    d. **Epistemic uncertainty (modal complement)**:
      She suggested that John **may have left** right away.
    e. **Epistemic certainty (indicative complement)**:
      She suggested that John **had left** earlier.

A similar gradation can be seen with the verb 'agree'. A subjunctive complement is apparently incompatible with this verb (48a). With a modal complement, 'agree' may code either weak permission (48b) or low epistemic certainty (48c). Finally, with an indicative complement (48d) 'agree' codes higher epistemic certainty:

(48) a. *__Strong permission (subjunctive complement)__:
        *She agreed that John **leave** right away.
    b. **Weak permission (modal complement)**:
        She agreed that John **should leave** right away
    c. **Lower epistemic certainty (modal complement)**:
        She agreed that John **may have left** right away.
    d. **Higher epistemic certainty (indicative complement)**:
        She agreed that John **had left** earlier.

Prototypical P-C-U verbs such as 'think', 'know' and 'say' allow a similar transition by combining with various complement forms. But the gradation here again begins at a lower point on the complementation scale:

(49) a. **Preference (modal complement)**:
        He said/thought/knew that she **should leave**.
    b. **Lower epistemic certainty (modal complement)**:
        He said/thought/knew that she **might leave**.
    c. **Epistemic certainty (indicative complement)**:
        He said/thought/knew that she **had left**.

Another subtle transition may be seen in preference verbs such as 'wish', 'hope' and 'be afraid'. These verbs, combined with modal complements, are commonly used to code preference, as in:

(50) a. She hoped that he **would arrive** on time
    b. She was afraid that he **wouldn't arrive** on time
    c. She wished that he **would arrive** on time

The very same verbs may also code a variant of **epistemic uncertainty**. The semantic coloring of the verb shifts here subtly, from preference for a potential event to **epistemic anxiety** about an event that has already occurred, but whose epistemic status is still unclear:

(51) a. She hoped that he **did arrive** on time
      b. She was afraid that he **may not have arrived** on time

This portion of the complementation scale is somewhat of a *hybrid*, standing somewhere between the **valuative** modality of preference and the **epistemic** modality of uncertainty.

7.2.4. Tense agreement and integrated perspective

Tense-aspect restrictions, imposed on the complement clause by its main clause, is an important if subtle dimension at the very bottom of the complementation scale. This may also be an area where cognition verbs such as 'know' or 'think', on the one hand, and utterance verbs such as 'say', on the other, may exhibit subtle differences. From a semantic perspective, grammatical **tense agreement** is another reflection of event integration, in this case creating an **integrated perspective**. Cognition verbs such as 'know' and 'think' demand obligatory tense agreement, as in:

(52) a. **Past-past**:
          I knew (that) you **were coming**
      b. ***Past-present**:
          *I knew (that) you **are coming**
      c. **Past-past**:
          I knew (that) you **had come**
      d. ***Past-present**:
          *I knew (that) you **have come**

Utterance verbs such as 'say' seem, at least superficially, to *not* require obligatory tense agreement. Thus compare:

(53) a. I said (that) you **were coming**
      b. I said (?that) you **are coming**
      c. I said (that) you **had arrived**
      d. I said (?that) you **have arrived**

It may well be, however, that the seeming permissiveness of 'say' is due to the fact that the complement clauses in (53b,d) are interpreted as **direct quote** complements (see below). Such complements typically do *not* require tense agreement. In other words, (53b) and (53d) may really be intended as, respectively:

(54) a. I said: "You **are coming**"
    b. I said: "You **have arrived**"

A fact that seems to supports this interpretation is that the subordinator *that* can be used only with indirect-quote complements. When *that* is used in (53b,d), they both become rather odd.

Tense agreement — imposed by the main clauses on its indirect-quote complement — is an indication of a more general phenomenon — **unified perspective**. In indirect-quote complements, the perspective of *the speaker* who uttered the main clause also persists in the complement clause (rather than the perspective of the *subject* of the main-clause). As we shall see directly below, direct-quote complements allow maximal detachment between the speaker's perspective (prevailing in the main clause) and the perspective of the quoted subject of 'say', which prevails in the complement clause.

7.2.5. From indirect to direct quote: The de-coupling of point-of-view

The last transition on the complementation scale, from indirect-quote to direct-quote complement form, signals the final de-coupling of the two propositions in the main and complement clause. No constraints on temporal, spatial or referential contiguity bind the two propositions. The point-of-view of the speaker retains its sway over the main clause, while the point-of-view of the *subject* of the main verb takes over the complement clause.

In addition to the de-coupling of tense-agreement, the ceding of the perspective of the complement clause to the subject of the utterance verb is also reflected in the interpretation of personal pronouns and other **pointing ('deictic') expressions** inside the complement clause. As an illustration of this, consider:

(55) **Pointing personal pronouns**:
    a. **Indirect quote**:
        She said that **I** was a crook
            (I = me, who's telling this to you)
    b. **Direct quote**:
        She said: "**I** was a crook"
            (I = she, who said that)

(56) **Pointing spatial demonstratives**:
a. **Indirect quote**:
She said that **this** book is good
(this book = the one **we**'re looking at **now**)
b. **Direct quote**:
She said: "**This** book is good"
(this book = the one **she** was looking at **then**)

(57) **Pointing time adverbs**:
a. **Indirect quote**:
She said that **now** is as good a time as any
(now = when **we** are talking **now**)
b. **Direct quote**:
She said: "You better quit **now**"
(now = when **she** was talking **then**)
c. **Indirect quote**:
She said (that) he left **yesterday**
(yesterday = the day **before today**)
d. **Direct quote**:
She said: "He left **yesterday**"
(yesterday = the day **before when she was talking**)

The control of tense agreement is also subtly shifted in direct quote complements, revealing tense to be part and parcel of the point-of-view system. Thus consider:

(58) a. **Indirect quote**:
Last night she said (that) he **had** disappeared
(> He disappeared **before she spoke**)
b. **Direct quote**:
Last night she said: "He **had** disappeared (before I could start looking for him)"
(> He disappeared **before she started looking for him**)

The de-coupled point-of-view seen in direct-quote complements is an indication of **maximal separation** between the events coded in the main and complement clauses. By opening a direct quotation, the speaker initiates another **universe of discourse**. This new universe is now governed by — i.e. presented from — the perspective of the subject of the utterance verb ('say'), but it is still *embedded* within another universe (the main clause) and another perspective (the speaker's).

7.2.6. Summary

In terms of its underlying semantic sub-dimensions, our complementation scale (10) seems to shift gradually along the following major steps:

(59) **Main steps on the complementation scale**:
   a. successful causation
   b. intended manipulation
   c. preference/aversion
   d. epistemic anxiety
   e. epistemic certainty/uncertainty
   f. quotation under speaker's perspective
   g. quotation detached from speaker's perspective

The overlap of lexical verbs — or of syntactic complement forms — along the mid-section of the scale is an argument for suggesting that the scale is a unified scale. The suggestion that the scale is unified is also supported by diachronic considerations.[10]

7.3. THE SYNTAX OF CLAUSE INTEGRATION

7.3.1. Preamble

In the preceding section we dealt primarily with the semantic parameters of event integration. In this section we will discuss the syntactic correlates of event integration — the grammatical integration of two clauses into a single complex clause. In particular, we will deal with four **grammatical coding devices** used in signaling the degree of event integration. These devices are not applied uniformly across the complementation scale. Rather, along particular portions of the scale, a particular syntactic device may be used more prominently than others. The four devices are:

(60) **Coding devices in the grammar of complementation**:
   a. **Co-lexicalization** (or 'adjacency') of the complement verb with the main verb[11]
   b. **Case-marking** of the subject of the complement clause
   c. **Verb morphology** of the complement verb
   d. **Physical separation** of the complement clause from the main clause, by either:
      (i) a **subordinating morpheme**, or
      (ii) a **intonational break** (i.e. a pause).

What emerges from the study of the syntax of complementation, perhaps more clearly than in any other area of grammar, is the profoundly **non-arbitrary** nature of the coding relation between grammar and meaning.

7.3.2. Verb adjacency or co-lexicalization

Consider again the contrast at the top of our complementation scale (10) between 'let' and 'make', both implicative-manipulative verbs:

(61) a. Mary **let-go** of John's arm
      b. Mary **let** John **go**
      c. Mary **made** John **go** (to the store)

The complementation structure of (61a), with the complement verb being **directly adjacent** to the main verb, is rare in English. It is found only at the very top of the scale, and with restricted complement verbs such as 'go', 'fly' or 'loose'.[12] This is the highest degree of structural integration between main and complement clause in English: The two verbs are, to all intent and purpose, **co-lexicalized** as a single verb.

The use of co-lexicalization to code the highest degree of semantic integration of the two clauses may be expressed as the following prediction:

(62) **Co-lexicalization and event integration**:
      a. "The higher a main verb is on the semantic scale
          of event integration, the more likely it is to co-
          lexicalize with its complement verb".
      b. "If a complement-taking verb is co-lexicalized,
          all the verbs above it on the scale of event inte-
          gration scale will also be co-lexicalized".

Both predictions (62a,b) are upheld in the grammar of English complementation, where only the verb highest on the event-integration scale, 'let', co-lexicalizes with its complement verb.

The natural **iconicity** that motivates the use of co-lexicalization in the grammar of complements is fairly transparent, and may be given as follows:[13]

(63) **The proximity principle**:
      "The closer two linguistic entities are in meaning,
      the more they will exhibit temporal proximity at
      the code level".[14]

7.3.3. Case-marking of the complement-clause subject

The second device used systematically in coding the complementation scale is the case-marking of the subject of the complement verb. To illustrate the use of this device along our complementation scale (10), consider again the transition from 'let' through 'make', 'tell' and 'want' to 'wish':

(64) a. She let-go **of him**   (GEN)
     b. She made **him** go   (DO)
     c. She told **him** to go   (DO)
     d. She wanted **him** to go   (DO)
     e. She wished that **he** would go (SUBJ)

At the top of the scale, with 'let' in (64a), the subject of the complement verb 'go' is marked as a *genitive* ('possessive'). In (64b,c,d) it is marked as *direct object*. Only when moving further down the scale, in the transition from the direct-manipulative 'want' (64d) to the non-manipulative 'wish' (64e), does the subject of 'go' acquire the case-marking characteristic of main-clause *subject*.

The correlation between the grammatical case-marking of the complement subject and the degree of semantic integration of main and complement clauses may be given as the following implicational-hierarchic prediction:

(65) **Event integration and case-marking of complement-clause subject**:
     a. "The more integrated the complement clause is semantically with the main clause as a single event, the less likely is the subject of the complement clause to receive the case-marking typical of the subject-agent of a main clause".
     b. "The hierarchy of case-roles in terms of typical subject marking is:
        (i) **Semantic role**: AGT > DAT > PAT > OTHERS
        (ii) **Grammatical role**: SUBJ > DO > OTHER".

The hierarchies in (65b) indeed look familiar. The first, (65b(i)), ranks the **access to subjecthood** — or 'topicality' — of the major semantic case-roles (see chapter 3). The second, (65b(ii)), expresses the same facts in terms of grammatical case-roles.

Prediction (65a) may be also re-cast as:

(66) **Event integration and agent-like marking of
the complement-clause subject**:
"The more integrated the complement clause is
semantically with the main clause as a single
event, the less likely is the subject of the complement clause to resemble a prototypical main-
clause agent in its case-marking".

In a language like English, with a **nominative** grammatical-case system,[15]
marking a clausal participant as subject also marks it as more agent-like.

7.3.4. Verb morphology: Degree of finiteness

The third grammatical device used in coding the complementation
scale is verb morphology. Here the scale stretches between the most **finite**
form — the prototype main-clause verbal form — and the most **non-finite**
form. As noted in chapter 6, the less finite a verb is, the more **noun-like** —
nominal, nominalized — it will appear.

Of the various features that code the non-finite or nominal status of
clauses, three concern us most in the grammar of complementation:

(a)   Derived **nominal form** of the verb
(b)   Reduction of **tense-aspect-modality** marking
(c)   Reduction of **verb agreement**

As an illustration of how the verb-forms partake in the grammatical
coding of the complementation scale, consider the following major steps in
scale (10):

(67) a. She let-**go** of him   (BARE STEM)
      b. She made him **leave**   (BARE STEM)
      c. She had him **leave** the room   (BARE STEM)
      d. She told him **to leave**   (INFINITIVE)
      e. She wished that he **would leave** (MODAL)
      f. She hoped that he **could have left** (MODAL+ASPECT)
      g. She knew that he **was leaving**   (TENSE, RESTRICTED)
      h. She said: "He **is leaving**"   (FULLY FINITE)

The bare-stem form of the verbs (67a,b,c) is the least finite — i.e. least
verb-like — on the complementation scale in English. It is used only in
complements of main verbs that occupy the very top of our event-integra-

tion scale. The infinitive form (67d) is a bit more verb-like. The modal form (67e) is more verb-like. And with the addition of aspect and tense (57f,g,h), one moves toward the bottom of the scale.

An even finer gradation in the finiteness of verb-forms is seen at the top of the complementation scale of modality verbs (see further below):

(68) a. She finished **her work**   (NOMINALIZED)
      c. She started **working**   (*-ing* INFINITIVE)
      d. She wanted **to work**   (*to* INFINITIVE)

The nominalized form (68a) is clearly the least finite, essentially a noun with a possessive determiner. The *-ing*-infinitive form (68b) a bit more finite; and the *to*-infinitive form (68c) a more finite yet. This gradation conforms to the one seen in chapter 6.

The use of verb-form as coding device along the complementation scale may be summarized with the following implicational-hierarchic prediction:

(69) **Event integration and nominal form**:
      "The higher a main verb is on the scale of event
      integration, the more nominal — or less finite —
      will its complement verb be".

The scale of finiteness of verb-forms in English is:[16]

(70) **Scale of finiteness of English verb-forms**:
      least finite

lexical-nominal	(remov*al*)
bare-stem	(remove)
-ing-infinitive	(remov-*ing*)
to-infinitive	(*to* remove)
modal	(*may* remove)
aspectual	(*having* remov-*ed*)
tense	(remov-*ed*)

      most finite

7.3.5. Physical separation: Subordinators and pause

The fourth type of grammatical means used to code the degree of clause integration in the grammar of complementation, physical separation, is used only at the bottom portion of the scale. Physical separation involves two separate sub-devices, one of them used higher on the scale (10l-q), the other at the very bottom (10r) with direct-quote complement. The two are:

    (a) the presence (vs. absence) of the **subordinator** *that*;

    (b) the use of an **intonational break** (pause).

Either one of these functions as a physical gap between the main and complement clause.

The use of either the subordinator or a pause in coding the degree of event integration may be summed up in the following implicational-hierarchic predictions:

(71) **Event integration and physical separation**:

    a. "The lower the main verb is on the event integration scale, the more likely it is that the complement clause be separated from the main clause by either a subordinator or a pause".

    b. "If physical separation is used at a certain point on the complementation scale, it will also be used at all points lower on the scale".

The relation between the use of the subordinator *that* and a pause is an exclusion relation. The subordinator is used only at the higher portion of the scale, where no intonational break occurs, i.e. when the two clauses fall under a **unified intonation contour**. Thus, *that* becomes significant in coding the transition from manipulation and modality verbs to P-C-U verbs. The pause, on the other hand, is used to code the final transition, from indirect-quote to direct-quote.[17]

7.4.   MODALITY VERBS

7.4.1. Definition of modality verbs

We turn now to the third class of complement-taking verbs, modality verbs. This class spans the upper section of the complementation scale, paralleling manipulation verbs. The parallelism between the two classes is both semantic and syntactic. The semantic characterization of modality verbs is:

(72) **Semantic characterization of modality verbs:**
     a. The main-clause verb codes the inception, ter-
        mination, persistence, success, failure, attempt,
        intent, obligation or ability — to bring about the
        state/event coded in the complement clause.
     b. The subject of the main clause must be co-refer-
        ential with the subject of the complement
        clause.

The syntactic relation between modality verbs and their complement
clauses may be given in tree diagram (74), representing (73):

(73) John wanted to leave

(74) **Tree diagram for modality-verb complementation:**

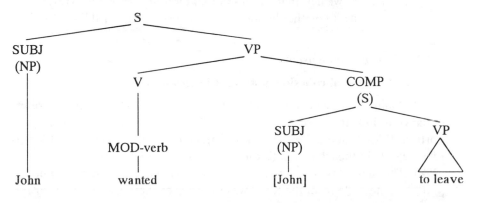

In (75) below we illustrate the scale of modality verbs, including the
portion where modality verbs shade into P-C-U verbs.

(75) **scale of modality verbs**   **syntax of complement**

   a. She finished **her work** late   NOMINAL COMP

   b. She finished **building** the house   *-ing*-INF. COMP

   c. She managed **to build** the house
   d. She was able **to build** a house
   e. She had **to build** a house   *to*-INF. COMP
   f. She tried **to build** a house
   g. She planned **to build** a house
   h. She wanted **to build** a house

   i. She knew **how to build** a house   *how-to* COMP
  (j. She wished that he **would build** a house   MODAL COMP)
  (k. She knew that he **had built** a house   FINITE COMP)

7.4.2. Semantic dimensions

7.4.2.1. Referential cohesion and event integration

Modality verbs contrast with P-C-U verbs along the dimension of **referential cohesion**. In the scale (75) above, all the modality verbs in the upper portion (75a-i) abide by the **equi-subject** condition. This condition is relaxed only in the transition through preference verbs (75j) to P-C-U verbs (75k). The hierarchy of referential cohesion (41) is thus preserved, ranking points on the scale from the top down in terms of their requirement for referential cohesion:

(41) **Hierarchy of referential cohesion**:
    SUBJECT CO-REFERENCE >
    ANY CO-REFERENCE >
    NO CO-REFERENCE

7.4.2.2. Implicativity

The top of the modality-verb scale is occupied by **implicative** verbs such as 'finish', 'start', 'continue', 'complete', 'manage' or 'fail'. We have already noted the correlation between successful manipulation and co-temporality of the main and complement events. In English, the less finite *-ing*-infinitive form tends to be used in complements of implicative verbs. Some, like 'finish' and 'stop', can only take this complement form. Verbs that can take both the *-ing* and the *to-* infinitive forms display a subtle contrast in implicativity. Consider for example 'try':

(76) a. (After everything else failed),
          he tried **reciting** the pledge of allegiance,
          but the child kept crying.
     b. He tried **to recite** the pledge of allegiance,
          but no sound came out.

In (76a), the inference is that the complement event was performed, though it didn't achieve the desired effect. In (76b), the inference seems to be that the complement event was attempted but not successfully performed.

A similar contrast can be seen between the two complement forms of 'start':

(77) a. John started **doing** the dishes every evening,
          but then changed his mind.
     b. John started **to do** the dishes every evening,
          but then changed his mind.

In (77a), the probability is higher that John changed his mind *after* doing the dishes for a spell. In (77b), the probability is higher that John changed his mind *before* doing any dishes.

7.4.2.3. Strength of intent

The non-implicative verbs that occupy the lower portion of the scale may be ranked in terms of **strength of intent**, with the rank-order being roughly:

(78) **Ranking of strength of intent**:
          try > plan > want

This ranking, while technically involving non-implicative verbs, relates intent to accomplishment through the following probabilistic inference:

(79) **Inferring success from intent**:
          "The stronger is the agent's intent to accomplish
          a task, the higher is the likelihood that the task
          will be accomplished".

7.4.2.4. *How-to* complements

The contrast between *to*-infinitive and *how*-to complements codes another transition on the scale. This can be illustrated with verbs that take both complement types, such as 'remember'. With a *to*-infinitive complement, 'remember' is an implicative verb. With a *how-to* complement, it is not implicative:

(80) a. **Accomplishment**:
              She remembered **to lock** the house
                  (> She locked the house)
       b. **Know-how**:
              She remembered **how to lock** the house
                  (*> She locked the house)

7.4.2.5. From self-directed intent to other-directed preference

As noted earlier above, the final transition along scale (75), from self-directed intent or ability (75f-i) to other-directed preference (75j), involves the relaxation of the equi-subject condition. As in the parallel transition from manipulation to preference verbs, the complement form changes from the less-finite *to*-infinitive to the more finite *modal* complement. This is illustrated by the transition from 'want' to 'wish':

(81) a. **Self-directed intent**:
              He wanted **to leave**
       b. **Other-directed preference**:
              He wished that **she would leave**

A more wide-ranging transition with a single lexical verb is seen with 'decide', as in:

(82) a. **Self-directed intent**:
              She decided **to do** it
       b. **Other-directed preference**:
              She decided that **Joe should do** it
       c. **Cognition**:
              She decided that Joe **did** it

And a wider-ranging transition yet is seen with 'forget':

(83) a. **Accomplishment (negative)**:
    She forgot **to run**
  b. **Self-directed ability**:
    She forgot **how to run**
  c. **Other-directed ability**:
    She forgot **how one could run**
  d. **Other-directed preference**:
    She forgot that **Joe should run**
  e. **Cognition**:
    She forgot that Joe **ran**

7.5. FOR-TO COMPLEMENTS

We have already noted the existence of this peculiar complement form. Syntactically, it may be characterized by three salient features:

(a) Like manipulative verbs, the subject of the complement clause must be coreferent with the *object* of the main clause.

(b) The subject of the complement clause is coded as the *benefactive* object of the main clause, with the preposition 'for'.

(c) The complement verb takes the *to*-infinitive form.

The combination of these features mark *for-to* complements as an intermediate, mid-scale form. And indeed, the verbs that take such complements are semantically in the middle of our scale, covering the transition portion of **other-directed preference**. Verbs either higher or lower on the scale tend to reject *for-to* complements. Thus compare:

(84) a. **Up-scale (manipulation)**:
    *She **told** for you to come at 8:00
    *She **wanted** for you to come at 8:00
  b. **Mid-scale (preference)**:
    She **said** for you to come at 8:00
    She**'d like** for you to come at 8:00
  c. **Down-scale (cognition)**:
    *She **thought** for you to come at 8:00
    *She **knew** for you to come at 8:00

Whenever a verb — or two closely-related verbs — can take both the *to*-infinitive and the *for-to* complement forms, the contrast is clearly between direct vs. indirect manipulation (or preference). Thus compare:

(85) a. **Direct order**:
          She told **him** to wait,
              but he said "No!"
      b. **Indirect order**:
          She said **for him** to wait,
              *but he said "No!"

(86) a. **Direct request**:
          She asked **him** to bring the file,
              *but they couldn't find him.
      b. **Indirect request**:
          She asked **for him** to bring in the file,
              but they couldn't find him.

(87) a. **Direct manipulation**:
          She sent **him** to buy supplies,
              *but they forgot to tell him.
      b. **Indirect manipulation**:
          She sent **for him** to buy supplies,
              but they forgot to tell him.

(88) a. **Direct order**:
          She ordered **him** to cook their meal,
              *and sent them to bring him over.
      b. **Indirect order**:
          She ordered **for him** to cook their meal,
              and send them to bring him over.

The difference between the two complement forms can be further illustrated by contrasting active and passive complements. Passive verbs with prototypical (non-human) patients are compatible with *for-to* complements of indirect manipulation, but incompatible with *to*-infinitive complements of direct manipulation. Thus compare:

(89) a. *She told **the car** to be washed
      b. She said **for the car** to be washed
      c. *She asked **the file** to be brought in
      d. She asked **for the file** to be brought

    e. *She sent **George** to be brought before the court
    f. She sent **for George** to be brought before the court
    g. *She ordered **their dinner** to be served at 6:00
    h. She ordered **for their dinner** to be served at 6:00

7.6. CONDITIONAL COMPLEMENTS

A distinct group of P-C-U verbs can take an alternative complement form, with 'if' or 'whether' instead of the subordinator 'that'. Semantically, these are verbs of **doubt** or **low certainty**. P-C-U verbs of high certainty seem to resist 'if' complements. Thus compare:

(90) **Lower certainty**:
    a. She **doubts** if he can do it
    b. She **asked** if he would do it
    c. She **wondered** if Joe was home
    d. He **inquired** if she was ill

(91) **Higher certainty**:
    a. *She's **sure** if he can do it
    b. *She **said** if he would do it
    c. *She **suspected** if Joe was home
    d. *He **knew** if she was ill

While a verb of higher certainty may reject 'if' complements, its negative or interrogative counterparts — both *non-fact* modalities — may accept it. Thus compare:

(92) a. *She **said** if he was there
    b. She **didn't say** if he was there
    c. **Did** she **say** if he was there?
    d. *He **knows** if she was home
    e. He **doesn't know** if she was home
    f. **Does** he **know** if she was home?
    g. *She **remembered** if it was Tuesday
    h. She **didn't remember** if it was Tuesday
    i. *She **saw** if it was Joe
    j. She **didn't see** if it was Joe
    k. **Did** she **see** if it was Joe?
    l. *She **was sure** if he was there
    m. She **wasn't sure** if he was there

Conditional complements may also be fronted, and if such fronting takes place, the subordinator 'if' must be replaced by 'whether', its less colloquial variant. This is true at least for the more formal register of English. Thus compare:

(93) a. { **Whether** } it was Tuesday (or not) I don't know
          { **?If**   }

      b. { **Whether** } he was there (or not) she didn't say
          { **?If**   }

7.7.   WH-COMPLEMENTS

Many P-C-U verbs can also take another complement form, marked by a WH-pronoun ('question word')[18] These verbs tend to be either high certainty verbs or their negative or interrogative counterparts, but not low certainty verbs. For example:

(94) **High certainty**:
      a. He **knows** where she is
      b. He **doesn't know** where she is
      c. **Does** he **know** where she is?
      d. She **remembers** who did it
      e. She **doesn't remember** who did it
      f. **Does** she **remember** who did it?

(95) **Low certainty**:
      a. *He **thinks** where she is
      b. *He **doesn't think** where she is
      c. ***Does** he **think** where she is?
      d. *She **doubts** who did it
      e. *She **doesn't doubt** who did it
      f. ***Does** she **doubt** who did it?

While superficially resembling WH-questions, WH-complements differ from those in some important respects. In particular, the word-order inversion that is characteristic of WH-questions in English is not found in WH-complements. Thus compare:

(96) **True WH-question**:
      a. What **can** you see there?
      b. *What you **can** see there?
      c. Why **did** you do it?
      d. *Why you **did** it?

(97) **WH-complements**:
- a. *Tell me what **can** you see there.
- b. Tell me what you **can** see there.
- c. *I don't know why **did** you do it.
- d. I don't know why you **did** it.

7.8. POST-POSED P-C-U VERBS

In informal spoken English, many P-C-U verbs appear in a seemingly parenthetic construction, following rather than preceding their complement clauses. Typically, the subject of the P-C-U verb in such constructions is restricted to certain personal pronouns. And in most cases it could be only a specific pronoun. Typical examples of this pattern are:

(98) a. He's back, $\left\{ \begin{array}{l} \textbf{I hear} \\ \text{*you hear} \\ \text{*they hear} \end{array} \right\}$

b. It's raining back East, $\left\{ \begin{array}{l} \textbf{they say} \\ \text{*you say} \\ \text{?I say} \end{array} \right\}$

c. She's finished, $\left\{ \begin{array}{l} \textbf{I see} \\ \text{?you see} \\ \text{*they see} \end{array} \right\}$

d. He's ready, $\left\{ \begin{array}{l} \textbf{I suppose} \\ \text{*you suppose} \\ \text{*they suppose} \end{array} \right\}$

e. Now, this is a new gizmo, $\left\{ \begin{array}{l} \textbf{y'know} \\ \text{*I know} \\ \text{*they know} \end{array} \right\}$

f. It's ready, $\left\{ \begin{array}{l} \textbf{I guess} \\ \text{*you guess} \\ \text{*they guess} \end{array} \right\}$

The restrictions on specific subject pronouns in (98) reveal something about the function of these constructions. The post-posed P-C-U verb is in fact not the focus of the information being communicated. That focus has shifted to the complement clause. The post-posed P-C-U verb now functions as an **epistimic quantifier** on the information in the complement clause, indeed as a propositional **modality**. It may inform the hearer about the **evidential status** of the information — whether directly witnessed (98c), obtained via hearsay (98a,b), or inferred but not fully believed (98d). The post-posed P-C-U verb may also impart epistemic doubt (98f) or social uncertainty (98e).

Even without post-posing, P-C-U verbs may be used as epistemic quantifiers. The conventionalized subject pronoun is so specific to particular verbs, that it is often dropped in rapid speech:

(99) a. **(I) think** she's there.
  b. **(Do you) think** she'll show up?
  c. **(I) bet (you)** she's gone
  d. **(I) guess** you were right
  e. **(I'm) afraid** she's not in today
  f. **(Let's) suppose** you're right, then...
  g. **(Let's) say** we divide it in half

7.9. NON-VERBAL PREDICATES WITH VERBAL COMPLEMENTS

A number of predicates that fit into the semantic and syntactic frame of both modality verbs and P-C-U verbs are not verbs, but rather adjectives or even nouns. Some examples of adjectives that follow the complementation pattern of modality verbs are:

(100) a. She **was able** to do it
  b. He **was reluctant** to do it
  c. She **was eager** to please
  d. He **was ready** to quit
  e. She **was determined** to get his share
  f. He **was incapable** of rendering judgement
  g. She **was afraid** to leave
  h. He **was ashamed** to admit that...
  i. She **was anxious** to leave a good impression
  j. He **was happy** to comply

Examples of adjectives that follow the complementation pattern of P-C-U verbs are:

(101) a. He **was aware** that she didn't like him
  b. I **am sure** that it's alright
  c. She **was doubtful** that he would come
  d. He **was ecstatic** that it was all done
  e. She **was happy** that he wasn't there to see it
  f. I'**m sorry** that you feel this way
  g. I'**m afraid** this is all a big mistake

Some non-verbal predicates follow the syntactic pattern of modality verbs, as in (100), but are semantically more akin to P-C-U verbs. Others yet are simply of various and sundry semantic types. Many such predicates are **factive**, i.e. used when the truth of the complement clause is presupposed.[19] Some examples of those are:

(102) a. He **was sorry** to see her leave
         (> He saw that she was leaving, and he was sorry about that)
      b. He's **a darling** to do this
         (> He's doing this, and so he's a darling)
      c. She **was smart** to decline
         (> She declined, and that was smart of her)
      d. She **was an idiot** to accept his offer
         (> She accepted his offer, and that was idiotic)

The very same predicates may be used with a modal operator, whereby the truth value of their complement shifts predictably toward irrealis:

(103) a. You**'d be crazy** to accept this
         (> If you accept this, you'd be considered crazy)
      b. You**'d be mad** to pass up this opportunity
         (> If you pass it up, you'd be considered mad)
      c. She**'d be an imbecile** to do such a thing
         (> If she did this, she'd sure be an imbecile)

Some of the predicates that follow superficially the syntactic complementation pattern of modality verbs impart, semantically, a sense of **ease of performance** of the complement verb. As an illustration, compare the modality-type predicate 'eager' with the superficially similar 'easy' and 'hard':[20]

(104) a. Mary **is eager** to please
         (> **Mary** would please **someone**)
      b. Mary **is easy** to please
         (> **Someone** can please **Mary**)
      c. This book **is hard** to read
         (> **Someone** finds it hard to read **this book**)

The semantic structure of (104b) and (104c) is better paraphrased in (105b,c), respectively, a paraphrase that cannot apply to (104a):

(105) a. *(For one) to please Mary **is eager**
      b. (For one) to please Mary **is easy**
      c. (For one) to read this book **is hard**

The relationship between the surface syntactic structures of (104b,c) and the semantically more revealing paraphrases given in (105b,c) may be represented in the tree diagrams (106) and (107) below, respectively:

(106) **Surface syntactic structure**:

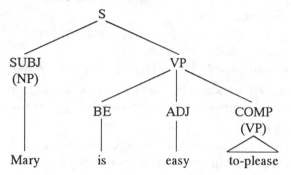

(107) **Semantically revealing ('deep') structure**:

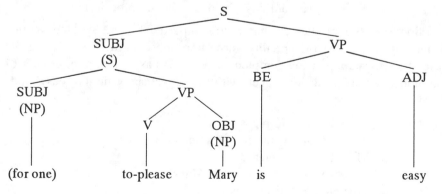

Another semantically revealing paraphrase of structures such as (104b,c) and (105b,c) involves post-posing the sentential subject of the deep structure (107) and replacing it with the pronoun 'it', as in (108b,c) below. Again, the paraphrase cannot apply to 'be eager':

(108) a. *It **is eager** (for one) to please Mary
     b. It **is easy** (for one) to please Mary
     c. It **is hard** (for one) to read this book

The surface syntactic structure of (108b,c) may be represented by the tree diagram (109) below:

(109)

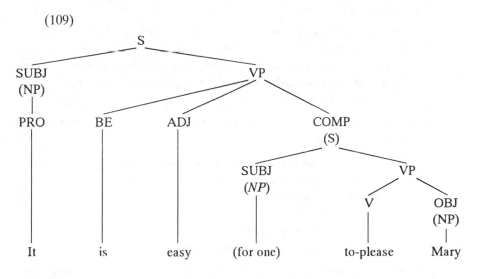

It   is   easy   (for one)   to-please   Mary

Finally, another group of predicates follow, superficially, the syntactic pattern of modality verbs. Their semantic structure is again complex and involves reversal of subject-object relations. These predicates tend to code **valuative judgement**, either of the surface subject as a person, or of the state/event clause within which the surface subject is logically the object. Some examples of these are:

(110) a. This **is too dreadful** to contemplate
     b. She **was gorgeous** to look at
     c. This issue **is too important** to overlook
     d. The hall was **too small** to accommodate the crowd

Semantically more revealing paraphrases of (110a-d) may sometimes be found. First, the erstwhile 'complement' in (110) can appear as a sentential subject, with the erstwhile subject now appearing as the object. However, this paraphrase captures the meaning of only (110a), and is totally inappropriate for (110b,c,d):

(111) a. (For one) to contemplate this **is too dreadful**
       b. *(For one) to look at her **was gorgeous**
       c. *(For one) to overlook this issue **is too important**
       d. *(For one) to accommodate the crowd in the hall
           was too small

The sentential subject can also be post-posed, as in:

(112) a. It **is too dreadful** (for one) to contemplate this
       b. *It **was gorgeous** (for one) to look at her
       c. *It **is too important** (for one) to overlook this issue
       d. *It **was too small** (for one) to accommodate the crowd
           in the hall

Constructions (110b,c,d) are better paraphrased in (113), a structure that is inappropriate for (110a):

(113) a. *This **is too dreadful**, so one contemplates it.
       b. She **was gorgeous**, when one looked at her.
       c. This issue **is (too) important**,
           so one must not overlook it.
       d. The hall **is (too) small**,
           so one cannot accommodate the crowd in it.

Some of the structures in paraphrases (113) are better discussed under the heading of **syntactic raising**.[21]

NOTES

1) In addition to verbs, some adjectives also take clausal complements; see section 7.9.

2) See section 3.3.8.

3) For arguments in support of a unified scale, see Givón (1990, ch. 13).

4) Contrasts such as those between (17) and (18) are not universally applicable, since they depend heavily on the type of verb in the complement clause. A much better test would be a detailed quantified study of the use of 'cause' and 'make' in natural text.

5) For participial ADV-clauses, see chapter 13. The co-reference constraints on the subject of ADV-clauses is used here as a diagnostic of subjecthood of the manipulee.

6) Example (32) also illustrates the compatibility of the no-contact preference verb 'wish' with the counter-fact modality. When one manipulates by communicating one's wish directly, the desired state/event falls under the modality of *irrealis*. When the wish is not communicated, and thus remains a private preference, the desired state/event can assume the *counter-fact* modality, as in (32a), in addition to the *irrealis* modality in (32b).

7) Until one can find contexts in which co-temporality and logical implication do *not* coincide, it is impossible to argue with absolute conviction that the crucial feature is co-temporality rather than logical implication.

8) See further discussion of referential cohesion and inter-clausal connectivity in chapter 13.

9) For non-declarative speech-acts, see chapter 12.

10) The extension of either meaning or form over time tends to proceed gradually, spreading along contiguous portions of a semantic space. Such extension is driven by judgements of *similarity*. The pervasive overlap in lexical and/or syntactic forms along the mid-section of the scale thus suggests a slow semantic gradation.

11) Other traditional names for co-lexicalization of verbs are 'predicate raising', 'predicate attachment' or 'clause union'.

12) Co-lexicalized verb combinations such as 'let-go', 'let-fly' or 'let-loose' have probably become *idioms*, i.e. single lexical verbs. This is a common historical fate of co-lexicalized verbs, given enough time.

13) For discussion of iconicity in grammar, see Haiman (1985, ed. 1985); Givón (1985; 1990, ch. 21).

14) In the written language, temporal proximity translates into spatial proximity.

15) English has a *nominative*-type case-marking system, whereby the subject of clauses is marked the same way — as a pre-verbal NP without a preposition — regardless of whether the clause is transitive or intransitive. Since the subjects of most clauses in texts that pertain to normal human affairs tend to be *human agents*, there is a strong statistical association in spoken English between what is "subject" and what is "agent".

16) See again the discussion of nominalization in chapter 6.

17) Coding clause separation vs. clause integration with intonation contours and intonation breaks is universal cross-linguistically, highly iconic and 'natural', and is acquired early by chil-

dren, long before the acquisition of other grammatical devices that code the same contrast. Most likely, the use of intonation also represents here an earlier stage in the *evolution* of grammar. For discussion see Chafe (1987) and Givón 1991a).

18) For WH-questions and other non-declarative clauses, see chapter 12.

19) For the original study of factive verbs in English, see Kiparsky and Kiparsky (1968).

20) These observations are due to Chomsky (1957).

21) See chapter 11.

8 | VOICE AND DE-TRANSITIVIZATION

8.1. INTRODUCTION

In this chapter we deal with clauses that diverge from the simple clause along the dimension of **transitivity**. As noted in chapter 1, the reference-point — 'theme' — for syntactic description is the **active-transitive** clause. The constructions we deal with in this chapter diverge from the theme in terms of either being less active or less transitive. Some of them are characterized traditionally as part of the phenomenon of **voice**, either **passive voice** or **middle-voice**. Others, while traditionally considered active, are nonetheless related to the phenomenon of **de-transitivization** in a variety of ways.

We will approach the description of de-transitive constructions by first distinguishing between the two components of **transitivity** — semantic and pragmatic. While this distinction is fundamental to our approach, one would do well to remember that, as elsewhere in grammar, semantics and pragmatics are not totally insulated from each other, but rather interact and overlap at their margins. In this they resemble other prototype-like categories that occupy neighboring spaces along a continuum.[1] For each construction discussed below, we will attempt to distinguish its more semantic features from its more pragmatic features.

The constructions surveyed in this chapter are:
(a) passive
(b) impersonal
(c) antipassive
(d) reflexive
(e) reciprocal
(f) middle voice

8.2. FUNCTIONAL DIMENSIONS OF VOICE

8.2.1. The semantics of transitivity

We will begin by briefly recapitulating the discussion of the semantics of transitivity. Three semantic dimensions are central to our understanding of de-transitivity. They are the same ones that figure in the semantic definition of **active-transitive voice**.[2] Each dimension corresponds to one central aspect of the prototypical **transitive event**:

(1)   **Semantic definition of transitive event**

    a. **Agent**: The prototypical transitive clause involves a volitional, controlling, actively-initiating agent who is responsible for the event, and thus is its **salient cause**.

    b. **Patient**: The prototypical transitive event involves a non-volitional, inactive non-controlling patient who registers the event's changes-of-state, and thus is it's **salient effect**.

    c. **Verb**: The verb of the prototypical transitive clause codes an event that is compact (non-durative), bounded (non-lingering), sequential (non-perfect) and realis (non-hypothetical). The prototype transitive event is thus a fast-paced, completed, real, and perceptually and/or cognitively **salient change**.

When we talk about the semantics of de-transitivity, we talk about constructions that involve a decrease in either

    (a) the agentivity of the agent,

    (b) the affectedness of the patient, or

    (c) the compact, bounded, sequential or realis-like nature of the verb.

8.2.2. The pragmatics of voice

8.2.2.1. Perspective and topicality

When confined to the active-passive distinction, the traditional notion of voice turns out to be primarily discourse-pragmatic. By 'pragmatic' one means here that the very same semantically-defined transitive event, coded by the very same combination of verb, agent and patient, may be rendered from more than one **perspective**. By 'discourse' we mean the **discourse context** within which the semantically-transitive clause is embedded. Most commonly, the relevant context controlling the pragmatics of voice involves the **relative topicality** of the agent and patient participants of the event.

8.2.2.2. Active voice

In the prototypical active clause, the agent — the apex of the generic topicality hierarchy[3] — is the **primary referent-topic** of the clause. Consequently, in the prototypical active-voice clause, the agent is the **grammatical subject**. The other participants in the active clause then occupy other available grammatical roles, such as direct object, indirect object etc. Most typically in English, the patient occupies the **direct-object** role in the active-voice clause.

8.2.2.3. Passive voice

In the prototypical passive clause, the agent is *not* the most topical. Rather, some non-agent is the primary referent-topic, and is thus also the grammatical subject. The competitive access of non-agents to the subject role in the passive clause follows the same generic topicality hierarchy (minus the agent):

$$(AGT >) \ DAT/BEN > PAT > OTHERS$$

However, since most transitive verbs in English have a patient but no dative participant, the typical subject of the passive clause tends to be its patient.

8.2.2.4. Antipassive voice

In the prototypical **antipassive** clause, the agent retains its high topicality — thus subjecthood — as in the active clause. However, the topicality of the *patient* is much lower than it is in the active clause. Patients of antipassive clauses tend to be thematically unimportant, redundant, predictable, unspecified or non-referring. In pragmatic terms, the patient of the antipassive clause thus departs from the patient of the transitive prototype in very much the same way as the agent of the passive departs from the agent of the prototypical active clause.

In terms of grammatical role assignment, the patient of an antipassive clause tends to lose some or all of its direct-object properties, and the clause is often *objectless* and thus effectively intransitive-like. This again parallels the treatment of the agent in passive clauses, where the agent is neither subject nor direct-object, and the clause is thus effectively objectless.[4]

8.2.3. Demotion, promotion and resulting state

We turn now to a more detailed exposition of the three main functional dimensions of de-transitive voice, using either the passive or other constructions as salient examples.

8.2.3.1. Agent demotion

In the passive clause, the agent of a semantically-transitive event is *demoted* from its pragmatic role of main topic, as well as from its more normal role of grammatical subject. The exact motivation for such demotion (or 'suppression') may vary. The agent may, for example, be unknown or unrecoverable, as in:[5]

(2)   "...He was killed in the Boer war..."

The agent may be anaphorically predictable from the preceding discourse, as in:

(3)   **The soldiers** invaded the village;
      soon the entire place was burned down

The agent may be cataphorically given in the subsequent discourse, as in:[6]

(4)   "...There was no telling what might have happened
      if he had not been interrupted. **The dog** had been
      whimpering and whining..."

The agent may be predictable on general grounds, i.e. stereotypical, as in:

(5)   The plane was brought down safely

Planes are habitually flown and landed by their *pilots*.

The agent may be universal and thus left unspecified, as in:[7]

(6)   "...as **everybody** knew, dogs were psychic...
      Now, it was known that these were actually
      fifth-dimensional objects..."

The agent may be deliberately suppressed in order to avoid culpability, as in:[8]

(7)   "...Finally she said: "A long, long time ago, before I was
      born... **He** got into a fight then, when he was young,
      and a man was killed. But **he** was a wild boy then,
      and drunk. Now **he** is an old man. **He** doesn't drink now.
      Not for years"..."

In examples (2) through (7) above, the de-transitive construction used to affect agent demotion was the passive clause. But other de-transitive constructions may share with the passive the feature of agent demotion, while not sharing its other features. A cluster of such constructions may be called **impersonal-subject** constructions, and are often used to code semantically-transitive or active events with a generic subject or agent. As illustrations, consider:

(8)   a. **One** used to work hard in those days
      b. **You** build a log house around here
      c. **They** don't make them like that any more

The agent of the de-transitive clause may also be predictable as the author of the text, as in:[9]

(9)   "...**Enough has been said here** of a subject
      which will be treated more fully in a subsequent
      chapter..."

The agent of a de-transitive clause may simply be unimportant or irrelevant in the discourse context. Thus, in example (5) above, the pilot is not topical enough to merit specific mention. Impersonal-subject constructions such as (8) above are often used to code events in such a context, as in:

(10) **They** found her nude body on the beach last night

Even when the agent is overtly mentioned in a bona-fide passive construction, it tends to be of low thematic import, and frequently non-human, as in:[10]

(11) a. "...the house was struck **by lightning**..."
      b. "...his son was run over **by a motorcar**..."

While the BE-passive in English makes it possible to mention the agent of the event, such overt mention is rather infrequent in passive clauses in texts. As an illustration of this, consider the frequency distributions of agentless vs. agent-including passives in two English texts:[11]

(12) **Frequency distribution of agentless and agent-including passive clauses in two English texts**

	agentless		agent-incl.		total	
text	N	%	N	%	N	%
LL	15	84%	3	16%	18	100%
GO	58	79%	15	21%	73	100%

On occasion there may be personal, social or cultural reasons for pro-scribing the overt mention of the agent responsible for an event. This may be seen in children's frequent use of various **middle voice** de-transitives or their equivalents, as in the ubiquitous:

(13) a. It broke
      b. It fell
      c. It got lost

8.2.3.2. Promotion of a non-agent

The second major functional domain of de-transitive voice is to some extent a predictable correlate of the first. In clauses in connected discourse, most typically one nominal referent is the main topic. Thus, if the agent is downgraded or demoted from that role, for whatever pragmatic reason and by whatever syntactic means, some other participant in the clause is inter-preted *by default* as the topic. The non-agent topic of the de-transitive clause is thus promoted to topicality, and often also to grammatical subject-hood. Or as Jespersen (1924) puts it:

> "...the passive turn is preferred if one takes naturally greater interest in the passive than in the active subject..." (1924, p. 168)

The syntactic means by which a non-agent can be promoted to topical-ity in a de-transitive clause may vary. In the four constructions in (14) below, the non-agent topic is promoted to full grammatical subjecthood:

(14) **Promotional de-transitive constructions**:
      a. **BE-passive**:
          John was killed in an accident
      b. **GET-passive**:
          Mary got elected on her second try
      c. **Middle voice**:
          The window suddenly broke

d. **Potential middle**:
This book is eminently readable

Other de-transitive constructions in English do not involve the promotion of the non-agent to full grammatical subjecthood. In such clauses, one may say that the non-agent is identified as the topic *by default*, in the absence of an overt agent. Impersonal-subject clauses in English are of this type:

(15) **Non-promotional de-transitive constructions**:
a. They found **him** lying on the beach half dead
b. One doesn't chew **tobacco** in polite company
c. You can find **cheap housing** there

In (15a,b,c) the patient of the event, while topical, remains the direct object of the clause; and the clause thus retains the syntactic character of a transitive clause in English.

8.2.3.3. Verb stativization

The third major functional dimension of de-transitive voice is primarily semantic. It involves the **stativization** of what otherwise would have been a semantically transitive verb. An event that is framed in the active voice is typically an agent-initiated, sharply-bounded, fast-changing **process**. In the passive voice, the same event can be re-framed as a **resulting state**. Such stativization is not a necessary ingredient of all de-transitive constructions. It is found most commonly in constructions that involve the syntactic promotion of a non-agent to grammatical subjecthood, such as those in (14) above. In contrast, stativization is less likely to be associated with impersonal-subject constructions such as those in (15), where the non-agent topic is not promoted to grammatical subjecthood.

The stativization of a de-transitive clause may manifest itself in a number of ways, some of which are predictable from the diachronic source of the de-transitive construction. BE-passive clauses in English in fact exhibit two of the most common grammatical devices used to code stativization:

(a) The use of **the auxiliary verb 'be'** as the main verb in the passive construction.
(b) The use of a **less-finite — adjectival, perfect, participial** — verb-form.

The stative-resultative nature of the BE-passive construction, i.e. the fact that the event is framed more as a resulting state, may be demonstrated by various tests. For example, manipulation verbs — particularly those that code requests and commands — tend to reject semantically-stative verbs in their complements, and accept only active verbs. As illustration of this selective preference, compare the active complement in (16a) with the stative ones in (16b,c,d):

(16) a. **Active**:
          She told him to **go to sleep**
      b. **Adjectival-stative**:
          *She told him to **be asleep**
      c. **Adjectival-stative**:
          *She told him to **be tall**
      d. **Progressive-stative**:
          *She told him to **be going to sleep**

In the same vein, manipulative verbs reject passive-voice complements, preferring the equivalent actives. Thus compare:

(17) a. She made John **chop the wood**
      b. *She made the wood **be chopped (by John)**
      c. They asked her to **leave her husband**
      d. *They asked her husband to **be left (by her)**
      e. John, go **find Mary**!
      f. *Mary, go **be found (by John)**!

The incompatibility of manipulative verbs with passive complements is presumably due to the fact that requesting or commanding requires that the manipulee has some control — i.e. the freedom to act.[12] But in re-framing an event as a resulting state, its patient-topic has no control.

8.3. THE FREQUENCY-DISTRIBUTION OF VOICE IN TEXT

We have assumed all along that the active (main, declarative, affirmative) clause is the basic, simple, **unmarked** clause-type. As noted in chapter 1, this assumption is associated, among other things, with the prediction that the unmarked member of a binary distinction has a wider distribution in communication; i.e. that it is more frequent in text. Distributional figures that support this can be seen in table (18).

(18) **Relative frequency of active and passive voice in main-declarative-affirmative clauses in four written English texts**[13]

	clause-type			
	active		passive	
text-type	N	%	N	%
academic	49	82%	11	18%
fiction	177	91%	18	9%
news	45	92%	4	8%
sports	64	96%	3	4%

The highest percentage of passives (18%) is found in academic non-fiction text, whose thematic orientation tends strongly towards abstract themes, non-human topics, generic referents and timeless states. The lower frequency of passives in action-oriented fiction, front-page news and the sports pages is no doubt much more representative of the human-universal norm.

The higher text-frequency of active-voice clauses is probably due to the conflation of the following factors:

(a) Agents are overwhelmingly human.

(b) Humans tend to talk mostly about humans.

(c) Agents thus tend to be the most topical —
— talked about — of all semantic roles.

(d) The subject position tends to be occupied by the most topical referent in the clause.

(e) In de-transitive clauses, a non-agent is more topical.

8.4.   THE SYNTAX OF DE-TRANSITIVE CLAUSES

8.4.1. Syntactic coding devices

Three major syntactic devices collaborate in making up the structure of de-transitive clauses:

(19) **Major syntactic devices used to code de-transitivity**
a. **The syntactic treatment of the non-topical agent**:
The extent to which the non-topical agent in the de-transitive clause is *demoted* down the grammatical case-hierarchy SUBJ > DO > IO, including downright *absence* from the passive clause.

b. **The syntactic treatment of the topical non-agent**:
The extent to which the topical non-agent is *promoted* up the case-hierarchy, including full promotion to subjecthood.

c. **The syntactic treatment of the de-transitive verb**:
The extent to which the de-transitive-clause verb retains grammatical features of the prototypical active-transitive verb, or conversely, acquires features of a stative-intransitive verb.

These three coding devices stand in an isomorphic relation to the three main functional components of de-transitive voice, respectively:

(a) agent suppression
(b) non-agent promotion
(c) verb stativization.

The syntactic structure of the various de-transitive constructions of English can be described in terms of the three syntactic devices outlined above. We will begin the discussion by outlining two extreme types.

8.4.2. Promotional vs. non-promotional de-transitives

In this section we will contrast the syntactic properties of two de-transitive constructions in English: (a) the promotional BE-passive ('canonical passive'), and (b) the impersonal-subject clause.

The three major syntactic features (19) most commonly associated with de-transitive clauses are not altogether independent of each other. Rather, they tend to exhibit strong associations, which may be expressed as follows:

(20) **Associations of the grammatical properties of de-transitive clauses**:
If (a) the topical non-agent is fully *promoted* to subjecthood, then
(b) the non-topical agent is *demoted*, either by being *absent* altogether or by being coded as *prepositional object* with 'by'; and
(c) the verb is coded as *stative* (and is also semantically stative); and further
(d) the range of non-agent roles that can become the subject of the de-transitive clause is severely restricted.

To illustrate the difference between the promotional BE-passive and the non-promotional impersonal subject construction, consider:

(21) a. **Active**:
        John discovered her body on the beach.
      b. **BE-passive (promotional)**:
        Her body **was** discover-**ed** on the beach (**by** John)
      c. **Impersonal subject (non-promotional)**:
        They found her body on the beach

In the promotional BE-passive (21b), all the grammatical properties listed in (20) are present: The non-agent topic is fully promoted to subjecthood; the agent is demoted, either by absence or by marking as a prepositional object; and the verb is marked by both the stative 'be' and perfect-participle-adjectival morphology. In the impersonal subject clause (21c), a *dummy* agent pronoun occupies the subject position and the actual agent is absent; the topical non-agent retains the same grammatical case-role as it had in the active-transitive clause (21a) (that is, it is *not* promoted); and the verb retains the same grammatical form as in the active clause. The only common structural thread running through both extreme types of de-transitivization is the demotion of the agent. One may thus consider agent demotion as the syntactic common denominator of de-transitivization.

The syntactic difference between the active (21a), the promotional BE-passive (21b), and the non-promotional impersonal-subject construction (21c) is represented in the treediagrams (22a,b,c) Respectively:

(22) a. **Active**:

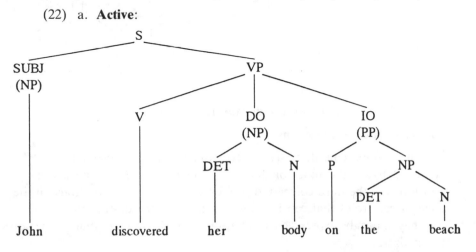

b. **Promotional BE-passive**:

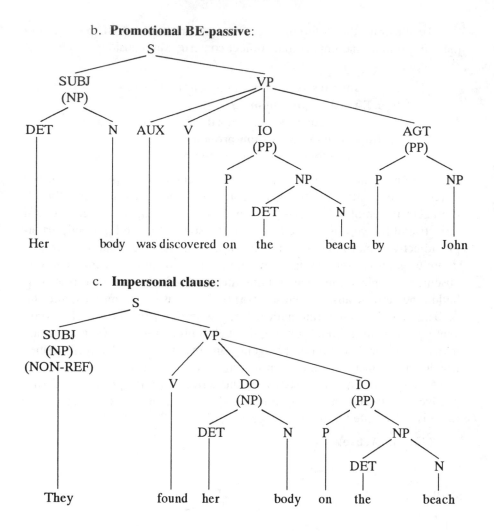

c. **Impersonal clause**:

8.4.3.   Case-role restrictions in de-transitivization

8.4.3.1. Case-role restrictions

The two extreme de-transitive types in English, the promotional BE-passive (21b) and the impersonal-subject construction (21c), contrast sharply in terms of the third correlated property (20d) — the restrictions on the range of case-roles that can become the topic of the de-transitive clause. This may in turn be expressed as a restriction on clause-types that can be de-transitivized.

In the promotional BE-passive (21b), the promotion of non-agents to full grammatical subjecthood is rigidly constrained to, primarily, either the patient or the dative-benefactive, and most commonly to the direct-object of the corresponding active clause. The promotional BE-passive is thus restricted to, primarily, active transitive clauses. As illustrations of this restriction, consider:

(23) a. **These shells** are found on the beach   (PAT, DO)
      b. **We** were told to cool it   (DAT, DO)
      c. **Mary** was given a new job   (DAT-BEN, DO)
      d. *__The new boss__ was worked for   (BEN, IO)
      e. *__The movie__ was gone to   (LOC, IO)
      f. *__The pen__ was written a letter with   (INSTR, IO)
      g. *__The kids__ were gone there with a lot   (ASSOC, IO)
      h. *__A pig__ was eaten like   (MANNER, IO)
      i. *__Real cheap__ can be lived here   (MANNER, ADV)

In contrast, the impersonal-subject construction (21c) has an unrestricted distribution in terms of either the case-role of its topical referent or clause-type. Thus compare:

(24) a. They find **these shells** on the beach   (PAT, DO)
      b. They told **us** to cool it   (DAT, DO)
      c. They gave **Mary** a new job   (DAT-BEN, DO)
      d. One works **for a new boss** now   (BEN, IO)
      e. One goes **to the movies** a lot here   (LOC, IO)
      f. You write letters **with a pen**   (INSTR, IO)
      g. You go there **with your kids**   (ASSOC, IO)
      h. One eats **like a pig** there   (MANNER, IO)
      i. You can live **real cheap** here   (MANNER, ADV)

8.4.3.2. Understanding promotional passives: Semantic vs. pragmatic case-marking

The syntactic treatment of the non-agent topic of the de-transitive clause, whether promotional or not, occupies a privileged status in the grammar of de-transitive voice. Among other things, this feature is responsible for the **functional bind** that arises from the promotion of a non-agent to the role of grammatical subject in the de-transitive clause. This functional bind arises from a simple fact about case-marking morphology in English: The grammatical subject (also the direct object) is morphologically *unmarked*, and thus does not code semantic case-role. The functional bind of promotional de-transitives may be now defined as follows:

(25) **Functional bind of promotional de-transitives**:
   a. If the non-agent topic of the de-transitive clause retains the same case-marking as it had in the corresponding active clause, and if that case-marking codes primarily *semantic* role (dative, benefactive, instrumental, associative, manner etc.), then the non-agent topic can not at the same time be also case-marked for its new pragmatic status as topic, i.e. as grammatical subject.
   b. Conversely, if the non-agent topic of the de-transitive clause is to be marked for its new *pragmatic* role as topic, i.e. as grammatical subject, then it cannot at the same time be also marked for its semantic role.

Given this dilemma, the promotional BE-passive in English represents one type of solution to the functional bind, i.e. (25a): it opts for marking the pragmatic role of the topic of the de-transitive clause. The various impersonal-subject constructions of English, on the other hand, represent the other solution (25b): they opt for marking the semantic role of the topic of the de-transitive clause.

One may now describe the strategy used by English hearers (or readers) in trying to decide the semantic case-role of the grammatical subject in active and BE-passive clauses as follows:

(26) **Semantic case-role assignment and voice**:
   a. If the verb is marked as *active*, then interpret the subject as *agent*;
   b. If the verb is marked as *passive*, then
      (i) interpret the subject as *patient* or *dative-benefactive* (pending on other considerations); and
      (ii) interpret the prepositional object marked with 'by', if present, as the *agent*.

8.4.3.3. Exceptions that reaffirm the rule

The restrictions on clause-type or case-role observed in the promotional BE-passive (23) may be now viewed as part of a **compensatory strat-**

egy designed to cope with the potential for **semantic-role confusion**. In English, the topic-subject of the promotional BE-passive is usually the direct object of the corresponding active clause. This assures that the interpretation of the semantic role of the subject of the BE-passive clause is mainly that of a *patient*, the prototypical direct-object of the active clause. The general restriction, for the moment disregarding exceptions, is then:

(27) "Only the direct object of the corresponding active can
be made the subject of the promotional BE-passive".

The relatively few exceptions to restriction (27) involve mostly *dative-benefactive* objects of a small set of verbs. These exceptions are easily understood in terms of the high **semantic specificity** of these verbs (most commonly 'give', 'show', 'tell', 'bring', 'send' and 'teach'). As noted in chapter 3, these verbs most commonly have their dative-benefactive participant as direct object. That is, in actual text the variant (28b) is preferred overwhelmingly over (28a):

(28) a. **Patient DO**:
      She gave **the book** to him
   b. **Dative DO**:
      She gave **him** the book

As we shall see directly below, there is a close parallel in English between restrictions on the promotion of a non-patient participant to direct-object ('dative-shifting'), as in (28b), and the promotion of such a participant to subject of the BE passive. But be that as it may, the fact that the direct-object-only restriction (27) is relaxed only when the semantics of the verb guarantees role transparency, reinforces the view that restriction (27) is in essence a compensatory strategy, designed to avoid semantic role-confusion.

To illustrate the interaction between restrictions on the BE-passive and semantic-role confusion, consider first:

(29) a. He gave the book **to her**   (DAT = IO)
   b. He gave **her** a book   (DAT = DO)
   c. **She** was given a book   (DAT = SUBJ-OF-PASS)

(30) a. She showed the house **to us**   (DAT = IO)
   b. She showed **us** the house   (DAT = DO)
   c. **We** were shown two houses   (DAT = SUBJ-OF-PASS)

(31) a. He told the story **to her**   (DAT = IO)
     b. He told **her** the story   (DAT = DO)
     c. **She** was told the story   (DAT = SUBJ-OF-PASS)

The verbs 'give', 'show' and 'tell' tend to select a *human dative* and a *non-human patient*. Promoting the dative to direct-object of the active, or to subject of the BE-passive, creates no case-role confusion; the human argument — whether DO, IO or subject-of-passive — is interpreted as a dative.

Consider next the verb 'send' whose non-patient object could be either a human *dative* or a non-human *location*. When the patient is non-human and the other object a human-dative, 'send' mimics the behavior of 'give', 'show' and 'tell':

(32) a. We sent the book **to John**   (DAT = IO)
     b. We sent **him** a book   (DAT = DO)
     c. **He** was sent two books last week   (DAT = SUBJ-OF-PASS)

On the other hand, when the patient and non-patient objects are *both* human, restrictions begin to appear:

(33) a. We sent the girl **to John**
     b. We sent **him** the girl
     c. ?**He** was sent two girls

And the restrictions are even more rigid when both objects of 'send' are non-human:

(34) a. We sent the book **to the store**
     b. *We sent **it/the store** a book
     c. ***It/the store** was sent two books

It appears then that only a human-dative goal can be promoted to the more topical grammatical roles of direct-object and subject. And further, the more similar the two objects are semantically, the less likely it is that the goal argument be promoted to direct-object or subject.

A similar pattern may be seen with the verb 'bring', whose goal argument can again be either a human *recipient* or a non-human *location*. When the two objects are well differentiated semantically — human dative vs. non-human patient — restrictions are minimal:

(35) a. We brought the book **to John**
     b. We brought **him** the book
     c. **He** was brought two books

Restrictions begin to appear when both objects are human:

(36) a. We brought the boy **to Mary**
     b. We brought **her** the boy
     c. ?**She** was brought two boys

And the restrictions are maximal when both objects are non-human:

(37) a. We brought the boy **to the playground**
     b. *We brought **the playground** the/a boy
     c. ***It/the playground** was brought two boys

The restrictions are more stringent when the dative-benefactive participant is only optional, i.e. is not part of the conventional semantic frame of the verb. To illustrate this, consider first transitive verbs that require an animate patient:

(38) a. He cured the cat **for her**   (BEN = IO)
     b. *He cured *her* the cat   (*BEN = DO)
     c. ***She** was cured a cat   (*BEN = SUBJ-OF-PASS)

(39) a. He washed the floor **for her**
     e. *He washed **her** the floor
     d. ***She** was washed a floor

Neither 'cure' nor 'wash' require a benefactive participant. Both are inherently transitive rather than bi-transitive. Further, in both verbs a human benefactive may easily be confused with the animate patient. Promoting the human benefactive to either direct-object or subject-of-passive is thus problematic, since its semantic role would be hard to compute.

Consider now transitive verbs that take typically an inanimate patient:

(40) a. He cooked a steak **for her**   (BEN = IO)
     b. He cooked **her** a steak   (BEN = DO)
     c. ***She** was cooked a steak   (*BEN = SUBJ-OF-PASS)

(41) a. He built a house **for her**   (BEN = IO)
     b. He built **her** a house   (BEN = DO)
     c. ***She** was built a house   (*BEN = SUBJ-OF-PASS)

Neither 'cure' nor 'wash' require a benefactive participant. Both are inherently transitive rather than bi-transitive. Further, in both verbs a human to direct object would create no semantic confusion here. Nevertheless, proceeding to promote the benefactive to the subject-of-passive is apparently too much of a processing burden, perhaps because of either the gruesome reading implicit in (40c) or the total nonsensical interpretation of (41c) — if the subjects were to be interpreted as *patients*.

A number of intransitive verbs typically take a benefactive object. In some, the verb-preposition combination has become at least partly idiomatic. When the idiomatic sense is used, promotion of the indirect object to subject-of-passive is allowed. When the non-idiomatic sense is used, it is not. Thus consider:

(42) **Idiomatic**:
    a. They cared **for her** well during her last year
    b. **She** was well cared **for** during her last year

(43) **Non-idiomatic**:
    a. John cared **for her** deeply
    b. ***She** was (deeply) cared **for** (by John)

One may explain the contrasting behavior of the idiomatic vs. non-idiomatic sense by noting that idiomatic verb-preposition combinations, as in (42), are perceived as *single lexical items*, so that the object acquires properties of a *direct* object. In contrast, the object of 'for' in (43) is an indirect object, and thus abides by the general restriction (27) which bars indirect objects from becoming subjects-of-passive.

Consider next the case of transitive verbs with an optional *instrumental* argument. As either direct object or subject-of-passive, the typically inanimate instrumental could have been equally well interpreted as the *patient* of these verbs. Consequently, neither promotion seems natural:

(44) a. John typed the letter **with the typewriter**
    b. *John typed **the typewriter** a letter **with**
    c. ***The typewriter** was typed a letter **with**

On the other hand, if the verb is used as intransitive with only an instrumental object, and has no competing patient direct-object, passivization seems more natural:

(45) a. John typed **with the typewriter**
    b. **The typewriter** was typed **with**

Likewise, when the verb and preposition form an idiomatic combination, passivization is less problematic, as in:

(46) a. They tampered **with the lock**
    b. **The lock** was tampered **with**

Consider next bi-transitive verbs with an obligatory *locative* indirect object. The inanimate locative — if promoted to either direct-object or subject-of-passive — could be confused with the inanimate patient. For this reason perhaps, neither promotion is natural:

(47) a. Mary put the knife **in the box**   (LOC = IO)
     b. *Mary put **the box** a knife **in**   (*LOC = DO)
     c. ***The box** was put a knife **in**   (*LOC = SUBJ-OF-PASS)

At least for some intransitive verbs with no patient that could be confused with the inanimate locative, passivization seems more natural, as in:

(48) a. Mary slept **in the bed**
     b. **The bed** was slept **in**
     c. They lived **in the house**
     d. **The house** seemed lived **in**

However, it may well be that the naturalness of the passives (48b,d) may be due to the fact that a bed and a house in such expressions are in some way *affected* by the sleeping or living, that is are patient-like. Thus compare:[14]

(49) a. Many people slept **in the street**
     b. ***The street** was slept **in**
     c. They lived **in Rome**
     d. ***Rome** appeared lived **in**

Consider finally the group of bi-transitive verbs that allow two alternant forms, one with a *locative* indirect object, the other with an *instrumental*, as in respectively:[15]

(50) a. They loaded the potatoes **on the truck**
     b. They loaded the truck **with potatoes**

Passivization of either variant is unproblematic, since either the instrumental (50a) or the locative (50b) is the direct object of the clause. Thus, respectively:

(51) a. **The potatoes** were loaded **on** the truck
     b. **The truck** was loaded **with** potatoes

In sum, the direct-object-only restriction on passivization (27) is relaxed in contexts where assignment of semantic roles is more transparent, given the conventional semantic frame of the verbs. This reinforces the idea that restriction (27) is motivated by considerations of semantic role transparency and the need to prevent role confusion.

As a final illustration of how the foregoing dispensing with the restrictions on passivization may lead to difficulties in interpreting a passive clause — or at the very least to a double-take reaction — consider the following passage from a high-brow editorial essay:[16]

> (52) "...**A considerable respect is owed the reality** that none of us has any substantial knowledge whatever, or any experience, of how to turn a command economy into a free one..."

The corresponding active clause from which such a passive would have been derived is presumably:

> (53) One/we owe(s) considerable respect *to* the reality...

Three features of this 'active' construction make it an unlikely source for passivization in English: (a) the indirect object of the active ('reality') is not a human dative-benefactive; (b) The object of the active is *indirect*; and (c) The active construction is *impersonal* to begin with. All three factors make (53) a rather atypical transitive clause, thus a rather poor candidate for de-transitivization.

The tendency to extend the scope of passivization toward verbs that are semantically stative but syntactically transitive, thus technically having a direct object, is apparent in example (54) below, taken from the more low-brow writing in the sports section:[17]

> (54) "...**The Braves were cost a run** on a poor throw to home plate in the third inning by left fielder Lonnie Smith. **They were cost another run** when Mark Lemke was thrown out at third base with none out in the fourth while trying to stretch a two-base error into a three-base miscue..."

8.5. OTHER DE-TRANSITIVE CONSTRUCTIONS

8.5.1. Preamble

In addition to the promotional BE-passive, English has several other de-transitive constructions whose functional definition overlaps, at least to some degree, with that of the BE-passive. Like the BE-passive, some of these de-transitives seem to apply primarily to semantically-transitive verbs. Many also seem to share the main pragmatic properties of the BE-passive: (a) topicalizing the patient, and (b) demoting the agent. While partially overlapping with it, these de-transitives diverge from the BE-passive either syntactically, semantically or pragmatically. In this section we discuss three types of de-transitive constructions:

(a) the GET-passive
(b) the impersonal-subject clauses
(c) middle-voice constructions

8.5.2. The GET-passive

8.5.2.1. Historical development

Compared to the BE-passive, the GET-passive is a relatively recent addition to the syntactic arsenal of English. Nonetheless, its relatively recent emergence owes much to a protracted series of gradual changes that can be traced back all the way to Chaucerian Middle English. The first set of changes involved the move from the original active-transitive sense of 'get' — 'obtain' — to a **bi-transitive locative** usage, where the patient is **caused-to-move** to a location. This early development may be represented schematically as:[18]

(55) a. **Externalizing the implicit self-beneficiary**:
He got a horse ===>
He got a horse **for himself**
b. **Extending self-beneficiary to other-beneficiary**:
He got a horse **for himself** ===>
He got a horse **for her**
c. **Making the beneficiary a directional-locative object**:
He got a horse **for her** ===>
He got the horse **to her**
d. **Extending the directional-locative to non-human goals**:
He got the horse **to her** ===>
He got the horse **to the barn**

In the next set of changes, the non-verbal prepositional-locative complement, as in (55d), was extended to active verbal complement, winding up with a **causative** construction followed by a verbal complement. This may be represented schematically as:

(56)   a. **From locative object to verbal locative complement**:
He got her **into the house** ===>
He got her **to go into the house**
    b. **From verb + locative-object to locative verb alone**:
He got her **to go into the house** ===>
He got her **to go**
    c. **From causative-locative verb to unrestricted causative**:
He got her **to go** ===>

He got her $\left\{ \begin{array}{l} \textbf{to leave} \\ \textbf{to stay} \\ \textbf{to work} \\ \textbf{to kill the goat} \end{array} \right\}$

The next set of changes involves first the extension of the causative construction, from active verbal complement to a **BE-passive** verbal complement, then the use of a **reflexive** version of that construction, and finally a re-analysis of the reflexive as an **inchoative-intransitive** clause. This may be represented as, schematically:

(57)   a. **From causative with BE-passive complement**
to REFL-causative with BE-passive:
She got him **to be admitted** ===>
She got **herself to be admitted**
    b. **From reflexive-causative to intransitive-inchoative**:
She got **herself to be admitted** ===>
She got **to be admitted**
    c. **Morphological simplification into GET-passive**:
She got **to be admitted** ===>
She got **admitted**

The full-fledged GET-passive (57c) begins to appear in written English toward the end of the 18th Century, although one suspects that it had existed in the colloquial much earlier.[19]

8.5.2.2. Agentivity, intent and control

Syntactically, the GET-passive is at first glance deceptively similar to the BE-passive. In both, the patient is fully promoted to grammatical subjecthood. In both, the demoted agent either does not appear at all, or else appears as a prepositional object with 'by'. In both, the verb is morphologically marked by the same perfect-participle form. Only the auxiliary verb — 'be' vs. 'get' — seems to differentiate the two constructions. But the syntactic — and pragmatic — similarity between the two constructions masks profound semantic differences, ones that are partially accounted for by the different diachronic history of the two constructions.

A major difference between the BE- and GET-passive involves the matter of control or intent, the very core transitivity feature of **agentivity**. In the BE-passive, the demoted agent — even when absent — is vested with purpose and control over event. In the GET-passive, it is the promoted patient that retains agentive control. This may be seen from the interpretation of purpose adverbs, as in:

(58) a. **BE-passive**:
John **was** shot by Mary *deliberately*
    (> Mary acted deliberately)
    (*> John acted deliberately)
  b. **GET-passive**:
John **got** shot by Mary *deliberately*
    (> John acted deliberately)
    (*> Mary acted deliberately)

The differential assignment of purpose — and responsibility — also explains the difference between the two passives in examples such as (following Lakoff, 1971):

(59) a. Criminals must $\left\{ \begin{array}{l} \textbf{get} \\ \textbf{?be} \end{array} \right\}$ arrested *to prove their machismo*

  b. Criminals must $\left\{ \begin{array}{l} \textbf{be} \\ \textbf{?get} \end{array} \right\}$ arrested *to keep the streets safe*

It likewise explains the differences between the BE- and GET-passive in (after Lakoff, 1971):[20]

(60) a. Mary **was** shot on purpose, the bastards!
  b. *Mary **got** shot on purpose, the bastards!

The use of other intent-related adverbs of manner also reveals similar differences:

(61) a. Six students **were** beaten savagely
  b. *Six students **got** beaten savagely

And this in turn correlates with the difference in the interpretation of manner questions, as in:[21]

(62) a. How **was** he killed?
          (> What did *someone* do to kill him?)
     b. How did he **get** killed?
          (> What did *he* do to get killed?)
     c. How **was** he caught?
          (> How did *they* catch him?)
     d. How did he **get** caught?
          (> How did *he* let them catch him?)

In (62b,d), the inference is that the subject of the GET-passive is somehow responsible for his own misfortune. In (62a,c) there seems to be no such inference about the subject of the BE-passive.

The active-agentive character of the GET-passive is also seen in the fact that, in contrast with the more stative BE-passive, it can be embedded under command verbs, as in:

(63) a. They told him to **get** fired
     b. *They told him to **be** fired

The agentive nature of the patient-subject of the GET-passive is of course a direct result of its relatively recent evolution out of a reflexive form of an active-agentive construction. In contrast, the BE-passive, which historically arose from a stative adjectival-resultative construction, retains more stative characteristics to this day.[22]

8.5.2.3. Human patient-subject

If intent, control and responsibility are vested in the patient-subject of the GET-passive, it is only natural to find a strong preference here for human subjects. Many examples seem to suggest just that, as in (from Lakoff, 1971):

(64) a. A house can **be** built of stone, brick or clay.
     b. *A house can **get** built of stone, brick or clay.

The GET-passive in fact seems odd even with a human subject when the resulting construction implies no intent or control on the part of the patient-subject:

(65) a. She **was** found wandering on the beach
     b. *She **got** found wandering on the beach

The preference for human subject in the GET-passive, as compared to the BE-passive, has been documented in a recent distributional study of spoken English. The results of this study may be summarized as follows:[23]

(66) **Distribution of human and non-human subjects in BE- and GET-passives**
(after Herold, 1986)

subject type	BE-passive		GET-passive	
	N	%	N	%
human	240	**54%**	124	**89%**
non-human	205	46%	16	11%
total:	445	100%	140	100%

While the subjects of BE-passives divide roughly equally between human and non-human ones, the GET-passive shows a lopsided 9:1 preference for human subjects.

8.5.2.4. Involvement and adversity

In spite of the strong preference for human subjects, inanimate subjects do crop up in GET-passives. However, the conditions under which they appear suggest a natural extension of the notion of **responsibility** towards other manners of human **involvement**. Thus, Lakoff (1971) has observed that when the subject of the GET-passive is inanimate, therefore incapable of responsibility, *some* human associated with the subject, or with the event in some other capacity, may either retain responsibility, be emotionally involved, or adversely affected. This involved human need not be the subject, and is often its possessor, as in (Lakoff, 1971):

(67) a. My cache of marijuana **got** found by Fido, the police dog
          (> I was remiss)
      b. My cache of marijuana **was** found by Fido, the police dog
          (> Fido was smart)

The involvement, and in this case responsibility, may in fact be vested in the *hearer*, as in (Lakoff, 1971):

(68) a. How did this window **get** opened?
          (> I'm holding *you* responsible)
      b. How **was** this window opened?
          (> *whoever* is responsible)

And similarly:[24]

> (69) a. Did that letter **get** mailed today?
>   (> Did *you* take care of it?)
>   b. **Was** that letter mailed today?
>   (> Did *anybody* take care of it?)

The strong tendency to use the GET-passive in spoken English as an **adversive** construction, i.e. with the inference that the patient-subject was adversely affected by the event, has also been documented in a text-distribution study of spoken English. The results are summarized in:[25]

(70) **Distribution of the adversive sense
      in the BE- and GET-passives**
      (after Herold, 1986)

sense of passive	BE		GET	
	N	%	N	%
adversive	95	**40%**	98	**82%**
neutral	143	60%	21	18%
total:	238	100%	119	100%

While only 40% of the BE-passives in the sample involved an adversive use, fully 82% of the GET-passives involved such use.

8.5.2.5. Register and social class

The GET-passive, being a relatively recent construction in written English, is still found primarily in the spoken register. This is confirmed by its frequency distribution in the spoken register of working vs. upper class American speakers. A summary of the distribution is given in:[26]

(71) **Distribution of the BE- and GET-passive
      according to social class**
      (after Herold, 1986)

passive type	social class				total
	working		upper		
	N	%	N	%	
GET-passive	89	**49%**	30	**17%**	119
BE-passive	91	51%	147	83%	238
total	180	100%	177	100%	357

It is in general true that the language of educated middle and upper class speakers, even in their spoken register, departs more sharply from the colloquial register. The fact that the GET-passive comprises roughly 50% of the total passive usage of working-class speakers, as against only 17% in upper class speech, underscores the relatively recent emergence of the GET-passive, and its lingering confinement to the informal colloquial register.

8.5.3. Impersonal-subject clauses

8.5.3.1. Non-referring subject pronouns

The most common impersonal-subject constructions in English involve either the subject pronoun 'one', 'you' or 'they'. The subject pronouns are considered **impersonal** in the sense that in this construction they do not refer to any particular entity. Thus, examples (72a,c,e) below represent the referring use of these pronouns, while examples (72b,d,f) represent the impersonal-subject construction with a non-referring use of the same pronouns:

(72) a. **REF**:   There were three guys sitting there,
               and **one** offered her his seat.
      b. **NON-REF:** **One** always offers **one**'s seat to a lady.
      c. **REF**:   The boss says **you** can start tomorrow.
      d. **NON-REF**: When **you** start, they usually tell **you**...
      e. **REF**:   I asked them, and **they** told me to keep going.
      f. **NON-REF**: He disappeared on Saturday, and a week later
               they found his body downstream near the...

8.5.3.2. Pragmatic demotion and promotion

We noted earlier that impersonal subject clauses share with the BE-passive the pragmatic feature of agent suppression — in this case more broadly **subject suppression**. It is not clear, however, whether and to what extent promotion to topicality of some remaining non-subject is associated with these constructions.[27]

8.5.3.3. Intent and control

Impersonal-subject clauses are clearly agentive, as long as the verb used is an active verb. As in the BE-passive (but unlike the GET-passive), intent, control and responsibility are vested here in the suppressed *agent* of the clause. To illustrate this, compare the interpretation of adverbs of intent used with the three de-transitive constructions:

(73) a. **BE-passive**:
          The stray dogs were shot *deliberately*
              (> Whoever shot them acted deliberately)
      b. **GET-passive**:
          John got shot *deliberately*
              (> John acted deliberately)
      c. **Impersonal**:
          They shoot stray dogs *deliberately* around here.
              (> 'They' do that deliberately)

Likewise, compare the interpretation of 'accidentally':

(74) a. **BE-passive**:
          The stray dogs were shot *accidentally*
              (> *Whoever* shot them did not mean to do it)
      b. **GET-passive**:
          John got shot *accidentally*
              (> *He* may not have expected the outcome,
                  but is still somehow responsible).
      c. **Impersonal**:
          They sometimes shoot stray dogs *accidentally*
              (> 'They' do it without intending to)

8.5.3.4. Semantically-active status

Impersonal-subject clauses in English are not semantically stative. In this way, they resemble the GET-passive but differ from the BE-passive. This is evident from the wide semantic range of active verbs that can fit in an impersonal clause (see 8.5.3.6.2. below), as well as from the use of adverbs of intent (see (73) above).

8.5.3.5. The distribution of impersonal-subject clauses

8.5.3.6.1. Modality

There are three dimensions along which the three impersonal-subject pronouns in English seem to differ. The first dimension is semantic, and has to do with the *modality* of the event. Both the impersonal pronouns 'one' and 'you' seem to be used with a habitual-irrealis modality, whereby no specific event is referred to, but only a habitual or customary event. In contrast, the impersonal 'they' can also cover specific events that occurred at some real past time, and are thus cast in the realis, perfective-preterite mode. Thus, compare:

(75) a. **Irrealis**:   **One** eats well there **usually**
      b. **Realis**:   ?**One** ate well there **on our last trip.**
      c. **Irrealis**:   **You** eat well there **usually**
      d. **Realis**:   ?**You** ate well there **on our last trip**.
      e. **Irrealis**:   **They** shoot stray dogs there **all the time**
      f. **Realis**:   **They** shot my pet goat **yesterday**

8.5.3.6.2. Transitivity

Unlike the BE-passive, impersonal-subject clauses in English are not restricted by verb-type. They can be formed with active or stative, transitive or intransitive verbs. This is of course a direct consequence of the fact that the topical non-agent is not promoted syntactically, and thus retains the same morphology and syntactic position as in the active clause. Its semantic role thus remains as obvious as it is in the active clause. In principle, it seems, any clause-type may be used with an impersonal subject, as in:

(76) a. **Active-transitive**:
          One does such a thing at **one**'s peril.
      b. **Stative**:
          "...Then **one** is invulnerable..."[28]
      c. **Passive**:
          One is not expected to move fast.
      d. **Active-transitive**:
          When **you** buy a house there, **you** often find out later...
      e. **Intransitive**:
          You don't sleep on the job here.
      f. **Passive**:
          Nowadays **you** are expected to carry **your** own weight.
      g. **Active-transitive**:
          They shoot horses, don't they?
      h. **Intransitive**:
          They sure live well around here.

It is not clear, however, whether 'they' in intransitive expressions such as (76h) is interpreted as a non-referring ('impersonal') pronoun, rather than a simple anaphoric one.

8.5.3.6.3. Register

Another dimension along which the three impersonal pronouns vary has to do with **social register**. The use of both 'you' and 'they' tends toward the colloquial informal register. In contrast, the impersonal 'one' — at least in American English — is more characteristic of educated, academic, written or formal styles. This tendency is not always easy to pin down. Thus, for example, in the following passage from a detective novel, the impersonal 'you' and 'one' alternate:[29]

> (77) "...It would be unreasonable to fear that. I am not so unreasonable. Once **you** have lost the fear of death — absolutely lost it — then all the other fears are meaningless. Nothing can touch **you**. All that is necessary is to keep the means of death to hand. Then **one** is invulnerable..."

In another example from the same author, an exaggerated use of detransitive voice and a plethora of 'one's seem to aim at depicting the speaker as prissy or pretentious:[30]

> (78) "..."If there's any swimming to be done, my dear Adam, **one** must leave it to you. **One** has **one**'s asthma, alas". He gave Dalgliesh a sly elliptical glance, and added deprecatingly, "Also, **one** cannot swim"..."

8.5.4. Middle-voice constructions

8.5.4.1. Preamble

Jespersen (1924) treats the category middle-voice as a highly language-specific one, and at first blush his denial of its universality seems to apply to English:

> "...On the "middle voice" as found, for instance, in Greek there is no necessity to say much here, as it has no *separate notional character* of its own: sometime it is purely reflexive, i.e. denotes identity of subject and (unexpressed) object, sometimes a vaguer reference to the subject, sometimes it is purely passive and sometime scarcely to be distinguished from the ordinary active..." (1924, p. 168; emphases added)

While in some way perceptive, Jespersen's denial of the coherence of mid-dle-voice as a notional category has probably a lot to do with its incoher-ence as a *grammatical* category. Still, there are a few coherent things that can be said about middle-voice constructions, provided one accepts two fundamental facts about them:

(a) They are most likely to involve a *family* of constructions.
(b) They are often a *transitional diachronic* phenomenon, rather than stable synchronic one.[31]

In this section we will survey a number of middle-voice constructions, defining them by the following cluster of criteria:

(79) **Criteria for inclusion in middle-voice**:
    a. The verb involved is inherently a *transitive* verb.
    b. The grammatical subject is a *patient*.
    c. There is no clearly discernible *responsible agent*, and thus no *action*.
    d. While a discernible agent is absent, the construction is *not* used primarily as an *agent-demoting* device.

Criterion (79a) separates middle-voice constructions from prototypical predicate adjective clauses. Criterion (79b) separates them from imper-sonal-subject constructions. Criterion (79c) separates them from both the promotional BE-passive and the prototypical reflexive (see below). Crite-rion (79d) separates them from both the BE-passive and impersonal-subject constructions.

8.5.4.2. Reflexive-GET middle voice

It is not entirely an accident that the de-transitive construction closest to the middle-voice definition is the GET-passive. This is because the his-torical evolution that gave rise to the GET-passive — from a transitive-causative, through its reflexive, and on to an intransitive ('inchoative') product of that reflexive — typically gives rise to middle-voice constructions. In English, two other GET-marked constructions travelled this route in very much the same sequence of steps, one prior to the GET-passive, one later. The relevant portion of the parallel steps may be given schematically as:[32]

(80) **GET-locative** (earliest)
    a. **Causative**:   He got **her** into the house
    b. **Reflexive**:   He got **himself** into the house
    c. **Intransitive**: He got into the house

(81) **GET-passive** (later)
   a. **Causative**:   He got **her** rescued
   b. **Reflexive**:   He got **himself** rescued
   c. **Intransitive**: He got rescued
(82) **GET-adjective** (latest)
   a. **Causative**:   He got **her** ready
   b. **Reflexive**:   He got **himself** ready
   c. **Intransitive**: He got ready

Given our criteria (79), the intransitives (80c), (81c) and (82c) can all be considered middle-voice. And in many current usages, the reflexives (80b), (81b) and (82b) are semantically nearly indistinguishable from their corresponding intransitives.[33]

8.5.4.3. Non-agentive middle-voice

In this section we survey four middle-voice constructions that abide by definition (79):

(83) **Non-agentive middle-voice**
   a. **Middle-voice intransitive**:
      The glass **broke**
   b. **Adjectival-lexical passive**:
      The glass was **broken**
   c. **Potential adjective**:
      This glass is **breakable**
   d. **Potential middle**:
      This glass **breaks** real easy
   e. **Corresponding active**:
      She **broke** the glass

Of these four middle-voice constructions, one — (83a) — in fact depicts an event, but with no agent. And like the other three, it rejects the overt mention of an agent. That is:

(84) a. *The window broke **by John**
   b. *His steak was well-done **by Mary**
   c. *Mary was visible **by John**
   d. *The book reads real easy **by everybody**

In using the potential adjective (83c), one may mention overtly a potential agent, at least in some cases:

(85) a. Mary was visible **to John**
    b. ?The book is readable **to any intelligent person**
    c. ?This code may be decipherable **to anybody**

It is not clear, however, whether 'John' in (85a) is the subject of a particular event of seeing, rather than a potential subject of a potential event.

In the case of the middle-voice variant (83d), an overt agent is impossible, regardless of the referentiality of the agent or specificity of the event:

(86) a. *The book read(s) real easy **to John**
    b. *The book read(s) easy **to anybody**

8.5.4.4. Syntactic, lexical and perfect passive

The English BE-passive arose historically from an adjectival construction. In such a construction, 'be' is the main verb, followed by a predicate adjective that is the **perfect-participle** product of a transitive verb. The original usage of this construction survives to this day, as in the **adjectival-lexical passive** in (83b). Another usage that survives to this day is the **perfect passive**, which was probably an intermediate step in the transition from the adjectival-lexical to the promotional BE-passive. The three constructions, in their historical order, are illustrated in:

(87) a. **Adjectival-lexical passive**:
    (They looked carefully, and indeed)
    The window **was broken**
        (> It was *in a broken state*)
    b. **Perfect passive**:
    (Then they discovered that)
    The window **had been broken**
        (> Someone *had broken* the window)
    c. **Promotional BE-passive**:
    The window **was broken** at three o'clock
        (> Someone *broke* the window)

Constructions (87a,b,c) diverge gradually in their pragmatic perspective on the event. The adjectival-lexical passive (87a) depicts a state, with no hint of either some past event or a responsible agent. The perfect passive (87b) displays a stative perspective that is clearly the result of some past event. Finally, the promotional BE-passive (87c), while sharing the resultative perspective of the perfect passive, depicts an event much more explicitly, though still an event with a pragmatically-suppressed agent.

8.6.   THE ANTIPASSIVE VOICE

8.6.1. Pragmatic dimensions

The passive and the antipassive voices constitute the two extreme cases in the pragmatics of de-transitivization. They each contrast with the active-transitive in pragmatically suppressing one argument of the prototypical transitive clause. In the passive, the suppressed (non-topical) argument is the agent. In the antipassive it is the patient. The relationship between the three pragmatic voices may be given schematically as:[34]

(88) **Relative topicality of agent and patient in the
      active, passive and antipassive voice:**

voice	topicality gradient	pragmatically suppressed
active	AGENT > PATIENT	/
passive	PATIENT >> AGENT	AGENT
antipassive	AGENT >> PATIENT	PATIENT

8.6.2. The syntax of patient demotion

There is not a single construction in English that can be labeled 'the' antipassive. Nevertheless, the antipassive pragmatic function is alive and well. And the various syntactic means by which the patient is demoted in the antipassive clause are far from arbitrary. To some extent, in fact, they are reminiscent of the syntactic means used in demoting the agent in the passive-like constructions. Some of these syntactic means also have the overall effect of making the antipassive resemble, syntactically, an intransitive clause.

The most common, and clearly iconic, device for demoting the object in the antipassive is **deletion**. This effectively renders the clause objectless, thus syntactically intransitive. In English, this device is used when the object is generic, predictable, habitual or conventionalized. As illustrations, consider:

(89) **Antipassive by object deletion**:
     a. **Active**:   Mary ate **the apple**
     b. **Antipassive**: Mary ate (in a hurry)
                     (> object = food)
     c. **Active**:   John drank **a cup of coffee**
     d. **Antipassive**: John drinks (heavily)
                     (> object = alcohol)
     e. **Active**:   Mary taught **English**
     f. **Antipassive**: Mary teaches (for a living)
                     (> object = some subject matter)

Another common device — again transparently iconic — for demoting the patient is **object incorporation**. Here the patient-object of the transitive clause is incorporated into the verbal word in the antipassive clause. This again renders the clause objectless, thus syntactically intransitive. As illustrations, consider the paired active and antipassive expressions in (90) below; the object may be referring in the active, but is always non-referring (and non-topical) in the antipassive:

(90) **Antipassive by object incorporation**:
     a. **Active**:   They hunted **the deer**
     b. **Antipassive**: They went **deer**-hunting
                     (> object = deer in general)
     c. **Active**:   He disposed of **the garbage**
     d. **Antipassive**: He works at **garbage**-disposal
                     (> object = garbage in general)
     e. **Active**:   She sold **the books**
     f. **Antipassive**: She is a **book**-seller
                     (> object = books in general)

A strong feature of object incorporation in English is that it tends to involve **nominalized** verb phrases. Thus compare the antipassives in (90b,d,f) above with the rather infelicitous (though perfectly interpretable) finite versions:

(91) a. ?They **deer**-hunt every spring
      b. *He **garbage**-disposes for a living
      c. *She **book**-sells

A similar pre-verbal incorporation of constituents, probably under similar pragmatic conditions, involves *manner adverbs* and *instrumental objects*. These two case-roles are typically non-referring and non-topical, so that their association with an antipassive device is not surprising. As illustrations, compare:

(92) **Manner or instrument incorporation**:
    a. **Active**:   He fished **with a fly-rod**
    b. **Antipassive**: He went **fly**-fishing
    c. **Active**:   She stitched the blanket **cross-wise**
    d. **Antipassive**: She did a lot of **cross**-stitching

8.6.3. Semantic dimensions of antipassives

8.6.3.1. Preamble

Some ways of marking the antipassive voice in English are not, strictly speaking, syntactic. Rather, they can be understood in terms of two important clauses in the semantic definition of the prototypical transitive event:[35]

    (a) A transitive event must have a **salient patient**; and
    (b) a transitive event must be cast in the **realis modality**,
        i.e. be a real, **salient event**.

In this section we will survey antipassive devices that involve, in one way or another, tampering with these two features of the prototype of transitive event.

8.6.3.2. Plural objects

A common way of coding a demoted, non-topical patient is to code it as **un-individuated** — i.e. **plural object**. Most commonly, pluralization has the predictable effect of rendering the object non-referring and non-topical.[36] This is illustrated in:

(93) **Antipassives with un-individuated patients**:
    a. **Active**:   She read **the book**
    b. **Antipassive**: She used to read **books**
    c. **Active**:   He loved **this woman**
    d. **Antipassive**: He loves **women**

8.6.3.3. Non-referring objects

Another device used to mark the demoted patient in the antipassive voice is to mark it as **non-referring**, through appropriate articles. Thus consider:[37]

(94) **Antipassive with non-referring patients**:
   a. **Active**:   He wanted to buy **the magazine**
   b. **Antipassive**: He wanted to buy **a magazine**
   c. **Antipassive**: He wanted to buy **any magazine**
                       that could be found there

8.6.3.4. Antipassive voice and non-fact modalities

There is a strong frequency associated between plural and/or non-referring objects and the use of **non-fact modalities** — **habitual**, **negative** or **irrealis** — in antipassive clauses. Consider:

(95) **Antipassive with non-fact modalities**:
   a. **Active**:
      He **read** a terrific book
   b. **Antipassive-habitual**:
      He constantly **reads** books
   c. **Antipassive-negative**:
      John **never** read a book in his life
   d. **Antipassive/irrealis**:
      John **would rather** read a book

The naturalness of semantic antipassives such as (93), (94) and (95) can be understood in terms of the semantic definition of the prototypical transitive event (1). Pluralization and non-referentiality go against the prototype of a **salient object** (1b). And a non-fact modality goes against the prototype of **real event** (1c). In the antipassive voice, this decrease in the semantic saliency of the patient tends to go hand in hand with the pragmatic decrease of its topicality.

8.7.   RECIPROCAL CONSTRUCTIONS

8.7.1. General definition

Like the promotional BE-passive, the reciprocal construction applies primarily to transitive clauses containing a direct object. Some relaxation of this constraint is possible, so that one finds reciprocals of some intransitive clauses with indirect objects.

The most general definition of the reciprocal clause may be given as follows:

(96) **Definition of the reciprocal clause**:
   a. **Semantic**:
   Two like events occur, with the subject of
   one being the object of the other, and vice
   versa. The two participants thus *act upon*
   each other reciprocally.
   b. **Syntactic**:
   The two events are coded as a single clause
   with a conjoined (or plural) subject. The
   object of that clause is expressed as the reciprocal pronoun 'each other'.

8.7.2. Semantic features

As an illustration of the relation between conjoined simple event
clauses and their reciprocal counterparts consider:

(97) **Direct-object relation (transitive)**:
   a. **Conjoined simple clauses**:
   The woman saw **the child**
      and the child saw **the woman**
   b. **Corresponding reciprocal**:
   The woman and the child saw **each other**

(98) **Indirect-object relation (intransitive)**:
   a. **Conjoined simple clauses**:
   The man talked **to the woman**
      and the woman talked **to the man**
   b. **Corresponding reciprocal**:
   The man and the woman talked **to each other**

(99) **Indirect object relation (bi-transitive)**:
   a. **Conjoined simple clauses**:
   The woman gave a rose **to the man**
      and the man gave a rose **to the woman**
   b. **Corresponding reciprocal**:
   The woman and the man gave roses **to each other**

As noted earlier,[38] a reciprocal clause — much like other cases of conjoined NPs — is not the full semantic equivalent of two conjoined simple

clauses. Rather, the semantic context for coding two reciprocal acts as a single reciprocal clause demands two associated conditions:

(a) That the two events are roughly **simultaneous**; and

(b) That the two events are in some way **related**.

Under the scope of the *habitual* modality, condition (a) above may seem inapplicable. Thus, at least superficially the conjoined clauses in (100a) below seem to be semantically interchangeable with the reciprocal clause (100b):

(100) a. John loves **Mary** and Mary loves **John** $<===>$

b. Mary and John love **each other**

More clearly, event-pairs whose two members occurred at different times, at different places, or in other disparate contexts, do not show logical equivalence with their reciprocal counterparts. Thus compare:

(101) **Disjointed time**:

a. John hugged Mary **yesterday**
and she hugged him **today** $*<===>$

b. John and Mary hugged each other

(102) **Disjointed location**:

a. Mary saw John **in the street**
and he saw her **on the bus** $*<===>$

b. Mary and John saw each other

(103) **Disjointed circumstances**:

a. John consulted Mary **about his job**
and she consulted him **about her doctor** $*<===>$

b. John and Mary consulted each other

One must emphasize that the fundamental semantic issue here is neither time nor place nor circumstances *per se*, but rather the conceptual perspective of **event integration**. With some event types, a reciprocal perspective is not only possible but also typical — even under conditions of temporal and spatial separation. As illustrations, consider:

(104) **Reciprocals with disjointed location**:

John lived in **New York** and Mary in **Los Angeles**,

a. and they **wrote each other** regularly.

b. and they **called each other** every night.

c. and they **missed each other** terribly.

(105) **Reciprocals with disjointed temporality**:
Since they were both so incredibly busy,
they **left phone messages** to each other.
He called her early in the morning
and she called him late at night.

8.7.3.   The syntax of reciprocal clauses

8.7.3.1.   Tree-diagram description

The surface syntactic difference between two simple conjoined clauses
and their corresponding reciprocal clause is represented in the following
tree-diagrams. Respectively:

(106) **Conjoined simple clauses**:

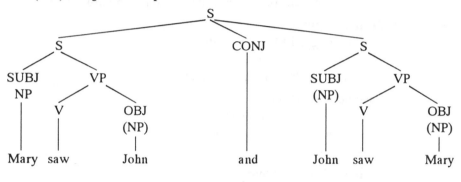

(107) **Reciprocal clause**:

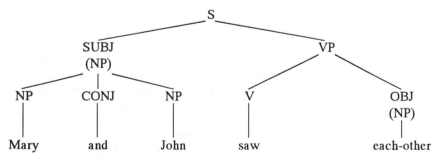

8.7.3.2.   Distributional restrictions

As noted above, reciprocal clauses may accommodate a reciprocal
relation between the subject and either a direct or an indirect object. While

this is true in principle, the distribution of reciprocal constructions across verb-types is far from being unconstrained. The most obvious constraint is on objectless intransitive verbs. Thus, the conjoined clauses in (108a) have no corresponding reciprocal:

(108) a. Mary slept and John slept
      b. *Mary and John slept **each other**

Another constraint has to do with the fact that many verbs select, rather specifically, a subject and an object that differ radically in semantic terms, such as concreteness, animacy, humanity, etc. As noted above, a crucial prerequisite for reciprocation is that the subject and the object switch their role from one clause to the other. In order for that to be possible, both subject and object must be of the same semantic type; and the semantic type of both the subject and object must be compatible with the semantic specificity imposed by the verb. To illustrate how such require-ments rule out many reciprocal constructions, consider first:

(109) a. John built the house
      b. *The **house** built **John**
      c. *John and the house built **each other**
      d. *John built **Mary**
      e. *Mary built **John**
      f. *John and Mary built **each other**

The inappropriateness of the reciprocal (109c) is the direct consequence of the inappropriateness of the simple transitive clause (109b). And the inap-propriateness of the reciprocal (109f) is the direct consequence of the inap-propriateness of the simple transitive clauses (109d,e). The same situation is seen in:

(110) a. *Mary talked to the **house**
      c. *The **house** talked to Mary
      d. *Mary and the house talked to **each other**

Some verbs are extremely permissive in the semantic selection of their arguments, so that almost any type of noun would fit in either the subject or the object slot. Consequently, the formation of reciprocal clauses is much less constrained with these verbs. One such verb is 'resemble', which selects both its subject and object with total disregard to concreteness, animacy, or humanity. Not only is it highly permissive in selecting subjects and objects, but it is also **inherently reciprocal**. That is, it abides by the bi-conditional logical implication:

(111) X resembles Y <===> Y resembles X
("If X resemble Y, then Y also resembles X")

Thus:

(112) a. This cloud resembles that one <===>
      b. That cloud resembles this one

      c. <===> The two clouds resemble **each other**

(113) a. Mary resembles the cloud <===>
      b. The cloud resembles Mary

      c. <===> Mary and the cloud resemble **each other**

Similarly with 'be/stand near':

(114) a. John is standing next to Mary <===>
      b. Mary is standing next to John

      c. <===> John and Mary are standing **next to each other**

Other verbal constructions exclude reciprocation on just as rigid logical grounds. For example, the relationship 'be under' is logically non-reciprocal:

(115) a. The book is **under the magazine** *<===>
      b. The magazine is **under the book**

      c. *The book and the magazine are **under each other**

One must note, however, that reciprocation of 'be/stand next to', while semantically permissive as in (114), is pragmatically constrained. This becomes obvious when one of the two arguments is more important than the other. If that is the case, the more important argument can only be the subject, but not the object, of the simple clause. And this makes reciprocation untenable. This is illustrated in (116), where a human stands next to a non-human:

(116) a. **John** is standing next to **the house** *<===>
      b. **The house** is standing next to **John**

      c. *John and the house are standing **next to each other**

8.7.3.3. 'Light' vs. 'heavy' reciprocal marking

There is a group of verbs, or verbal constructions, that are **inherently reciprocal**. Some examples of those are:

(117) a. Joe and May *kissed*
   b. They *met* for lunch
   c. Her parents *fought* over her
   d. Their hands *touched*
   e. They *argue* all the time
   f. Mary and Jane *quarreled*
   g. They *made love*
   h. They *corresponded* regularly
   i. They *collaborated* on their book
   j. They *co-authored* the report
   k. They *resemble* each other
   l. They *are similar*
   m. They *are identical*
   n. They *are very close*

English, like many other languages,[39] has two distinct reciprocal grammatical patterns, one called 'light' with no distinct morphology, the other called 'heavy' with the more prominent reciprocal pronoun 'each other'. The 'light' pattern is used with inherently reciprocal verbs, as in (117).[40] The 'heavy' pattern seems to be unrestricted; it is obligatory with the common — non-inherent — reciprocals, but may also be added optionally to inherent reciprocals.

The semantic difference between the two patterns can be further amplified by noting that a 'light' reciprocal is more likely to be interpreted as a fully integrated **single event**, while a 'heavy' reciprocal may be interpreted, at least in some contexts, as a succession of separate events. For example:

(118) a. **Light pattern**:
      John and Mary kissed
         (i) Simultaneously
         (ii) *First he kissed her, then she him
   b. **Heavy pattern**:
      John and Mary kissed **each other**
         (i) Simultaneously
         (ii) First he kissed her, then she him

Non-inherent reciprocals can take only the 'heavy' pattern, and in this case both an integrated and a sequential interpretation of the complex event is possible. That is:

(119) a. **Light pattern**:
    *Mary and John hit
   b. **Heavy pattern**:
    Mary and John hit **each other**
       (i) Simultaneously
      (ii) First he hit her, then she him

At least for some verbs, the semantic distinction between the two patterns is not clear. Thus compare:

(120) a. **Light pattern**:
    They write regularly
       (i) He writes her regularly and she him,
           but not necessarily on the same day.
      (ii) He writes regularly, and so does she,
           but not necessarily to each other,
           and not necessarily the same day.
   b. **Heavy pattern**:
    They write **each other** regularly
       (> Each wrote regularly to the other,
          but not necessarily on the same day).

8.7.3.4. Reciprocal vs. joint action

As noted earlier, reciprocal clauses have either conjoined or plural subjects. But a plural subject — particularly when the reciprocal pronoun is left unexpressed — may also code **joint action**. This is indeed an option with the 'light' pattern of some English reciprocal verbs, as may be seen in (120a) above. But the option is not applied evenly across the verb lexicon, or even across the various contexts where a 'light' reciprocal pattern is used with the same verb. Thus compare:

(121) a. **Light**:   John and Mary fought regularly
            (> They fought **each other** regularly)
            (*> They fought **other people** regularly)
   b. **Light**:   John and Mary fought to save their marriage
            (> They fought **together**)
            (*> They fought **each other**)
   c. **Heavy**: John and Mary fought **each other**
            (*> They fought someone else together)

   d. **Light**: Mary and John wrote regularly
               (> They wrote **each other**)
               (> They wrote to **others**)
               (> They wrote **independent pieces**)
               (> They wrote **jointly**)
               (> They wrote **jointly** to **others**)
   e. **Light**: Mary and John wrote for magazines
               (> separately)
               (?> jointly)

In the non-inherently-reciprocal 'write', the light pattern may also code antipassive interpretations, as can be seen in both (121d) and (121e). Both semantic and real-world pragmatic considerations thus govern the interpretation of the 'light' reciprocal pattern, allowing it to code either reciprocal actions, or joint actions, or separate events.

8.8. REFLEXIVE CLAUSES

8.8.1. Preamble

In this section we deal with three types of constructions that may be called 'reflexive':

(a) Simple reflexive
(b) Emphatic reflexive
(c) Possessive reflexive

All three abide by the more general definition (122a) below. In addition, two of them — (a) and (c) — also abide by the more restricted definition (122b):

(122) **Definition of reflexive constructions**:
   a. "The same referent is *mentioned twice* in the same clause".
   a. "The same referent participates in the clause *in two different roles*".

Beyond this common definition, each of the three reflexive constructions involves different specific details as to what two roles the repeating referent occupies within the clause, and how the repetition is treated syntactically. The simple and possessive reflexives also exhibit a certain relation with transitivity.

8.8.2. The simple reflexive

8.8.2.1. Semantic and syntactic definition

The simple reflexive construction may be defined semantically and syntactically as follows:

(123) **Definition of the simple reflexive**

　　a. **Semantic**:

　　　　"The subject is **co-referent** with the object, and thus
　　　　acts upon itself — reflexively".

　　b. **Syntactic**:

　　　　"The object in the reflexive clause is represented by
　　　　a **reflexive pronoun**".

The syntactic difference between a simple transitive and a simple reflexive clause may be given in tree-diagrams (124) and (125) below, respectively:

(124) **Simple transitive clause**:

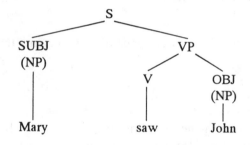

(125) **Simple reflexive clause**:

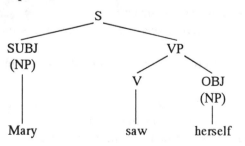

8.8.2.2. Distributional restrictions

The restrictions on the kind of verbs that can partake in the simple reflexive resemble the restrictions on reciprocals. Thus, the simple reflexive relation — of co-reference — can exist between the subject and either the direct or the indirect object:

(126) a. **Transitive (DO):**
        The woman saw **herself**
     b. **Intransitive (IO):**
        The man talked **to himself**
     c. **Bi-transitive (DO):**
        The woman gave **herself** a present
     d. **Bi-transitive (IO):**
        The woman told the man **about herself**

As in the case of reciprocals, a verb with no object — neither DO nor IO — cannot partake in a reflexive construction:

(127) a. *The woman slept herself
     b. *The man cried himself
     c. *The woman talked herself

As with reciprocals, the verb in the simple reflexive clause must allow the same semantic type of participants in both the subject and object position; otherwise reflexivization is not possible. Thus, the literal interpretations of (128) below are unacceptable, either in the simple-transitive or in the simple-reflexive form:

(128) a. *He broke her
     b. *He broke himself
     c. *She built him
     d. *She built herself
     e. *The house painted him
     f. *The house painted itself

8.8.2.3. Simple reflexives and de-transitivization

Because of semantic constraints of the type described above, simple reflexivization of transitive verbs is more common when the verb is *not* prototypically transitive. Typically, the object of verbs that undergo reflexivization is *not* a prototypical object — inanimate, salient patient — but rather a human *dative-benefactive* or *associative*. Examples of this kind are:

(129) a. She sent **herself** a letter
     b. She gave **herself** an A grade
     c. Do **yourself** a real favor and...
     d. We cooked **ourselves** a good meal
     e. He competed only **with himself**

Other verbs that allow reflexivization may depart from the transitive prototype by selecting a less prototypical patient as object and a dative as subject, as in:

(130) a. He knew **himself** only too well
     b. She hated **herself** for having done it
     c. They didn't trust **themselves** with the car
     d. You are afraid of **yourself**
     e. He looked at **himself** in the mirror
     f. She judges **herself** too harshly
     g. We consider **ourselves** lucky to have you

As noted in the case of reciprocals, above, stative verbs that are highly permissive in subject and object selection readily undergo reflexivization. Such verbs may be syntactically transitive, in having a direct object, but they are not prototypical transitives:

(131) a. The house still resembles **itself**
     b. A number must, at least trivially, equal **itself**
     c. A new idea suggested **itself** to him

Given this strong tendency toward semantic intransitivity, it is of course not an accident that the interpretation of reflexive clauses — especially with stative verbs and/or non-agentive subjects — often shade into de-transitivity. So that the reflexive is semantically akin to either a passive impersonal or middle-voice. To illustrate this, consider:

(132) a. **Reflexive**:   His suggestion **proved itself** useful
     b. **Middle**:   (> His suggestion **proved** useful)
     c. **Passive**:   (> His suggestion **was proven** useful)

(133) a. **Reflexive**:   A small rock **dislodged itself** from the cliff-face

     b. **Middle**:   (> ?A small rock **dislodged** from the cliff-face)

     c. **BE-passive**:   (> A small rock **was dislodged** from the cliff-face)

     d. **GET-passive**: (> A small rock **got dislodged** from the cliff-face)

(134) a. **Reflexive**: A small pebble **lodged itself** in the crack

     b. **Middle**:   (> ?A small pebble **lodged** in the crack)

     c. **Passive**:   (> A small pebble **was lodged** in the crack)

(135) a. **Reflexive**:   The argument eventually **resolved itself** in her favor

     b. **Middle**:   (> ?The argument **resolved** in her favor)

     c. **BE-passive**:   (> The argument **was resolved** in her favor)

     d. **GET-passive**: (> The argument **got resolved** in her favor)

The development of middle forms, as in examples (132b) through (135b) above, is presumably gradual and verb-specific. Many verbs do not yet admit this form, although to all intent and purpose it is semantically plausible. Thus, (133b), (134b), (135b) are perhaps marginal. And (136b) below is clearly not yet possible:

(136) a. **Reflexive**:   She **hurt herself** in an accident

     b. **Middle**:   (> *She **hurt** in an accident)

     c. **BE- passive**: (> She **was hurt** in an accident)

     d. **GET-passive**: (> She **got hurt** in an accident)

In a different grammatical context, however, a middle of 'hurt' is indeed acceptable, as in:

(137) She **hurts** real bad

Given the strong affinity of simple reflexives and de-transitivization, the historical development we considered earlier, of the three intransitive-middle constructions with 'get', seems rather natural:

(138) **GET-locative**
    a. **Reflexive**:   He got **himself** into trouble ===>
    b. **Middle**:   He got into trouble

(139) **GET-passive**
    a. **Reflexive**:   She got **herself** admitted to the Bar ===>
    b. **Middle**:   She got admitted to the bar

(140) **GET-adjective**
    a. **Reflexive**:   They got **themselves** ready ===>
    b. **Middle**:   They got ready

8.8.3. Emphatic reflexives

8.8.3.1. Historical development

The very same reflexive pronouns of simple reflexives are also used in emphatic reflexives. Historically, in fact, the emphatic use of these pronouns is much older. So that in Chaucerian English, the simple object pronoun ('him', 'her', 'them') were used for both anaphoric objects pronouns and simple reflexives, as in:[41]

(141) ...and [he] born **hym** well...
    '...and (he) carried **himself** well...'

                                      (*Canterbury Tales*, Prologue; p. 87)

As Haiman (1992) notes, such usage survives all the way into Shakespearean English, in context of non-emphatic ('expected') reflexive co-reference, as in:

(142) ...There he harms **hym**...
    ...'There he harms **himself**...'

                                    (*Troilus and Cressida, 1:2:260*)

The emphatic pronouns ('himself', 'herself', 'themselves') spread into the grammar of simple reflexives first in restricted — emphatic, unexpected — contexts, a change that is already evident in Chaucer, as in:

(143) ...And eek delivere **hymself** out of prisoun...
    '...And also to get himself out of prison...'

                                         (*Knight's Tale*, 1767-9)

It was presumably uncommon for a person to deliver *themselves* out of prison. Haiman (1992) notes, finally, that the use of anaphoric object pronouns as simple-reflexive pronouns has survived into spoken modern English, in cases of extreme **self alienation**. Thus, the alleged victim of a recent rape trial in Palm Beach assessed her own credibility after losing the case in the following words:[42]

(144) "...The prosecutor believed me,
    the grand jury believed me,
    I believe **me**..."

Self-alienation is a metaphoric separation between the subject and the object, even though they are logically co-referential.

8.8.3.2. Semantic and pragmatic features

The function of emphatic reflexives is **emphasis** or **contrast**, two notions that will for the moment remain informal.[43] Briefly, a contrasted referent is **compared**, explicitly or implicitly, with another referent that partakes in a similar event or state. Or the contrasted referent may be compared with itself under different circumstances. And further, the speaker using a contrastive device assumes that the contrasted item is **unexpected** or goes **against the hearer's likely belief**.

8.8.3.3. Syntactic features

8.8.3.3.1. Constraints on grammatical role

There seems to be a strong preference for using emphatic reflexives on subjects but not on objects:

(145) a. Joe **himself** saw Mary
    b. ?Joe saw Mary **herself**
    c. Mary **herself** killed Joe
    d. ?Mary killed Joe **himself**
    e. We **ourselves** resent it
    f. ?We resent it **itself**
    g. I **myself** refused to vote for Joe
    h. ?I refused to vote for Joe **himself**
    i. You **yourself** said it to Mary
    j. ?You said it to Mary **herself**

It may well be that the preference for subject emphasis is not absolute, but rather lexical-specific, so that particular verbs — or event types — allow object contrast even if the majority don't. It may well be that the preference for subject contrast is inherently pragmatic, having to do with the higher topicality — thus importance — of the subject vis a vis the object.[44] Thus for example, object emphasis seems a bit more natural when the object is an important human participant:

(146) a. *I put it on the table **itself**
       b. I gave it to the President **himself**

And if the object is also a subject of a closely-bound clause, the acceptability of object emphasis seems to increase:

(147) a. *I saw Mary **herself**
       b. ?I saw Mary **herself** do it
       c. ?I saw Mary do it **herself**
       d. I saw Mary doing it **herself**
       e. I saw Mary as she **herself** was doing it

8.8.3.3.2. Constraints on order

The reflexive pronoun used for subject emphasis need not be adjacent to the subject, but may be displaced to other locations in the clause; but such displacement is not unconstrained:

(148) a. Mary **herself** has come to recognize this
       b. Mary has **herself** come to recognize this
       c. ?Mary has come **herself** to recognize this
       d. ?Mary has come to **herself** recognize this
       e. *Mary has come to recognize **herself** this
       f. Mary has come to recognize this **herself**

While different clause (and verb) types impose slightly different restrictions, the three most common positions for the emphatic reflexive pronoun seem to be:

(a) directly after the subject (148a)
(b) following an auxiliary (148b)
(c) at the end of the clause (148f)

Constraints on clause-final placement of the emphatic reflexive pronouns may be due to several factors, and those factors may interact. One likely constraint appears to involve the length of the gap between the subject and the reflexive pronoun. Consider, for example:

(149) a. She told him **herself**
 b. She told him the story **herself**
 c. ?She told him the story when they came home **herself**
 d. ??She told him the story when they came home about the terrible snow storm last winter **herself**

Another constraint seems to involve syntactic complexity: embedded clauses, their position within the main clause, and the addition of other participants. Consider first manipulative verbs with verbal complement:

(150) a. She **herself** told him to do it
 b. ?She told him **herself** to do it
 c. ??She told him **himself** to do it
 d. ??She told him to do it **herself**
 e. She told him to do it **himself**

Example (150a) is unproblematic, with the pronoun directly following its antecedent subject. Example (150b) is already odd: Due to gender, the reflexive 'herself' could only be co-referential with the main-clause subject 'she'. But its position directly following the object NP — and an object that is also co-referential with the subject of the complement clause — makes (150b) less natural than (150a). In (150c) equally no gender confusion is possible, but the pronoun — though co-referent with 'him' — follows the *object* of the main clause, which is co-referent to the zero-coded subject of the complement. Example (150d) is odd in spite of no gender confusion, presumably because the pronoun is placed at the end of a clause — the complement — in which it has *no* co-referent whatever. The clause-final placement in (150e) seems the only natural to emphasize the subject of the complement clause.

Another constraint seems to be due to transitive — or potentially transitive — verbs in a complement clause, and the odd semantic effect of having the subject-emphatic pronoun directly following them. This may be illustrated in:

(151) a. She **herself** asked him to relax
 b. *She asked him to relax **herself**
 c. She **herself** asked him to eat
 d. *She asked him to eat **herself**
 e. She **herself** asked him to join
 f. *She asked him to join **herself**

One suspects that the oddity of (151b,d,f) is due to a tendency to interpret emphatic reflexive pronouns directly following a (transitive) verb as **simple reflexives**.

8.8.4. Possessive reflexives

The possessive reflexive clause, with 'own' combining with the anaphoric possessive pronoun, abides by our general definition of reflexives (123). In addition, it also abides by a more specific definition:

> (152) **Definition of possessive reflexive**:
>   "The subject is the possessor of the object".

The possessive-reflexive pattern is restricted to emphatic, contrastive **counter-normative** contexts. As illustration of the interplay between norm and counter-norm, consider first the contrast between a simple possessive pronoun and a possessive-reflexive pronoun:

> (153) a. Mary adored **her** mother
>   b. ?Mary adored **her own** mother
>   c. Mary killed **her own** mother
>   d. Mary killed **her** mother

Adoring one's mother is the cultural norm, so that (153a) is used as a matter of course, while (153b) seems odd. But killing one's own mother is counter-normative, so that (153c) is appropriate, while (153d) is an oddly subdued way of expressing such a glaringly counter-normative event.

Consider next the following passage from a newspaper opinion column:[45]

> (154) "...Say what you like about Jimmy Carter, but grant
>   him the instinctive good judgement about the American
>   voter's distaste for Royalism. He ostentatiously carried
>   **his own** garment bag..."

Contrast now:

> (155) a. Joe carried **his** bags to the plane
>   b. ?Joe carried **his own** bags to the plane
>   c. The President carries **his own** bags to the plane
>   d. ?The president carries **his** bags to the plane

Regular folks normally carry their own bags to the plane, so that (155a) is matter-of-fact while (155b) is either odd or requires an expanded context to justify the contrast. Presidents, on the other hand, normally do *not* carry their own bags to the plane. This renders (155c) — as (154) — more natural and (155d) somewhat odd.

The co-reference relation of simple ('anaphoric') possessor pronouns is open, so that it may either refer to the subject and thus be used reflexively, or refer to some other NP. In contrast, the co-reference of the possessive-reflexive pronoun is always restricted to the subject of the same clause, and thus conforms to definition (152). This is illustrated in:

(156) a. Mary saw Cindy and then killed **her** mother
        (> killed *either* Cindy's or her own mother)
    b. Mary saw Cindy and then killed **her own** mother
        (> killed her *own* mother, but not Cindy's)

8.8.5. Reflexives and grammatical relations

As noted earlier above, the conditions under which all three types of reflexives occur are defined in terms of the two major grammatical case-roles — subject and object. Further, in all three reflexives — the simple reflexive, the emphatic reflexive and the possessive reflexive — the relevant roles of subject and object pertain to the same clause. Therefore, the co-reference relation between the reflexive pronoun and its antecedent should not, at least in theory, stretch across clause boundaries. This presumed restriction makes reflexive constructions an intriguing tool for probing the limits of the grammatical notions of clause, subject and object. In this section we will illustrate briefly some of the potentials of these tools for syntactic research.

Consider first the use of both simple possessive pronouns and possessive reflexive pronouns in the equi-subject complements of modality verbs:

(157) a. **Simple reflexive**:
       Joe wanted to kill **himself**
    b. **Possessive reflexive**:
       Mary began to hate **her own** mother

Since the subject of the complement verb is co-referential with the subject of the main clause, all proper constraints on co-reference in reflexivization are obeyed.

Consider next the use of simple reflexives in the complements of manipulation verbs, whose subject is co-referential with the *object* of the main clause:

(158) a. Mary told Joe to kill $\left\{ \begin{array}{l} \textbf{himself} \\ \textbf{*herself} \end{array} \right\}$

Joe in (158) is the subject of a complement clause in which Mary plays no role. The constraint on reflexivization is still defined strictly in terms of grammatical relations within the same clause.

As noted above, without the reflexive 'own' co-reference of the possessive pronoun is more open:

(159) a. Mary told Joe to ignore **his** mother
     b. Mary told Joe to ignore **her** mother

And 'own' again restricts co-reference to the proper subject of the same (complement) clause:

(160) a. Joe told Mary to ignore **her own** mother
     b. *Joe told Mary to ignore **his own** mother

The clause-internal definition of reflexivization seems to also apply when the reflexive pronoun occurs in the complement of perception-cognition-utterance verbs. Simple possessive pronouns are again unrestricted:

(161) Joe knew that Mary loved $\left\{ \begin{array}{l} \textbf{his} \\ \textbf{her} \end{array} \right\}$ mother

And both explicit reflexive pronouns 'self' and 'own' again constrain co-reference to the subject of the same clause:

(162) a. Joe knew that Mary loved $\left\{ \begin{array}{l} \textbf{herself} \\ \textbf{*himself} \end{array} \right\}$
     b. Joe knew that Mary loved $\left\{ \begin{array}{l} \textbf{her own} \\ \textbf{*his own} \end{array} \right\}$ mother

The strict clause-internal definition of the possessive-reflexive relation becomes problematic with transitive, complement-taking utterance verbs. This is evident in:

(163) Joe told Mary that $\left\{ \begin{array}{l} \textbf{his own} \\ \textbf{her own} \end{array} \right\}$ mother was sick

Example (163) reveals three startling deviations from the strict definition of the possessive-reflexive relation (152):

  (a) The reflexive pronoun is now the *subject* of a clause,
       rather than its object.

(b) The reflexive pronoun may now refer to *either* the subject
or the object.

(c) The co-referent subject or object are *in another clause*,
i.e. across the clause boundary.

The situation is even more baffling when added complexity is introduced, e.g. when the complement clause is transitive, as in:

(164) Joe told Mary that **her** mother killed $\left\{ \begin{array}{l} \textbf{her own} \\ \textbf{*his own} \end{array} \right\}$ brother

$(>$ killed $\left\{ \begin{array}{l} \textit{the } \textbf{mother's } \textit{own} \\ \textbf{*Mary's } \textit{own} \\ \textbf{*John's } \textit{own} \end{array} \right\}$ brother$)$

(165) Joe told Mary that **his** mother killed $\left\{ \begin{array}{l} \textbf{her own} \\ \textbf{his own} \end{array} \right\}$ brother

$(>$ killed $\left\{ \begin{array}{l} \textit{the } \textbf{mother's } \textit{own} \\ \textbf{Joe's } \textit{own} \\ \textbf{*Mary's own} \end{array} \right\}$ brother$)$

Example (164) seems to conform to the strict definition of the possessive-reflexive relation. That is, the object is possessed, by the subject, and all within the same clause. In (165), however, another interpretation is tolerated: The reflexive pronoun can be co-referent with 'Joe', who is the subject of the *main* clause.

A possible explanation of the difference between (164) and (165) involves the observation that in (164) Joe is the subject of the main clause, and Mary is the possessor-of-subject in the complement. While in (165) Joe is *both* — subject of main clause and possessor-of-subject in the complement. The conflation of both subject related roles into one referent (Joe) now makes the referent more **subject-like** vis-a-vis the complement clause. What this does to a strict theory of grammatical relations remain to be assessed.[46]

Finally, note the contrast, in possessive-reflexivization, between the complements of two manipulative verbs, 'let' (at the top of the binding hierarchy, with a co-lexicalized complement verb) and 'make' (one rung below with no co-lexicalized complement verb):[47]

(166) a. She let-go of $\left\{ \begin{array}{l} \textbf{her own} \\ \textbf{*his own} \end{array} \right\}$ hand

b. She made him drop $\left\{ \begin{array}{l} \textbf{his own} \\ \textbf{*her own} \end{array} \right\}$ hand

The subject of 'let' in (166a) behaves like the subject of a *single* co-lexicalized verb ('let-go'). Co-lexicalization thus seems to entail complete **clause union**, joining the two verbal clauses into a single grammatical unit. The subject of 'make' in (166b), on the other hand, remains only the subject of the main clause. The complement clause, while truncated, retains some of its independent status, at least so far as grammatical subjecthood is concerned.

NOTES

1) For a discussion of the prototype approach to categories, see chapter 2.

2) See discussion in chapter 3. The approach pursued here owes much to observations made by Hopper and Thompson (1980).

3) We discussed the generic topicality hierarchy of the semantic case-roles of clausal participants (AGT>DAT/BEN>PAT>OTHERS) in chapter 3. By *generic* we mean that in natural human discourse, the overwhelming *statistical* tendency is for the agent to be more topical than the dative/benefactive, the latter more topical than the patient, and so on.

4) As noted in chapter 3, the main syntactic diagnostic of transitivity in English is whether the clause does or does not have a direct object.

5) Jespersen (1924, p.167).

6) Trout (1974, pp. 39-40).

7) Trout (1974, p. 40).

8) Hillerman (1990, p. 38).

9) Jespersen (1924, p. 167).

10) Cited from Jespersen (1924, p. 168). Prototypical agents tend to be human.

11) Reproduced from Givón (1979a, ch. 2). The two texts studied were L'Amour (1965, pp. 1-25) and Orwell (1945, pp. 5-14).

12) See discussion of manipulative verbs in chapter 7.

13) Reproduced from Givón (1979a, chapter 2). One must note that the passive clauses counted in this study did *not* include other types de-transitive clauses, so that to some extent the frequency of overall de-transitive voice is under-represented.

14) John Haiman (in personal communication).

15) This variation in bi-transitive verbs is a form of dative-shifting, and was described in chapter 3.

16) William Pfaff, "Well meaning advice to East ignores the economic realities", Ed-Op section, **The Eugene Register-Guard**, Eugene, OR, 6-8-91. The typical dative-benefactive *human* object of 'owe' is readily promoted to direct object, and somewhat less readily to subject, as in:
> She owed a lot of money *to various banks*
> She owed *the banks* a lot of money
> ?*The banks* were owed a lot of money

17) Bill Plaschke, "Braves cop a flop in NL opener", **The Eugene Register-Guard**, 10-10-91, p. 2D.

18) For details see Givón and Yang (1991).

19) Grammatical change takes place, overwhelmingly, in spoken language, and only later on — sometimes never — penetrates the written register. The GET-passive is to this day considered primarily a spoken construction. See Herold (1986), Givón and Yang (1991).

20) One suspects that the reference in Quirk *et al* (1985, p. 161) to the effect that:
"...the *get*-passive...puts the emphasis on the subject rather than the agent..."
is directed at this semantic property of agentivity.

21) Dwight Bolinger (1966, unpubl.; in personal communication).

22) For the history of the BE-passive, see Visser (1973).

23) Re-computed from Herold (1986); see also Givón and Yang (1991).

24) Dwight Bolinger (1966, unpubl.; in personal communication).

25) Re-computed from Herold (1986); see also Givón and Yang (1991).

26) Re-computed from Herold (1986); see also Givón and Yang (1991).

27) Since the remaining referent is not syntactically promoted to subjecthood, one suspects that pragmatic promotion — even by default — is not a necessary feature of these constructions.

28) P.D. James, **The Black Tower** (1975, p. 263)

29) P.D. James, **The Black Tower** (1975, p. 263)

30) P.D. James, **Unnatural Causes** (1967, p. 218). The speaker in this case is also described as a homosexual.

31) For an extensive review of middle-voice constructions and their diachronic connections, see Kemmer (1988).

32) For more details see Givón and Yang (1991).

33) Lakoff (1971) writes: "...many languages are like English in having two morphologically and semantically distinct passives. The one that corresponds to the English *get*-passive in some languages has the form of a reflexive. Other languages have 'middle' constructions, which fulfil the role of both the *get*-passive and reflexives of certain types..." (1971, p. 149)

34) Following Cooreman (1982). For more details see Givón (1990, ch. 14).

35) See section 8.2.1., above. For the original discussion see again Hopper and Thompson (1980).

36) We noted in chapter 5 that plurals are used systematically to code *non-referring* objects.

37) See again chapter 5, as well as Hopper and Thompson (1980).

38) See chapter 6, section 6.6.2.

39) See Haiman (1985), Kemmer (1988).

40) The verb 'resemble' in English is a conspicuous exception to this generalization, seemingly requiring 'each other'. Thus:
   *John and Mary *resembled*

41) See Haiman (1992).

42) In a TV interview during which Ms Bowman exhibited obtrusive mannerisms of self-detachment.

43) The full discussion of the pragmatics of contrast is deferred to chapter 10.

44) Many of the contrastive devices discussed in chapter 10 are also topicalizing devices.

45) W. Safire, Ed-Op section, p. A-15, **The New York Times**, 6-20-91

46) The facts noted here suggest that subjecthood — or subject properties — is sometime a matter of degree. This conforms to the suggestion made by Keenan (1975).

47) See chapter 7.

9 | RELATIVE CLAUSES

9.1. INTRODUCTION

Relative clauses are **subordinate clauses** that are embedded, as noun modifiers, inside a noun phrase. Functionally, they are part of the grammar of referential identification.[1] The most common type of embedded relative clause falls under the unified intonation contour of the entire noun phrase. Some types of relative clause, however, are unembedded and retain their own intonation contour.[2]

It has become common over the past 30 years to view the relationship between a relative clause (henceforth REL-clause) and its corresponding simple clause as a **transformational relation**, described as the process of **relativization**. The input to this process is a simple clause acting as a post-nominal modifier in the NP, and the output is a post-nominal REL-clause. While this description may be theoretically problematic,[3] it is a useful descriptive strategy, allowing us to understand the structure of REL-clauses in terms of the structure of simple clauses that convey the same propositional-semantic information.[4]

9.2. FUNCTIONAL ASPECTS OF RELATIVIZATION

9.2.1. Restrictive relative clauses

9.2.1.1. Preamble

Restrictive relative clauses (henceforth RRCs) are considered the prototype REL-clauses. They are the most common in text, as well as the most common among languages. We will begin the discussion by outlining their use in the grammar of referential identification.

9.2.1.2. Referent tracking, grounding and presupposition

Like other restrictive modifiers such as adjectives and determiners, RRCs are used in the grammar of **referential coherence**. In other words, they are used in **grounding** the referent noun to the knowledge-base that is already represented in the mind of the hearer.

Most typically, a RRC is used when the speaker assumes that the referent's identity is **accessible** to the hearer — but **not easily accessible**. As noted in chapter 5, when a referent is maximally accessible, a pronoun or zero anaphora is used; and when it is less accessible, a full noun is used. Modifying a full noun with a RRC is one of several strategies used when a referent is less accessible. Each of these strategies is used under specific discourse conditions.

The use of RRCs as a referent-tracking strategy — or as an **anaphoric grounding device** — may be outlined as follows:

(1)   **RRCs as a referent tracking strategy**:
    (a) The speaker assumes that a certain state or event is known, familiar or **mentally accessible** to the hearer.
    (b) The proposition corresponding to that familiar state/ event is thus pragmatically **presupposed**.[5]
    (c) The referent to be identified is a participant — subject, direct object, indirect object etc. — in the state or event coded in the proposition.
    (d) The familiar proposition thus helps guide the hearer toward identifying the referent in his/her mentally-stored knowledge. It **grounds** the referent in the hearer's knowledge-base.
    (e) The proposition used for such grounding is coded syntactically as a RRC.

The use of strategy (1) may be illustrated informally by the following example. Suppose you and I have just entered a dark bar; we stop at the door to let our eyes adjust to the dark. There are five people inside, all but one clustered around a pool table. You lean over and say either (2a) or (2b):

(2)   a. That guy **standing next to the bar** is packing a gun.
     b. The gal **I told you about** is not here yet.

In trying to identify a person to me, you've used a RRC in both (2a) and (2b). For the RRC in (2a) to do its purported job, you must assume that I noticed the man — either on my own or due to your intervention. Likewise, for the RRC in (2b) to do its job, you must assume that I remember what you told me earlier. Your use of a RRC either way is successful only if such assumptions were correct.

A tighter definition of RRCs may be divided into two parts. The first is semantic and applies to all relative clauses. The second is pragmatic and applies only to restrictive relative clauses.

(3)   **Definition of RRCs**:
    a. **Semantic**:
        "A REL-clause codes a state/event one of whose participants is **co-referential** with the head noun modified by the REL-clause".
    b. **Pragmatic**:
        "The speaker assumes that the state/event coded by a RRC is **familiar, known** or **accessible** to the hearer, or otherwise is **unlikely to be challenged** as new information".

As illustration of how definition (3) works, consider the RRC modifying of 'man' in (4) below:

(4)   The man **who married my sister** is a crook
    (a) **Main clause**:
        The man [ ] is a crook
    (b) **RRC**:
        [who married my sister]
    (c) **Proposition implicit in the RRC**:
        The man married my sister

Sentence (4) above is made out of the main clause (4a) and the embedded RRC (4b). The RRC (4b) modifies the subject noun of the main clause, 'man'. The full propositional meaning of the RRC — if it were not used as an embedded modifier — is given in (4c). In (4) above, the head noun modified by the RRC was co-referential with the subject of the RRC (4c). But the head noun can also be co-referential with the direct object of the RRC, or with its indirect object; as in respectively:

(5) **Head noun coreferent with the DO of the RRC**:
The man **(whom) my sister married** is a crook
a. **Main clause**:
The man [ ] is a crook
b. **RRC**:
[(whom) my sister married]
c. **Proposition implicit in the RRC**:
My sister married the man

(6) **Head noun coreferent with the IO of the RRC**:
The man **(who) my sister lives with** is a crook
a. **Main clause**:
The man [ ] is a crook
b. **RRC**:
[(who) my sister lives with]
c. **Proposition implicit in the RRC**:
My sister lives with the man

9.2.1.3. Referring-indefinite heads and cataphoric (anticipatory) grounding

In the preceding section we described the prototypical RRC as modifying a **definite head noun**. The definitiness of the head noun, sginalling its accessibility, obviously contributed to our suggestion that the REL-clause is involved in tracking the referent in the **anaphoric** mental representation of text. Definition (3), particularly its pragmatic clause (3b), characterized such a prototypical situation.

But RRCs are also used to modify **referring-indefinite head nouns**. And the existence of such constructions raises serious questions about the universal applicability of the pragmatic portion (3b) of our definition. The problem may be illustrated with the following examples:

(7) a. A man **who had no shoes on** came into the office yesterday.
b. I know a woman at work **who you'd enjoy meeting**.
c. There's a man **you ought to talk to** here.

The head nouns in (7a,b,c) are all REF-indefinite, introduced into the discourse for the first time. They are not assumed to be anaphorically accessible to the hearer. Likewise, the events or states depicted by the RRCs in (7) cannot be presupposed by the speaker as part of the accessible anaphoric text represented in the mind of the hearer. The information coded in the

RRCs in (7) is just as new as the information coded in the main clauses in (7). But if the states/events coded in the RRCs in (7) are not presupposed, what is their precise informational status? Are they then asserted? Let us test two hypotheses about this issue.

First, we may propose that what unifies all RRCs, regardless of definiteness of their heads, is their informational status as **unchallengeable background information**. In order to test this hypothesis, consider the appropriateness of a hearer's challenge to examples (2a,b) above. In both examples, the RRC modified a definite head noun:

(8) **RRCs modifying a definite head**:
   a. The guy **standing next to the bar** is packing a gun.
   b. The gal **I told you about** is not here.
   c. **Challenge**:
       How do you know?

The most likely interpretation of challenge (8c) is to the assertion in the main clause in (8a) or (8b); respectively:

(9) a. How do you know he's packing a gun?
   b. How do you know she's not here?

A much less likely, indeed strange, interpretation of (8c) would be as a challenge to the propositions coded in the RRCs; respectively:

(10) a. ?How do you know he's standing next to the bar?
    b. ?How do you know you told me about her?

There is nothing wrong in challenging the propositions in (10a,b) *per se*. The strangeness of the challenge is only due to the position of those propositions as RRCs — i.e. as shielded, unchallengeable background information that is not being asserted.

Consider now similar challenges to sentences with an RRC modifying a REF-indefinite head:[6]

(11) **RRCs modifying REF-indefinite heads**:
    a. A man **who had no shoes on** collapsed in the bread-line.
    b. A woman **begging in the street** was arrested yesterday.
    c. **Challenge**:
        How do you know?

If the RRCs in (11a,b) indeed code shielded, unchallengeable background information, as in the case of definite head nouns, the interpretation of the hearer's challenge (11c) ought to reveal a similar pattern of discrimination.

But in fact, the information in both main clauses and RRCs in (11a,b) seems to be equally challengeable. So that (11c) is equally plausible as:

(12) a. How do you know he collapsed in the bread-line?
      b. How do you know he had no shoes on?
      c. How do you know she was arrested yesterday?
      d. How do you know she was begging in the street?

But if the RRCs in (11a,b) are just as challengeable as their respective main clauses, are they asserted?

Another way of approaching this dilemma lies in the notion of **grounding**. The discourse-pragmatic function of the RRCs that modify REF-indefinite nouns may be the same as that of RRCs modifying definite nouns: In both cases, the information in the RRC serves to ground the referent to some mental text-structure. The common function thus remains that of establishing **referential grounding** or **referential coherence**. However, the information structure into which definite and REF-indefinite referents are grounded is crucially different. A definite referent is grounded **anaphorically** by its modifying RRC, i.e. grounded into existing mental structure. In contrast, a REF-indefinite referent is grounded **cataphorically** by its modifying RRC, i.e. grounded into mental structure that is in the process of being organized, structure that is abuilding.[7]

To illustrate the difference between the two types of grounding, consider the use of the very same RRC in:

(13) a. **Definite referent**:
          The woman **you met last year** just called.
      b. **REF-indefinite referent**:
          A woman **you met last year** just called.

In both (13a) and (13b) the speaker is obviously talking about an event — coded in the RRC — that is familiar to the hearer, who after all is depicted as the conscious subject of that event. In (13a), the speaker must assume that the referent is still accessible in the hearer's pre-existing mental structure. The speaker thus cues the hearer with the definite article to launch an anaphoric referent-search. In (13b), the speaker judges the RRC-coded event sufficiently remote, and thus that the hearer does not have ready access to the referent in readily-available mental storage. Perhaps the event took place too long ago; perhaps it was unimportant; perhaps the referent was unimportant. Given such judgement, the speaker introduces the referent as REF-indefinite — as if it were brand new to the hearer. The RRC indeed relates the referent to the hearer's past experience. However, the referent is still grounded cataphorically. And so the combination of REF-indefinite NP plus RRC instructs the hearer to create a new structure, relative to which the referent must cohere.

The grounding of a REF-indefinite NP via a modifying RRC need not depend on the hearer's past experience. This is clearly indicated by examples (11a,b), where the newly-introduced referent was grounded to the hearer's general knowledge. Such generic grounding makes a newly-introduced referent salient and relevant to the unfolding discourse by grounding it to the hearer's cultural world.

The coherence and grounding properties of REF-indefinite nouns modified by RRCs may be summarized as follows:[8]

(14) **Coherence and grounding of REF-indefinite nouns modified by a RRC**:
   a. **Head noun grounded to**: generic-lexical knowledge
   b. **Relevance**: important topic
   c. **Grounding direction**: cataphoric (incoming discourse)
   d. **RRC grounded to**: (i) hearer's past experience
                            (ii) hearer's generic knowledge
   e. **Activation status**: experience is currently inactive
   f. **Accessibility**: experience is inaccessible (hearer needs 'reminding')

Of the six components of (14), five — (14a,b,c,e,f) — are cued by the REF-indefinite marking of the head noun. Only one, (14d), is cued by the modifying RRC.

As noted in Chapter 5, definite nouns may be grounded to three distinct mental structures:
(a) mind-stored text in episodic memory
(b) mental model of the current speech situation
(c) generic knowledge
Of the three sources, two — (a) and (b) may combine with RRCs, while the combination of frame-based definite nouns with RRC seems problematic:[9]

(15) a. **Episodic-text grounding**:
     The woman **I mentioned first**...
   b. **Situation-model grounding**:
     That woman **sitting at the end of the bar**...
   c. **Generic-knowledge grounding**:
     ?The President **who lives in the White House**...

The coherence and grounding properties of definite referents modified by RRCs may be summarized as:

(16) **Coherence and grounding of definite nouns modified by a RRC**:
   a. **Head noun grounded to**: specific knowledge
   b. **Relevance**: important topic
   c. **Grounding direction**: anaphoric
   d. **RRC grounded to**: (i) episodic-text memory
       (ii) speech-situation model
   e. **Activation status**: experience is currently inactive
   f. **Accessibility**: experience is accessible
       (hearer needs no reminding)

Of the six coherence and grounding components in (16), five — (16a,b,c,e,f) — are still cued by the definite marking of the head noun, and one, (16d), is cued by a combination of the definite determiner plus the RRC.

In sum, the function of the RRC is substantially the same in processing both definite and indefinite referents. It is the determiners ('articles') — definite vs. REF-indefinite — that cue the hearer toward grounding the referent in either an anaphoric or cataphoric direction.

9.2.1.4. The use of RRCs to ground frame-based referents

Restrictive REL-clauses may also partake, sometimes in combination with other grounding devices, in grounding referents to **generic knowledge**. This does not involve the grounding of unique generic-definite referents,[10] but rather to **frame-dependent** definite referents. As noted in chapter 5, such referents are grounded in a mixed fashion, partly to the generically-accessible 'frame' and partly to the anaphoric text. In the examples below, the RRC itself supplies the frame-based grounding information:

(17) a. The man **who married my mother** is a crook.
   b. The plumbing **in our house** never works right.
   c. The roof **on your summer cabin** is leaking.
   d. The chef **in our favorite restaurant** has just quit.

None of RRCs in (17), all modifying definite referents, serves to ground the referents anaphorically. In fact, expressions (17a,b,c,d) are all plausible discourse-initial introductions of a referent that has not been discussed before. The newly introduced referent is nevertheless definite — i.e.

judged accessible to the hearer — by virtue of the frame-based information supplied in the RRCs. The relevant portion of that information is roughly, respectively:

(18) a. A person has only one mother.
          One's mother may be currently unmarried.
          An unmarried woman may remarry.
          A woman can only marry one man at a time.
      b. A person typically has a house,
          typically only one.
          A house usually has plumbing.
      c. A cabin has a roof,
          typically only one.
      d   A restaurant tends to have a chef,
          typically just one.

9.2.1.5. Non-referring head nouns and strict co-reference

The semantic condition of our definition of restrictive REL-clauses (3b) also requires some modification. This condition requires a relationship of **co-reference** between the head noun and one argument in the REL-clause. But such co-reference could not be a strict logical relation if the head noun is itself non-referring. To illustrate the problem, consider:

(19) a. Anybody **who marries my sister** is asking for trouble.
      b. Any man **whom my sister marries** better think twice.
      c. I know no man **who would do this**.
      d. Women **who love too much**
          and the men **they marry**...
      e. The man **who would say this** is a cad.

Whether marked as indefinites (19a,b,c,d) or as definite (19e),[11] the non-referring head is just that — it has no particular reference. Further, the RRCs modifying such heads in (19) always fall under some **non-fact modality**, either irrealis or the habitual. That is, the RRCs code hypothetical states/events, within which the co-referent argument also is non-referring. In fact, a non-referring head noun would be incompatible with a *realis* modality in the RRC. To illustrate this, consider two examples patterned loosely after (19a). In the first, the RRC is in the *habitual* 'non-fact' modality. In the second, it is — at least superficially — in the *past/perfective* 'fact' modality:

(20) a. She said that anybody **who marries her sister**
          will be lucky.
      b. She said that anybody **who married her sister**
          would be lucky.

In spite of the use of the past-perfective in (20b), the modality remains non-fact, hypothetical, irrealis.[12] The non-referring head 'anybody' imposes this constraint.

Consider next a similar contrast, patterned on example (19e):

(21) a. The man **who would say this** is a cad.
      b. The man **who said this** is a cad.

Definite nouns are typically referring. They can be used as non-referring, as in (21a) — but only if the modality in the REL-clause is non-fact. When coupled with a fact modality, as in (21b), a definite head must be interpreted as referring.

The coherence function of the information coded in RRCs that modify non-referring heads may vary, depending on the referential status of the RRC's participants. The *non-fact* modal status of the RRC seems to have no bearing on the direction of coherence here. Thus, for example, the RRCs in (19a,b) presumably establish anaphoric coherence with an earlier discourse reference to 'my sister' and her marital predicaments. Likewise, the referring 'this' in (19c) establishes anaphoric coherence to the preceding discourse. In contrast, (19d) — taken as a book title — establishes either cataphoric or generic coherence vis-a-vis the non-referring head noun 'women'. And the RRC in (19e), again due to the referring 'this', establishes anaphoric coherence to the preceding discourse.

9.2.1.6. Restrictive REL-clauses with semi-referring heads

There is a class of **semi-referring**[13] indefinite relative pronouns that serve in so-called **headless REL-clauses**.[14] When the RRCs are under the scope of a *fact* modality and include referring participants, the unexpressed though implicit head noun is clearly referring, but not fully specified. Typical examples are:

(22) a. Whoever **stole my wallet** dumped it in the trash.
          (> **Somebody** stole my wallet)
      b. Whatever **she gave you**, get rid of it.
          (> She gave you **something**)
      c. Wherever **he went** must be a nice place.
          (> He went **somewhere**)

When the RRC is under the scope of a *non-fact* modality and the participants are non-referring, the implicit head noun may be non-referring:

(23) a. Whoever **finishes first** gets a bonus.
          (> I have no idea who that will be)
      b. Whatever **she gives you**, don't accept it.
          (> I don't know what she'll give you)
      c. Whenever **we talk**, we wind up disagreeing.
          (> I don't refer to any particular time)
      d. Wherever **he goes**, he spreads good cheer.
          (> I don't refer to any particular place)

In spite of the presence of referring participants in the RRCs (23b,c,d), the
non-fact modality seems to impose a non-referring interpretation on the
implicit head. In either (22) or (23), however, the modality by itself does
not determine the direction of the grounding function of the RRC. Rather,
it is the various referents inside the RRC that seem to do that.

9.2.2. Non-restrictive relative clauses

9.2.2.1. The logic of restriction

We noted earlier (chapter 6, section 6.3.) that some noun modifiers
can be either restrictive or non-restrictive. The difference between the two
types of modification can also be seen in REL-clauses. Compare:

(24) a. **Restrictive**:
          Women **who love too much** are often disappointed.
          (> **Some** women love too much, and **those women** are
              often disappointed)
      b. **Non-restrictive**:
          Women, **who love too much**, are often disappointed.
          (> **All** women love too much, so **all** women are
              often disappointed)

In (24a), the restrictive REL-clause serves to single out a restricted sub-set
of the domain 'women'; it narrows the domain of reference. In (24b) the
REL-clause does not single out such a restricted sub-set; it does not narrow
the domain of reference.

Non-restrictive REL-clauses (henceforth NRRCs) are typically separated from their head noun by an intonational break or a pause, marked in
written English by a comma. They are thus **parenthetical** clauses that share
some of the functional and structural characteristics of restrictive REL-
clauses.

9.2.2.2. Presupposition, assertion and challenge

NRRCs abide by the semantic clause (3a) of our definition (3), but do not conform to its pragmatic clause (3b). That is, the head noun is indeed co-referential with some participant in the state or event coded in the REL-clause. But that state/event is typically **not presupposed**, even when the head is referring and definite and the clause is under the scope of a fact modality. This difference between non-restrictive and restrictive REL-clauses may be illustrated by the different potential for challenging the information in the two types. Consider:

(25) a. **Restrictive**:
          ...so after all this trouble
          the man **who went to call the police** comes back and...
      b. **Non-restrictive**:
          ...so after all this trouble
          the man, **who went to call the police**, comes back and...

Under typical circumstances, the speaker telling the story in (25a) would be miffed by a reaction such as (26a) below, and justified in responding to that reaction with (26b):

(26) a. **Challenge**:
          So now you're finally telling me someone did call them!
      b. **Response to challenge (appropriate to 25a)**:
          I thought I'd told you that earlier!
      c. **Response to challenge (appropriate to 25b)**:
          Well, yeah, I suppose I should have mentioned that
          earlier.

In contrast, the speaker telling the story in (25b) is likely to not be miffed by challenge (26a), and simply respond with the matter-of-fact (26c). This is so because the speaker uttering a NRRC does not assume that the information about the state/event is accessible to the hearer. However parenthetical, the contents of an NRRC is asserted as new information.

9.2.2.3. Coherence and grounding

While asserted, the information in NRRCs tends to be parenthetical, and thus somehow **backgrounded**. The speaker may judge the information to be useful or relevant at that point. They may, for example, deem the information **less central** for the main thematic line of the discourse. But the information is nevertheless produced at that point in order to ground the referent to some context. That grounding may again tie the reference to the anaphoric, cataphoric or generic context. These three main directions of grounding referents by the use of NRRCs may be illustrated as follows:

(27) a. **Anaphoric grounding (definite head)**:
          The woman, **who was standing next to the door**,
          pulled a gun and...

      b. **Cataphoric grounding (REF-indefinite head)**:
          A good friend of mine, **whom I hope you'll meet some day**,
          just called and said...

      c. **Generic grounding (topical generic head)**:
          Academics, **who tend to be somewhat abstract**,
          have a peculiar sense of...

In (27a), the speaker supplies the hearer with more information concerning a noun ('the woman') that has been mentioned previously; the referent, while currently inactive, is assumed to be anaphorically accessible. In (27b), the referent ('a good friend of mine') is being introduced for the first time; the information in the NRRC gives the referent cataphoric coherence, it grounds it to the incoming discourse. In (27c), the information in the NRRC grounds 'academics' to the hearer's generic knowledge.

9.2.2.4. Restriction and reference

As shown in (27), NRRCs can modify, definite, REF-indefinite, and at least some generic head nouns. Unlike RRCs, however, NRRCs cannot modify strictly non-referring nouns. To illustrate this, compare (19a,b,c) above with (28) below:

(28) a. *Anybody, **who marries my sister**, is asking for trouble.
      b. *Any man, **whom my sister marries**, better think twice.
      c. *I know no man, **who would do this**.

The incompatibility of NRRCs with non-referring heads is also shown by the contrast:

(29) a. The man **who would say this** is a cad.
      b. *The man, **who would say this**, is a cad.

With a RRC in a non-fact modality, it is easy to interpret 'the man' in (29a) as a non-referring expression, despite the definite article. With a NRRC as in (29b), that option is removed, and (29b) is ungrammatical; unless somehow a referring sense can be imparted to the head noun, as in:[15]

(30) The man, **who would visit every summer**,
      was well known on the island.

9.2.2.5. Generic head nouns and topicality

Non-restrictive REL-clauses can modify generic head nouns. As noted in chapter 5,[16] **generic subjects**, while semantically non-referring, are pragmatically topical. In being topical, generic subjects conform to the norm of clausal subjects. As an illustration of NRRCs modifying generic subjects, compare again:

(31) a. **Restrictive**:
          Women **who love too much** are often disappointed.
          (> **Some** women love too much; **those women** are
              often disappointed)
      a. **Non-restrictive**:
          Women, **who love too much**, are often disappointed.
          (> **All** women love too much; **all** women are often
              disappointed)

In addition, NRRCs can also modify **generic objects**. Thus compare:

(32) a. **Restrictive**:
          We study elephants **who live in the tropics**.
          (> **Some** elephants live in the tropics;
              we study **those**.
      b. **Non-restrictive**:
          We study elephants, **who live in the tropics**.
          (> **All** elephants live in the tropics;
              we study **all** elephants).

What all this boils down to is the fact that generic NPs are a peculiar species of referents — logically non-referring but pragmatically referring or topical. And the restriction on NRRCs is apparently motivated by the pragmatics of reference rather than by its logic. All REL-clauses, apparently including NRRCs, may thus be considered **topicalizing constructions**.[17] An unmodified generic object may indeed be non-topical, but a NRRC marks it as topical. Thus compare:

(33) a. **Non-topical generic object**:
      He used to go up to that valley and hunt **deer**,
      and fish and camp up the river and spend the
      whole summer unwinding...
   b. **Topicalized generic object**:
      He used to go up to that valley and hunt **deer**,
      which **abound** there and **are** real easy to **track**,
      spend the whole summer stalking **them** and...

In (33a) the non-topical 'deer' appears once and is never mentioned again. In (33b), the topical 'deer' keeps recurring in both the REL-clause and beyond.

9.2.2.6. Restriction and unique reference

The functional difference between restrictive and non-restrictive REL-clauses can also be illustrated by using referentially unique head nouns, such as proper names or pronouns. Such referents cannot be modified by restrictive REL-clauses, but only by non-restrictive ones. Thus compare:

(34) a. **Non-restrictive**:
      John, **who is my friend**, is a poet
   b. **Restrictive**:
      *John **who is my friend** is a poet
   c. **Non-restrictive**:
      I, **who you all know**, will speak now
   d. **Restrictive**:
      *I **who you all know** will speak now

Restrictive modification is superfluous with referentially unique NPs because such NPs are **uniquely identifiable** to the hearer. This exclusion further underscores the role of restrictive modifiers in the grammar of referential coherence.

9.3.   THE SYNTAX OF RELATIVIZATION

9.3.1. Embedding inside a noun phrase

Relative clauses can be embedded in NPs that occupy any syntactic position in the clause — subject, direct object, indirect object, adverb or predicate. In all these positions, the deleted coreferent noun inside the REL-clause may be, at least in principle, either the subject, direct object, indirect object, adverb or predicate. This distributional freedom of REL-clauses may be illustrated by the four combinations:

(35) a. **Subject REL-clause modifying a subject noun**:
          The man **who came to dinner** left.
      b. **Subject REL-clause modifying an object noun**:
          She liked the man **who came to dinner**.
      c. **Object REL-clause modifying a subject noun**:
          The man **she married** left her.
      d. **Object REL-clause modifying an object noun**:
          She liked the man **she married**.

The four combinations in (35) are represented in the tree diagrams below. Respectively:

(36) **Subject REL-clause modifying a subject noun**:

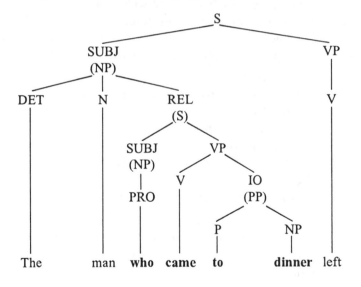

(37) **Subject REL-clause modifying an object noun**:

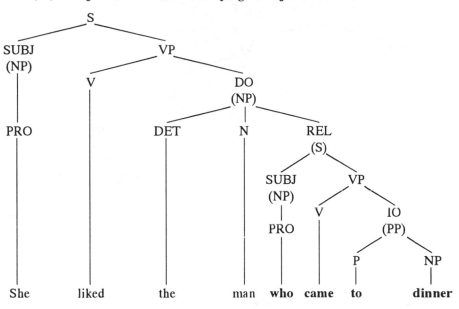

(38) **Object REL-clause modifying a subject noun**:

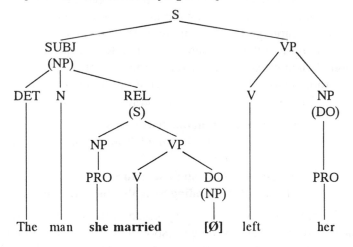

(39) **Object REL-clause modifying an object noun**:

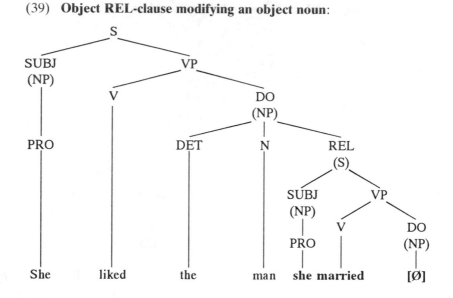

9.3.2. Deletion under identity and case-role recoverability

The syntactic difference between a simple clause and a REL-clause may be described as a **transformational process**, via which the syntactic structure of a simple clause is adjusted to its specific functional and syntactic environment — that of a noun modifier within an NP.[18] One of the most conspicuous features of such structural adjustment is the **deletion under identity** of the co-referent noun inside the REL-clause. In essence, this deletion eliminates redundancy ('repetition'). So that rather than saying the cumberstone (40a) below, with its double intonation contour, one says the shorter (40b) under a single intonation contour:

(40) a. **Simple clause (unadjusted) structure**:
          The man, I mean **the man is standing near the bar**,
          he is packing a gun.
      b. **REL-clause (adjusted) structure**:
          The man **[Ø] standing near the bar** is packing a gun.

The subject noun 'man', overtly expressed in the simple clause in (40a), is missing or **zero marked** in the corresponding REL-clause in the (40b). As an independent main clause, the subject-less REL-clause in (40b) would be odd:

(41)   *[Ø] standing near the bar

As a REL-clause, however, in the context of modifying a head noun inside an NP (i.e. (40b)), (41) is easy to interpret. Its zero-marked subject is co-referential with the head noun, and is thus recoverable from the immediate context.

Another crucial piece of information about the missing noun inside the REL-clause is not as easy to recover: Its **grammatical case-role** in the REL-clause. The head noun is not a reliable guide here, since it bears its *own* case-role (and case-marking) inside the *main* clause. In (40b), the head noun occupies the subject role in both the main and relative clause. But as noted above, the co-referent noun may occupy a variety of different case-roles in the REL-clause:

(42)   a. **Subject**:
        The man **who died**...
            (> **The man** died)
       b. **Direct object**:
        The woman **John saw**...
            (> John saw **the woman**)
       c. **Indirect object**:
        The man **Suzy gave the flower to**...
            (> Suzy gave the flower **to the man**)
       d. **Nominal predicate**:
        The sort of a person **she was**...
            (> She was **that sort of a person**)
       e. **Possessor**:
        The man **whose car I borrowed**...
            (> I borrowed **the man's** car)
       f. **Adverb**:
        The way **he did it**...
            (> He did it **this way**)

The diversity of case-roles that the zero-marked ('deleted') co-referent noun can play inside the REL-clause is an important ingredient of the function of REL-clauses. It allows speakers to ground referents with a large variety of states and events, within which the referent may participate in a variety of roles. However, when **deletion under identity** is used in forming REL-clauses, this diversity of possible case-roles incurs a penalty: It gives rise, at least in principle, to the conundrum of **case-role recoverability**.

The conundrum of case-role recoverability in relativization is:

(43) **The case-role recoverability conundrum**:
  (a) The **referential identity** of the zero-marked co-referent noun inside the REL-clause is recoverable from the head noun itself.
  (b) But the **case-role** of the zero-marked co-referent inside the REL-clause is not likewise recoverable.

The syntax of relativization, in English as elsewhere, may be viewed as the strategies by which the conundrum is solved. In English relativization, several strategies may be used, some specific to particular contexts, others allowing considerable choice and variation. In the next sections we will survey the major strategies.

9.3.3. The relative pronoun strategy

The first relativization strategy in English involves the use of case-marked **relative pronouns**. In most cases, these pronouns are derived historically from case-marked **interrogative pronouns**.[19] Typical though somewhat idealized examples are:

(44) a. **Subject**: The man **who** stopped by the house...
              (> **The man** stopped by the house)
     b. **Object**: The man **whom** she married...
              (> She married **the man**)
     c. **Place**:   The village **where** she lived...
              (> She lived **in the village**)
     d. **Reason**: (the reason) **why** he left...
              (> He left **for that reason**)
     e. **Time**:   (the time) **when** he arrived...
              (> He arrived **at that time**)
     f. **Manner**: (the way) **how** she did it...
              (> She did it **that way**)

In the case of subject and object (44a,b), the need to specify the case-role of the missing noun is real, given that typically 'a man' could be either subject, object or indirect object. In the case of examples (43c,d,e,f), the need for case-role assignment is to some extent superfluous. This is so because the head nouns themselves — 'village', 'reason', 'time', 'way' — are semantically constraining. By their very meaning they tend to suggest the case-role of the missing noun — location, reason, time, manner, respectively.[20]

In case of most indirect-objects, the REL-pronoun strategy must be supplemented by the use of prepositions (see section 9.3.6. below).

9.3.4. The relative subordinator strategy

Another relativization strategy in English dispenses with case-marked REL-pronouns, and employs the neutral **subordinator** 'that' at the beginning of the REL-clause. This strategy cannot be used freely for all case-roles. It is employed most commonly with direct and some indirect object roles, and less commonly with subjects and adverbial roles. Thus, compare (44) above with (45):

(45) a. **Subject**: The man **that** stopped by the house...
      b. **Object**:   The man **that** she married...
      c. **Place**:   *The village **that** she lived...
      d. **Time**:   *(The time) **that** he arrived...
      e. **Manner**:   ?(The way) **that** she did it...
      f. **Reason**:   (The reason) **that** he left...
      g. **Indirect object**: The woman **that** he lived with...

When this strategy is available, choosing the invariant 'that' over a case-marked REL-pronoun is a matter of considerable variation along lines of dialect, style, age, register and individual preference. What is more, the use of the invariant 'that' contributes nothing to recovering the case-role of the missing referent. Unlike REL-pronouns, 'that' is morphologically neutral, and yields no clue about the case-role of the missing co-referent noun.

9.3.5. The gap strategy

In both spoken and written English, the case-role of the missing referent inside the REL-clause can be recovered without any morphological clues. In such cases, it seems, the co-referent noun is deleted without any compensatory trace. In recovering the case-role of such a zero-marked referent, the following information is presumably available to the hearer:

(a) the lexical-semantic **case-frame** of the verb; i.e. the typical case-roles associated with the verb.
(b) the lexical identity of the zero-marked referent (identical with the head noun).
(c) both the case-roles and lexical identities of all the other participants in the REL-clause. Those are presumably left undeleted and fully case-marked in the REL-clause.

Given such information, the case-role of the missing referent — the gap in the array of arguments of the REL-clause — is inferred by subtraction.

In both spoken and written English, the gap strategy is used routinely in direct-object relativization, as in:

(46)   a. The woman **I met [Ø] yesterday**...
       b. The apple **Eve ate [Ø]**...
       c. The man **she married [Ø]**...

It is also used in indirect-object relativization, in conjunction with another strategy (see 9.3.6. below).

In addition to semantic information, the hearer may also rely on syntactic information in inferring the case-role of the missing referent. The entire computation may benefit from combining all available information:

(a) **Syntactic**:
    (i) The combination NP-NP-V under the same intonation contour cannot be interpreted as a simple clause, given the S-V-O (NP-V-NP) normal word-order of English.
    (ii) The subject NP in the REL-clause is not missing.
(b) **Semantic**:
    The verb — cf. 'meet', 'eat', 'marry' in (46) — requires both a subject and a direct-object.

In non-standard spoken dialects of English, the gap strategy can also be used in subject relativization, in combination with the proper intonation pattern. The following representative sample was culled from a detective novel by E. Leonard, a writer with a penchant for non-standard speech:[21]

(47)   a. "...it was the guy's wife **told you where he went**, huh?..." (p. 61)
       b. "...he looked more like a guy **drove a delivery truck or came to fix your air-conditioning**..." (p. 82)
       c. "...because he's not the type of guy **would take it with any degree of understanding**..." (p. 85)
       d. "...Tommy said yeah, he knew guys **talked to him personally, had Michael Weir to their club**..." (p. 139)
       e. "...so she goes to Lovejoy, tells him something important **will help him out**..." (p. 163)

f. "...I know guys **would cut Roxy in half with a chain saw**..." (p. 167)

g. "...so Lovejoy's the one **makes it happen**..." (p. 176)

h. "...Harry said there were guys in the picture business **had their secretaries call them here**..." (p. 194)

i. "...[Catlett] struck Chili as the type **wanted to be seen**..." (p. 194)

j. "...the type of guy [if he wasn't dealing drugs] **would be into some other kind of hustle**..." (p. 194)

Computing the case-role of the missing referents as subjects (rather than object) of the REL-clauses in (47) could again be done by combining semantic and syntactic information. The syntactic portion of the relevant information may be given as follows:

(a) The clause looks deceptively like a simple main clause, with the surface sequence S-V-O [NP-V-NP].

(b) But the intonation contour is not characteristic of a main clause, but rather resembles that of head-noun plus REL-clause.

(c) Judging by the semantic frames of the various verbs, no object referent is missing.

9.3.6. Indirect object relativization: Prepositions as clues

When the zero-coded co-referent noun inside the REL-clause occupies an indirect-object role, the recoverability strategy used in English always relies on the preposition that would mark that indirect object in the corresponding simple clause. Several variations of such a strategy are available:[22]

(a) The REL-pronoun strategy plus a fronted preposition

(b) The REL-pronoun strategy plus an unfronted preposition

(c) The subordinator strategy plus an unfronted preposition

(d) The gap strategy plus an unfronted preposition

Each of the four strategies is illustrated below across a number of indirect-object types. Respectively:

(48) **ASSOC-object REL-clauses**:
  a. John loves a woman **with whom** he went to school...
  b. John loves a woman **whom** he went to school **with**...
  c. John loves a woman **that** he went to school **with**...
  d. John loves a woman he went to school **with**...

(49) **DAT-object REL-clauses**:
  a. The woman **to whom** you gave the book...
  b. The woman **whom** you gave the book **to** ...
  c. The woman **that** you gave the book **to** ...
  d. The woman you gave the book **to**

(50) **BEN-object REL-clauses**:
  a. The man **for whom** I wrote the letter...
  b. The man **whom** I wrote thee letter **for**...
  c. The man **that** I wrote thee letter **for**...
  d. The man I wrote the letter **for**...

(51) **INSTR-object REL-clause**:
  a. The ladder **with which** I climbed...
  b. The ladder **which** I climbed **with**...
  c. The ladder **that** I climbed **with**...
  d. The ladder I climbed **with**...

(52) **LOC-object REL-clauses**:
  a. The house **under which** I stood...
  b. The house **which** I stood **under**...
  c. The house **that** I stood **under**...
  d. The house I stood **under**...

While all four strategies are in principle available, my hunch is that there is a growing preference, at least in the spoken informal register, for strategy (d). This strategy combines three attractive features:

  (a) It maintains the seeming preference for the gap strategy in object relativization, a strong feature of the spoken register. Presumably, it thus takes advantage of whatever computational habits are associated with the gap strategy.

  (b) It counters the worst effect of the gap strategy — lack of explicit information about the case-role of the missing referent — by leaving intact inside the REL-clause the preposition which codes that case-role.

(c) It leaves the preposition at the very same post-verbal position where, characteristically, the missing referent would be located in the simple main clause.

9.3.7. Possessive REL-clauses

9.3.7.1. Standard strategies

English has a special possessive REL-pronoun, 'whose', and a special relativization pattern associated with it. This pattern is used when the missing co-referent noun occupies the role of **possessor modifier** within some NP inside the REL-clause. The NP containing the possessor modifier can, in principle, occupy any grammatical position within the REL-clause. Thus consider:

(53) a. **Possessor within the subject NP in the REL-clause**:
The woman **whose** house burned down...
(> **The woman's** house burned down)

     b. **Possessor within the object NP in the REL-clause**:
The woman **whose** house he built...
(> He built **the woman's** house)

Examples (53a,b) above may be described as 'derived from' — or transformationally related to — the simple structures in (54a) and (55a) below, respectively:

(54) a.

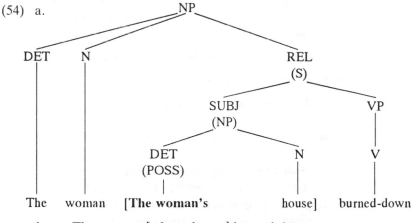

    b. ⇒ The woman [**whose** house] burned down

(55) a.

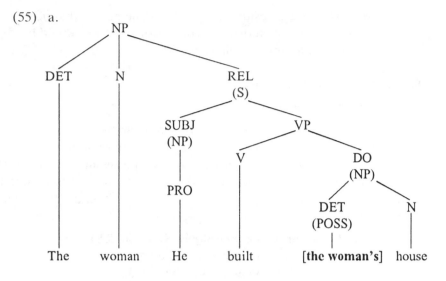

b. ⇒ The woman [**whose** house] he built

The 'derivation' in (54) and (55) involves replacing the possessor determiner with the REL-pronoun 'whose', then placing the entire NP, including
the possessor REL-pronoun, directly after the head noun.

The possessor determiner may also modify an indirect object within the
REL-clause. The four relativization strategies that can be used in such cases
follow the same four-way choice seen above for indirect-object relativization. Thus, the semantic configuration (or 'deep structure'):[23]

(56)   The woman [He went **to the woman's** house]

may be rendered, at least in theory, as either:

(57)   a. **REL-pronoun plus fronted preposition**:
           The woman [**to whose** house] he went...
       b. **REL-pronoun plus unfronted preposition**:
           The woman **whose** house he went **to**...
       c. **Subordinator plus an unfronted preposition**:
           *The woman **that** he went to the house **of**...
       d. **Gap strategy plus unfronted preposition**:
           *The woman he went to the house **of**...

Of these four strategies, (57c,d) are marginal at best; (57a) is either awk-
ward or stuffy; and (56b) is clearly preferred, at least in the spoken register.

9.3.7.2. The anaphoric pronoun strategy

In non-standard spoken English, another strategy for possessive REL-clauses is available. It involves the use of **anaphoric pronouns**. This strategy may be summarized as follows:

(a) The possessor modifier is replaced by a possessive ana-phoric pronoun that retains its normal location within the clause.

(b) The subordinator 'that' is placed between the head noun and the REL-clause.

Consider for example:

(58) a. **Possessor within the subject NP**:
          The woman **that** [**her** house] burned down last night...
      b. **Possessor within the direct-object NP**:
          The woman **that** he built [**her** house]...
      c. **Possessor within an indirect-object NP**:
          The woman **that** he went [to **her** house]...

While non-standard and perhaps jarring to the educated ear, the anaphoric pronoun strategy in fact bypasses rather elegantly the problem of recovering the case-role of the 'missing' possessor referent: The referent is not missing, it is coded by an anaphoric possessive pronoun that occupies the same position in the REL-clause as it would in the corresponding simple clause.

The anaphoric pronoun strategy is a profoundly **simplifying** strategy, in that it bypasses the major mental computation difficulty associated with relativization. A pronominal trace of the co-referent argument is left inside the REL-clauses. That 'trace' occupies the same syntactic position, and is case-marked the same way, as the missing co-referent argument would have been. To find this strategy employed in possessive relativization is not surprising, since possessive REL-clauses involve an extra level of complexity above and beyond the one found in subject, object and indirect-object REL-clauses. In the latter, co-reference holds between the head noun and some participant NP within the REL-clause. In possessive REL-clauses, the co-reference relation must reach into an NP inside the REL-clause, to a possessive modifier within that NP. This difference in syntactic complexity may be characterized through the following two tree diagrams.

(59) **Object REL-clause**:

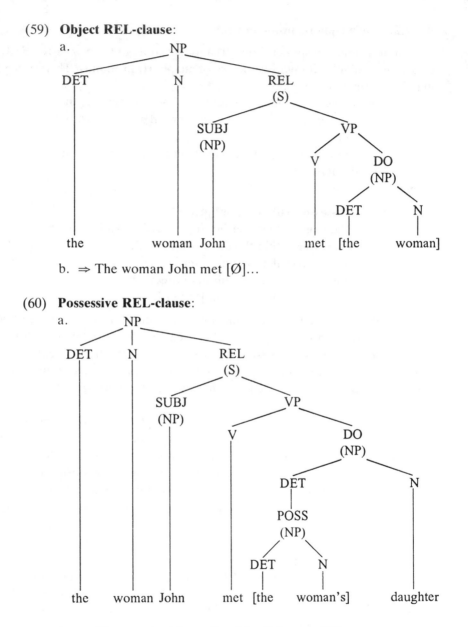

a.

b. ⇒ The woman John met [Ø]...

(60) **Possessive REL-clause**:

a.

b. ⇒ The woman **whose daughter** John met [Ø]...

We will return to the question of syntactic complexity and the use of anaphoric pronouns further below.

9.3.7.3. Relativization with complex locative prepositions

As noted in chapter 6, complex locative prepositions such as 'on top of', 'in front of', 'at the bottom of' etc. arise historically from possessive constructions, and so they retain the surface complexity of such constructions. In indirect-object REL-clauses involving such complex locative prepositions, the whole range of indirect-object relativization strategies are, at least in principle, available. Thus compare:

(61) a. **REL-pronoun plus fronted preposition**:
      The house **on top of which** he stood...

     b. **Possessive REL-pronoun plus fronted preposition**:
      ?The house **on whose** top he stood...

     c. **REL-pronoun with unfronted preposition**:
      ?The house **whose** top he stood **on**...

     d. **Subordinator 'that' plus unfronted preposition**:
      The house **that** he stood **on top of**...

     e. **Gap strategy plus unfronted preposition**:
      The house he stood **on top of**...

     f. **Anaphoric pronoun strategy**:
      The house **that** he stood **on top of it**...

Again, some of these relativization strategies are preferred over others. Both (61b) and (61c) are probably less than viable. In both the complex preposition 'on top (of)' is split down the middle, thus obscuring its new status as a single — albeit complex — lexical item. Option (61e) is probably the common colloquial choice, with the related option (61d) perhaps close behind. Option (61f), with the anaphoric pronoun, may again be confined to the non-standard colloquial register.

9.3.8. Relativization of adverbial roles: Semantically-specific head nouns

As noted earlier above, REL-clauses that involve certain **adverbial roles** — time, manner, reason, purpose or even place — have some unique characteristics. They often employ the gap strategy of relativization, with no concomitant problems of case-role recoverability. This is so because either the head noun or the REL-pronoun in such constructions is semantically specific, revealing through its meaning the likely case-role of the missing co-referent noun. Some examples of such REL-clauses are:

(62) a. The **time** he was supposed to meet me...
      b. **When** she finally showed up...
      c. The **place** we wound up staying...
      d. **Where** he went next...
      e. The **reason** she let it go was...
      f. **Why** I finally quit was...
      g. The **way** he did it was...
      h. **How** we propose to do it is...

9.3.9. Some problems with relative pronouns

9.3.9.1. 'Who' vs. 'whom'

> "...THE OMNIPOTENT WHOM
> [Will McDonough in the Boston Globe]
> Berry could get stubborn and pull out his contract that says he has complete control over playing personnel. He could make or veto any trade, decide *whom* is protected on the 37-man Plan B roster and *whom* is not, and *whom* is taken in the draft..."
> (Quoted from **The New Yorker**; emphases added.)

There is a growing tendency in standard American English, spoken as well as written, to dispense with the distinction between the subject REL-pronoun 'who' and the object REL-pronoun 'whom'. This is done by letting go of 'whom' altogether. The REL-pronoun 'who' is then retained for both subjects and objects — provided they are human. This development may be related to the growing tendency to use neither a REL-pronoun nor the invariant subordinator 'that' in object relativization.[24] Older educated speakers may still find this usage jarring. Still, the invariant 'who' is probably winning over 'whom'. Thus compare:

(63) a. The woman ({ **who** / ?**whom** }) I told it **to**...
      b. The guys ({ **who** / ?**whom** }) she grew up **with**...
      c. The woman ({ **who** / ?**whom** }) they finally appointed...

The demise of 'whom' is probably hastened by the conflation of the following factors:

(a) Subject REL-clauses are the most common in text, so that the form 'who' is bound to be the most frequent.

(b) Object REL-clauses are increasingly formed via the *gap strategy*, further reducing the text-frequency of 'whom'.

(c) Indirect-object REL-clauses increasingly combine the gap strategy with *stranded prepositions*, thus further reducing the text-frequency of 'whom'.

9.3.9.2. Animacy and relative pronouns

While English has been drifting toward neutralizing the distinction between the REL-pronouns 'who' and 'whom', the distinction between human and non-human REL-pronouns remains intact. The neutral subordinator 'that'[25] is obligatory for subject REL-clauses involving non-human heads, although it is also acceptable with human heads. Thus compare:

(64) **Subject REL-clause**:
   a. **Human**: The boy $\begin{Bmatrix} \textbf{who} \\ \textbf{that} \end{Bmatrix}$ got lost...
   b. **Non-human**: The letter **that** got lost...

The situation of object REL-pronouns is less problematic, given the wide currency of the gap strategy. Here too, the subordinator 'that' represents a neutral marker, equally acceptable with human and non-human head nouns:

(65) **Object REL-clause**:
   a. **Human**: The man (**that**) she was going to see...
   b. **Non-human**: The house (**that**) she was going to buy...

9.4. THE SYNTAX OF NON-RESTRICTIVE REL-CLAUSES

9.4.1. Parenthetic clauses, co-reference and coherence

As noted earlier above, NRRCs are parenthetical modifying expressions, separated from the head noun by an intonational break. Clearly, they are not embedded clauses in the strict sense. The presence of an intonation break makes for a less well-defined, more permissive syntactic environment, whereby many types of parenthetical expressions may occur. Thus consider:

(66) a. The woman, **who** was sitting at the bar,...
      b. The woman, **whom** I'd never seen before,...
      c. The woman — **she** was sitting at the bar — ...
      d. The woman — I'd never seen **her** before — ...
      e. The woman — and I have no idea who **she** was — ...
      f. The woman — now **this** is going to be real funny — ...
      g. The woman — hey buddy, now you shut up and listen! — ...

The first two parenthetical clauses (66a,b) are formally NRRCs. The next
two, (66c,d), contain a co-referent subject or object NP inside the parenthetic clause, roughly with the same semantic configuration as in (66a,b),
respectively. But the use of anaphoric pronouns renders these parenthetical
clauses syntactically unlike a REL-clause. In (66e,f), the distance — both
semantic and syntactic — between the parenthetic clause and typical NRRC
gets progressively wider. Thus the parenthetical clause in (66f) contains no
co-reference to the head noun, but an open-ended cataphoric referent
('this'). Finally, the parenthetical clause in (66g) has no discernible co-reference with 'woman', and is not even a declarative clause.

Examples (66) seem to suggest that there are no syntactic constraints
on what could be a parenthetical clause, but only pragmatic constraints on
coherence. The coherence may be referential, but it could be of other types.
The role of coherence in licensing a parenthetical clause after a noun is
illustrated in the following contrast:

(67) a. The woman — and **I** was sitting and waiting **there**
            so I know what happened **next** — got up and left.
      b. *The woman — and **the price of fish** was really going
            up fast that year — got up and left.

The parenthetical expression in (67a), with no co-reference to 'woman', has
many other elements of coherence ('I', 'there', 'next'). The one in (67b) has
none.

9.4.2. Morphology of NRRCs

The distribution of REL-pronouns and (the subordinator 'that') is also
different in non-restrictive REL-clauses. To begin with, the subordinator
'that' cannot be used in NRRCs. The distinction between 'who' (subject)
and 'whom' (object) can be maintained, and similarly the distinction
between 'who(m)' (human object) and 'which' (non-human object):

(68) a. **Subject, human**:

The man, $\left\{\begin{array}{l}\textbf{who}\\ \textbf{*that}\end{array}\right\}$ was sitting next to the back door,...

b. **Object, human**:

The woman, $\left\{\begin{array}{l}\textbf{who(m)}\\ \textbf{*that}\end{array}\right\}$ no one saw coming in,...

c. **Subject, non-human**:

The book, $\left\{\begin{array}{l}\textbf{which}\\ \textbf{*that}\end{array}\right\}$ was lying on the table,...

d. **Object, non-human**:

The book, $\left\{\begin{array}{l}\textbf{which}\\ \textbf{*that}\end{array}\right\}$ she saw as she came in,...

Another characteristic of NRRCs is that the gap strategy for object relativization, so productive in restrictive REL-clauses, cannot be used here. That is:

(69) a. *The woman, he met [Ø] at the office,...

(RRC: 'the woman he met at the office...')

b. *The cup, she drank from [Ø],...

(RRC: 'the cup she drank from...')

c. *The book, she gave him [Ø],...

(RRC: 'the book she gave him...'

9.4.3. NRRCs, adverbial case-roles and reference

Earlier above we noted that the head nouns modified by NRRCs cannot be non-referring. This may explain another skewing in the distribution of NRRCs: They can be readily used in relativization of the prototypically referring case-roles — subject, direct-object, indirect object. They are much less compatible with adverbial roles, which typically are non-referring. Thus compare:

(70) a. **Manner**:

RRC: The **way** he did it was...

NRRC: *The **way**, he did it, was...

b. **Reason**:

RRC: The **reason** he left was...

NRRC: *The **reason**, he left, was...

c. **Time**:
   RRC: The **time** I saw her last was...
   NRRC: *The **time**, I saw her last, was...
d. **Place**:
   RRC: The **place** you can find him is...
   NRRC: *The **place**, you can find him, is...

9.4.4. Double-headed parenthetical REL-clauses

English has another pattern of parenthetical expressions that seem to share REL-clause structure. The REL-clause in such a pattern seems **double headed**: Its lexically specified head is followed by a pause, but the REL-clause itself begins with a definite pronominal head. Most commonly, that second head is 'the one(s)', as in:

(71) a. The woman, **the one** who came last night,...
      b. The men, **the ones** you met last night,...
      c. The knife, **the one** I cut the meat with,...
      d. The tables, **the ones** they put the food on,...

In a limited number of cases, mostly with plural heads, the second head can also be a demonstrative. That is:

(72) a. The men, **those** who came late,...
      b. ?The man, **that** who came late,...

In relation to the pronominal second head, these REL-clauses seem to share the restrictive pattern. However, in relation to the first — lexical — head they seem to share the non-restrictive pattern. This is evident from the fact that the first head cannot be non-referring:

(73) a. **Restrictive**:
         I don't know **anybody** who can do it.
      b. **Non-restrictive**:
         *I don't know **anybody**, who can do it.
      c. **Double headed**:
         *I don't know **anybody**, the one who can do it.

(74) a. **Restrictive**:
         Nobody who can do that is altogether sane.
      b. **Non-restrictive**:
         ***Nobody**, who can do it, is altogether sane.
      c. **Double headed**:
         ***Nobody**, the one who can do it, is altogether sane.

(75) a. **Restrictive**:
      She's looking for **somebody** who could mow her lawn.
   b. **Non-restrictive**:
      *She's looking for **somebody**, who could mow her lawn.
   c. **Double headed**:
      *She's looking for **somebody**, the one who could mow her lawn.

Examples (75b,c) may be acceptable, but only if 'somebody' is interpreted as referring.

9.5.   HEADLESS RELATIVE CLAUSES

Thus far, we have dealt primarily with relative clauses that modify head nouns. But as noted above, a REL-clause can also be headed by a pronoun; and, at least in some patterns, it may appear **headless**. In English, headless REL-clauses employ unstressed REL-pronouns. The distribution of such REL-clauses is constrained by both animacy and case-role, so that the human 'who' and 'whom' do not appear in such constructions. As illustrations, consider:

(76) a. **Subject/non-human**:
      (i) **Headed**: **The thing** that happened then was strange.
      (ii) **Headless**: **What** happened then was strange.
   b. **Subject/human**:
      (i) **Headed**: **The man** who came to dinner left.
      (ii) **Headless**: ***Who** came to dinner left.
   c. **Object/non-human**:
      (i) **Headed**: **The thing** I saw there was strange.
      (ii) **Headless**: **What** I saw there was strange.
   d. **Object/human**:
      (i) **Headed**: **The man** I saw there was rather tall.
      (ii) **Headless**: ***Who(m)** I saw there was rather tall.
   e. **Indirect object/non-human**:
      (i) **Headed**: **The thing** he cut it **with** was a knife.
      (ii) **Headless**: **What** he cut it **with** was a knife.
   f. **Indirect object/human**:
      (i) **Headed**: **The woman** I gave it **to** is not here.
      (ii) **Headless**: ***Who** I gave it **to** is not here.

For the adverbial case-roles of place and time, the headless pattern seems unproblematic, with the REL-pronoun either stressed or unstressed:

(77) **Place**:
  a. **Unstressed**:
     From **where** she stood, she could see everything.
  b. **Stressed**:
     WHERE exactly she stood is unclear.

(78) **Time**:
  a. **Unstressed**:
     When I saw her last, she was leaving for work.
  b. **Stressed**:
     WHEN she's leaving is not yet decided.

There seems to be a correlation between the stressing of the REL-pronoun in (77), (78) above and a **non-referring status** of the time or place referent. With an unstressed REL-pronoun in (77a) and (78a), the place and time seem to be specified, thus referring. With the stressed REL-pronouns in (77b) and (78b), the place and time seem to be unspecified.[26] The correlation between stress and reference is further suggested by the behavior of the adverbial case-roles 'reason' and 'manner'. These are prototypically non-referring roles, and indeed seem to allow only the stressed REL-pronoun pattern. Thus compare:[27]

(79) **Reason**:
  a. **Unstressed**:
     ?**Why** she told it to me soon became clear.
  b. **Stressed**:
     WHY she told it to me remains a mystery.

(80)   **Manner**:
  a. **Unstressed**:
     *****How** she did it soon became clear.
  b. **Stressed**:
     HOW she did it remains a mystery.

In the informal spoken register, the unstressed REL-pronouns can be used with a specified lexical head noun, as in:[28]

(81) "...that's **the way how** this kind of monologue progresses..."

The association between stressed REL-pronouns in the headless pattern and non-referring interpretation of the missing heads is further upheld by surveying the environments in which other case-roles — the ones that are prototypically referring — exhibit this pattern. Thus compare:

(82) **Subject**:
  a. **Unstressed/realis/referring**:
     *Who came to dinner left early.
  b. **Stressed/irrealis/non-referring**:
     WHO comes to dinner here is none of your business!

(83) **Object**:
  a. **Unstressed/realis/referring**:
     *Who she saw there was Bill.
  b. **Stressed/irrealis/non-referring**:
     WHO she saw there is none of your business.

Stressed pronoun-headed REL-clauses are indeed typical of uncertainty irrealis environments, such as WH-complements of many perception-cognition-utterance verbs. For example:[29]

(84) a. You'll never guess **WHO** is coming to dinner.
  b. She doesn't know **WHO** I saw.
  c. They never said **WHO** she met there.
  d. Nobody knows **WHO** he left his fortune to.
  e. I never told her **WHAT** I did.
  f. It wasn't clear **WHERE** she went.
  g. She asked him **HOW** he did it.
  h. They don't understand **WHY** she left.

The non-referring nature of stressed REL-pronouns is further underscored by the fact that they are incompatible with non-restrictive REL-clauses. As noted earlier, NRRCs can only modify referring heads. Thus contrast:

(85) a. The man, **who** was standing near the bar,...
  b. *The man, **WHO** was standing near the bar,...
  c. The woman, to **whom** he left his house,...
  d. *The woman, to **WHOM** he left her house,...
  e. The book, **which** I left on the back seat,...
  f. *The book, **WHICH** I left on the back seat,...

A final note concerns the use of **augmented REL-pronouns** in headless REL-clauses. Augmented REL-pronouns are, for example, 'whoever', 'whatever', 'wherever', 'whenever', 'whichever' and 'however'. The '-ever' forms may be used in both realis and irrealis clauses, with the head being — at least logically — either referring or non referring. Thus, respectively:

(86) a. **Realis/referring**:
         Whoever did that must have been a saint.
               (> Someone did it, but I don't know who)
      b. **Irrealis/non-referring**:
         Whoever you see there, tell them to stop.
               (> You might see someone, so far unspecified)
      c. **Realis/referring**:
         I hope she gets **whatever** she asked for.
               (> She asked for something, but I don't know what)
      d. **Irrealis/non-referring**:
         Whatever you do, don't tell me.
               (> You might do something, but I don't know what)

The fact that the missing head of these headless constructions can be non-referring strongly suggests that the REL-clauses involved are semantically restrictive.

9.6.   SUBJECT REL-CLAUSES WITH THE MAIN VERB 'BE'

When the main or auxiliary verb in a subject REL-clause is 'be', it may be dispensed with. The REL-clause then appears without a main verb, as well as without a REL-pronoun or a subordinator. This pattern, found only in restrictive REL-clauses, can be seen with the locative main verb 'be', as in:

(87) a. **Without deletion**:
         The fiddler **who is on the roof**...
      b. **With deletion**:
         The fiddler **on the roof**...

It is also found with the progressive auxiliary 'be', as in:

(88) a. **Without deletion**:
         The woman **who is standing near the bar**...
      b. **With deletion**:
         The woman **standing near the bar**...

It is also found with the passive auxiliary 'be', as in:

(89) a. **Without deletion**:
Fish **that are caught after October 15th**...
b. **With deletion**:
Fish **caught after October 15th**...

It is also found with the copular verb 'be' followed by (at least some) adjectival predicates, as in:

(90) a. **Without deletion**:
The one **who is tall enough to touch the ceiling**...
b. **With deletion**:
The one **tall enough to touch the ceiling**...
c. **Without deletion**:
Anyone **who is qualified** may apply.
d. **With deletion**:
Anyone **qualified** may apply.

The pattern is, however, incompatible with nominal predicates following the copular 'be':

(91) a. **Without deletion**:
The woman **who was our teacher**...
b. **With deletion**:
*The woman **our teacher**...
c. **Without deletion**:
Anyone **who is an athlete**...
d. **With deletion**:
*Anyone **an athlete**...

9.7. EXTRAPOSED RELATIVE CLAUSES

The relative clauses discussed thus far directly follow their head nouns. This presumably makes the hearer's task of tracking the co-reference relation between the head noun and the missing noun inside the REL-clause more manageable. But there is a variant REL-clause construction in English that is not adjacent to its head noun, but rather is **extraposed** — placed at the end of the main clause. In this section we will outline some of the salient features of this construction.

9.7.1. Restrictiveness

Only restrictive REL-clauses may be extraposed:

(92) a. **Adjacent**:
          A man **who lost his wallet** came in yesterday.
      b. **Extraposed**:
          A man came in yesterday **who lost his wallet**.
      c. **Adjacent**:
          The woman **I told you about** came in yesterday.
      d. **Extraposed**:
          The woman came in yesterday **that I told you about**.

Pronoun-headed REL-clauses can also be extraposed, and we noted earlier that such REL-clauses are restrictive:

(93) a. **Adjacent**:
          The man, **the one who lost his wallet**, came in.
      b. **Extraposed**:
          The man came in, **the one who lost his wallet**.

In contrast, non-restrictive REL-clauses cannot be extraposed:

(94) a. John, **who lost his wallet**, came yesterday.
      b. *John came yesterday, **who lost his wallet**.
      c. Mary, **whom I told you about**, is here.
      d. *Mary is here, **whom I told you about**.

Another indication that extraposed REL-clauses are restrictive is the permissibility of the subordinator 'that' in such constructions. As noted earlier, this neutral subordinator cannot be used in NRRCs. Thus compare:

(95) a. **RRC, adjacent**:
          A man **that I met last year** came in yesterday and...
      b. **RRC, extraposed**:
          A man came in yesterday **that I met last year** and...
      c. **NRRC, adjacent**:
          *Mary, **that I told you about**, came in yesterday and...
      d. **NRRC, extraposed**:
          *Mary came in yesterday, **that I told you about**, and...

The restrictive nature of extraposed REL-clauses is also revealed from the fact that they reject uniquely-referring heads, such as names or pronouns. Thus:

(96) a. **Adjacent**:
    *John **who I saw yesterday** came in and...
  b. **Extraposed**:
    *John came in **who I saw yesterday** and...

9.7.2. Definiteness and reference

As noted by Bolinger (1991), extraposed REL-clauses can have either referring or non-referring head nouns:

(97) a. **REF-indefinite**:
    A guy came in **who offered to do it for less**,
    so we hired him
  b. **NON-REF**:
    If someone comes in **who offers to do it for less**,
    hire them.
  c. **NON-REF**:
    Nobody came in **who would do it for less**,
    so we hired the same guy as last year.

The fact that non-referring heads can take extraposed REL-clauses is another indication that these clauses are indeed restrictive.

Bolinger also suggests that the heads of extraposed REL-clauses tend to be indefinite. This is suggested by examples such as:

(98) a. **NON-REF**:
    Nobody ever came over **that John couldn't fool**.
  b. **REF-indef**:
    A man came over once **that even John couldn't fool**.
  c. **DEF**:
    ?The man came over once **that even John couldn't fool**.

(99) a. **NON-REF**:
    I've found no book by a new author
    that I think would please my sister.
  b. **REF-indef**:
    I've found a book by a new author
    that I think would please my sister.
  c. **DEF**:
    ?I've found the book by a new author
    that I think would please my sister.

Bolinger notes two exceptions to the seeming restriction on definite heads. First, a definite-marked head may be non-referring, as in:

(100) a. The man is yet to be born **that John could not fool**.
b. The problem is yet to be found **that Mary could not solve**.

Second, if a definite head is introduced with the appropriate **presentative verb**, it is compatible with extraposed REL-clauses. Thus, with the presentative verb 'come in':

(101) a. **Adjacent**:
The woman **I told you about** finally came in yesterday.
b. **Extraposed, presentative**:
The woman finally came in yesterday **that I told you about**.

Compare (101) now with the non-presentative verb 'got more and more upset':

(102) a. **Adjacent**:
The woman **they were talking about**
got more and more upset.
b. **Extraposed**:
*The woman got more and more upset
that they were talking about.

Examples such as (101) and (102) suggest that the preference for indefinite heads when the REL-clause is extraposed has nothing to do with definiteness *per se*. Rather, it has to do with the following two related facts:

(a) Extraposed REL-clauses have a **presentative** discourse function; and
(b) Presentative clauses tend to involve, typically, indefinite referents.

9.7.3. Extraposition and presentative function

We will discuss presentative clauses in more detail in chapter 11. Briefly, they are constructions used to introduce a new participant into the discourse for the first time. As such, they tend to be **paragraph-initial** (or episode-initial) rather than paragraph medial. And the introduced participant, being brand new, tends to be **indefinite**. Typically, presentative clauses display a strong bias toward verbs of **entry into the scene**. Most typically, the new participant is introduced as the subject of 'live, 'be', 'exist', 'appear', 'come in', 'enter'. But it may also be introduced as the object of '(I) have', '(we) met', '(we) got', (I) know', etc.

As can be seen from examples (92) through (102) above, typical extraposed REL-clauses tend to be those that make sense as presentative clauses. So that one could easily construct examples with infelicitous extraposed clauses with indefinite heads — by making the verb unlikely as a presentative verb. Thus consider (following Bolinger, 1991):

(103) a. **Typical presentative**:
A guy *came on stage* **that I used to know back in Milwaukee** and...
b. **Atypical presentative**:
?A guy *gave a long speech* **that I used to know back in Milwaukee** and...

As Bolinger notes, presentative predicates are finely adapted to specific nouns. Thus compare:

(104) a. **Typical presentative**:
A spot was materializing *that had pretty ominous look.*
b. **Atypical presentative**:
?A spot was getting bigger **that had a pretty ominous look**.
c. **Typical presentative**:
A pain was setting in **that I could hardly stand**.
d. **Atypical presentative**:
?A pain was getting worse **that I could hardly stand**.

The discussion above may be now summarized as follows:
(a) Restrictive REL-clauses can be a presentative device.
(b) Extraposed REL-clauses are always a presentative device.
(c) Being typically a presentative device, extraposed REL-clauses typically introduce a new participant into the discourse. That is why their head nouns are typically indefinite.
(d) But extraposed REL-clauses, unlike other presentative devices, may also re-introduce a known — definite — participant back into the scene. In such cases, which are less common, the head noun is definite.

9.7.4. Extraposition and syntactic complexity

The extraposition of REL-clauses is sometimes sensitive to considerations of **syntactic complexity**. In particular, longer REL-clauses are more likely to be extraposed, otherwise they tend to split the main clause down the middle and defer its processing. As illustration of this, compare:

> (105) a. **Long, extraposed**:
> He bought a rug from his uncle's estate **that cost him**
> **a small fortune that he couldn't really afford but went**
> **ahead and spent anyway**.
>   b. **Long, adjacent**:
> ?He bought a rug **that cost him a small fortune**
> **that he couldn't really afford but went ahead**
> **and spent anyway away** from his uncle's estate.
>   c. **Short, adjacent**:
> He bought a rug **he liked** from his uncle's estate.

The avoidance of **referential ambiguity** may also motivate restrictions on extraposition. Here semantic considerations often help in resolving potential ambiguities. Thus:

> (106) a. He gave a diamond ring to some woman
> **that he found at the party**.
>   b. He gave a diamond ring **that he found at the party**
> to some woman.
>   c. He gave a diamond ring to some woman
> **that was made for his wife years ago**.

In (106a), the REL-clause is at least in principle ambiguous, being semantically compatible with either 'diamond ring' or 'woman'. Given that potential ambiguity, the interpretation is most likely dictated by adjacency. That is, the REL-clause is more likely to modify 'woman'. An extraposed interpretation, with the REL-clause modifying 'diamond ring', is less likely. For the REL-clause to modify 'diamond ring' unambiguously, it must be placed adjacent to it, as in (106b). The REL-clause in (106c), on the other hand, is semantically compatible only with 'diamond ring' but not with 'woman'. An extraposed interpretation is thus acceptable.

Consider finally:

(107) a. He gave the ring to Mary **that he found at the party**.
      b. He gave a ring to her **that he found at the party**.
      c. He gave a ring to Mary, **whom he met at the party**.

Unlike in (106a), the REL-clause in (107a,b) could only be interpreted as extraposed, i.e. as modifying 'ring'. This is so because restrictive REL-clauses cannot be used with referentially unique heads. The REL-clause in (107c), being semantically incompatible with 'ring', is easy to interpret as a modifier of the adjacent 'Mary' — but only as a non-restrictive modifier.

9.8. RELATIVIZATION AND SYNTACTIC COMPLEXITY

9.8.1. Preamble

A restrictive REL-clause is embedded as noun modifier within a noun phrase, which in turn partakes — as subject or object — in another clause. By definition, embedding one clause within another increases the syntactic complexity of the host clause. If a language has the formal grammatical machinery for embedding one clause within another, it more likely also possesses the machinery — the very same ones — for re-doing the same process over again; that is, for embedding a clause within an embedded clause. This **recursive process** is called **multiple embeddings**.

While in principle available to the speaker, multiple embedding is severely constrained in natural communication, both oral and written. And like other limits on permissible syntactic complexity, constraints on multiple embedding are probably governed by considerations of **analytic complexity**. Such considerations are more apparent in speech perception, but probably also apply to speech production. In this section we will discuss two types of multiple embedding in relativization. Each, in its own domain, seems to suggest the cognitive consequences of syntactic complexity.

9.8.2. Ross's complex-NP constraint

There is a class of syntactic operations, including relativization, that can apply to an NP inside a main clause, but are rather problematic when applied to an NP inside an embedded clause. Ross (1967) has named the limit on such operations the **Complex-NP Constraint** (henceforth CNPC).

Ross's constraint applies to REL-clause as well as to several other complex modifiers in the noun phrase.[30] To illustrate Ross's constraint with REL-clauses, consider the embedding of clause (108b) below as a REL-clause modifying the object NP in clause (108a), yielding the once-embedded structure (108c):

(108) a. **Main clause**:
The woman saw **the dog**
　　 b. **Subordinate clause**:
The dog bit a man
　　 c. **Embedding configuration**:
The woman saw **the dog** [that [Ø] bit the man]

As noted earlier, the head noun can be co-referent with either the subject or the object of the REL-clause. So that the very same simple transitive clause, say (108a), can yield two possible REL-clauses. In one, it is a subject REL-clause modifying 'woman', as in (109a) below. In the other, it is an object REL-clause modifying 'dog', as in (109b):

(109) a. The **woman** [who [Ø] saw the dog]...
　　 b. The **dog** [(that) the woman saw [Ø]]...

The syntactic structure of (109a) may be given as (110):

(110)

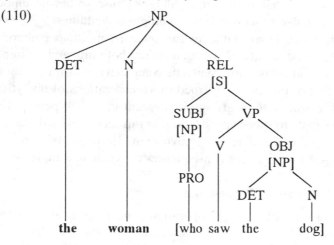

The syntactic structure of (109b) may be given as (111):

(111)

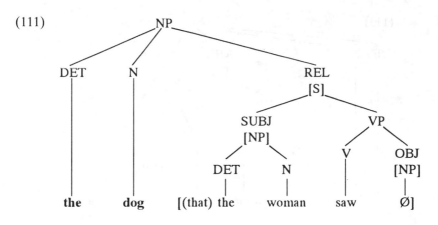

In the examples (109a,b) and (110), (111) above, the symbol [Ø] inside the REL-clause occupies the same grammatical position — subject or object, respectively — of the missing co-referent NP.

Suppose now that an NP in the main-clause is already modified by a REL-clause. One could increase the complexity of such a construction by modifying the same head noun with another REL-clause, as in:

(112) The **dog** [that the woman saw **Ø**] [that **Ø** bit the man]...

The twice-embedded structure in (112) is easily interpretable as the diagrammed structure in (113):

(113)

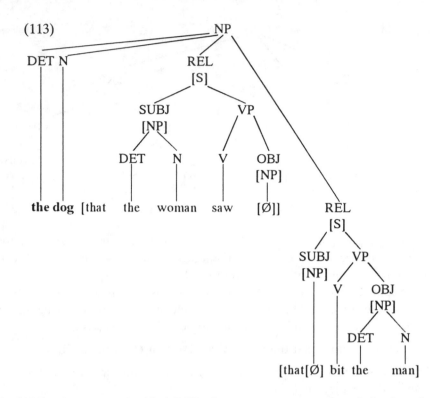

In (113), the two embedded REL-clauses are on a par, each having the same modifier status vis-a-vis the head noun.[31] Equally easy to interpret is a twice-embedded configuration where the second REL-clause modifies an NP inside the first one, as in:

(114) **The woman** [who [Ø] saw **the dog** [that [Ø] bit the man]]...

The syntactic structures of (114) may be represented in the tree diagram (115):

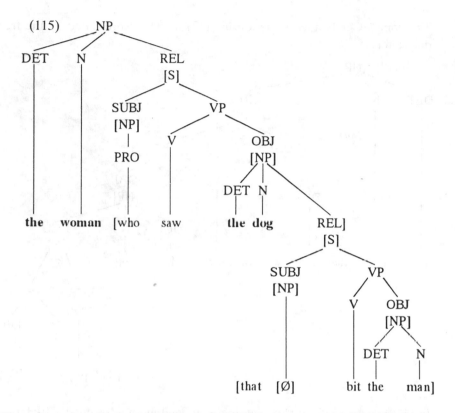

(115)

The type of multiple embedding of REL-clauses seen in (114)/(115) can proceed further without seeming problems of mental processability, as in:

(116) This is **the cat** [that [Ø] chased **the rat**
[[Ø] that ate **the cheese** [that [Ø] was.....]]]

The common denominator of all the permissible multiple embeddings above is that the coreference relation holds between a head noun and its 'missing' co-referent NP inside an **adjacent REL-clause**.

What seems to be much harder to process, it seems, are multiple embeddings where the coreference relations crosses over more than one clausal boundary. That is, embedding configurations whereby the REL-clause is not adjacent to its head noun. For example:

(117) ***The man** [that the woman saw **the dog** [that [Ø] bit [Ø]]]...

The complex embedded structure in (117) may be represented by the tree diagram (118):

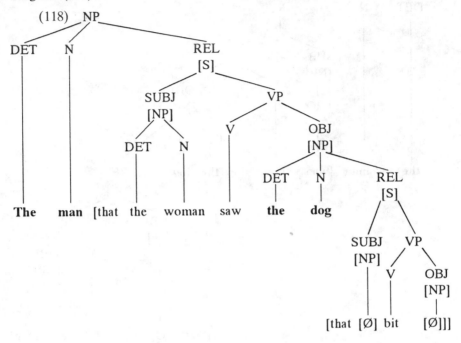

In (118), the co-referent to 'the dog' is indeed in an adjacent REL-clause. But 'the man' and its co-referent in the second REL-clause are not in adjacent clauses. Just as hard to process is the complex embedded structure in:

(119) ***The dog** [that the woman saw **the man** [that [Ø] bit [Ø]]]...

The complex structure in (119) may be represented by the tree diagram (120):

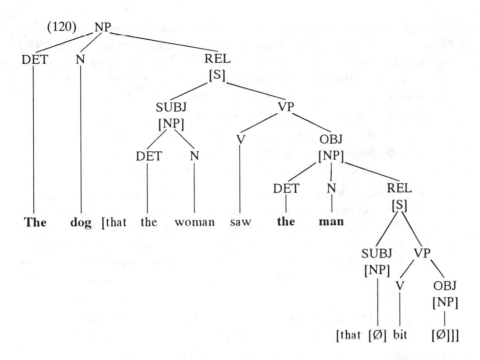

In (120) the co-referent to 'the man' is indeed in an adjacent REL-clause. But now 'the dog' is not adjacent to its co-referent inside the second REL-clause. In both (117/118) and (119/120), the co-reference relation spans over an intervening clause to reach inside a **non-adjacent REL-clause**. That is, it must cross two clause boundaries.[32]

In non-standard dialects of English, structures such as (117/118) and (119/120)) are in fact attested. However, they display one feature that seems to alleviate the processing difficulty: An **anaphoric pronoun** that marks the co-referent NP inside the non-adjacent REL-clause. Thus, respectively:

(121) a. **The man** [that the woman saw
             the dog [that [Ø] bit **him**]]]...
      b. **The dog** [that the woman saw
             the man [that **it** bit [Ø]]]]...
             or
      c. **The dog** [that the woman saw
             the man [that [Ø] bit **it**]

The zero-marked co-referent — 'dog' in (121a), 'man' in (121b) or 'dog' in (121c) — is now in a REL-clause that is adjacent to its head noun. The anaphoric pronoun — 'him' in (121a), 'it' in (121b) and 'it' in (121c) — is now in a clause that is not adjacent to its head noun. However, simple anaphoric reference can cross over one clause in English, as in:

(122) a. John wanted to talk to **Mary**, but he was so busy all
          day at the office, so he finally called **her** at home.
      b. **Mary** wanted to talk to John, who was just too busy
          all day at the office, so **she** finally got him at home.

The tendency to use anaphoric pronouns in complex but non-adjacent embedded structures is also found — in the spoken register — in structures that are judged acceptable even without such pronouns. Thus example (123a) below, where the intervening clause is a V-complement, is presumably acceptable in standard English without the anaphoric pronoun inside the non-adjacent REL-clause. But its equivalent (123b) is quite natural in the spoken register:

(123) a. **The thing** [that they said [that [Ø] was true]] wasn't.
      b. **The thing** [that they said [that **it** was true]] wasn't.

The structure of (123a,b) may be represented by the tree diagram (124):

(124)

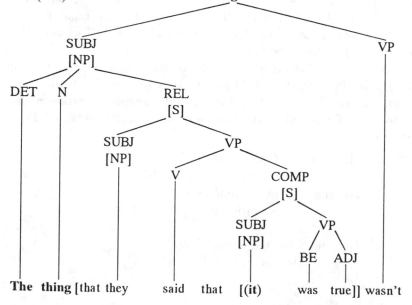

Similarly, a complex structure such as the standard (125a) can be heard in the spoken register as (125b):

(125) a. **The man** [that she thought [that they killed [Ø]]] lived.
    b. **The man** [that she thought [that they killed **him**]] lived.

The complex structure of (125a,b) may be represented by the tree diagram (126):

(126)

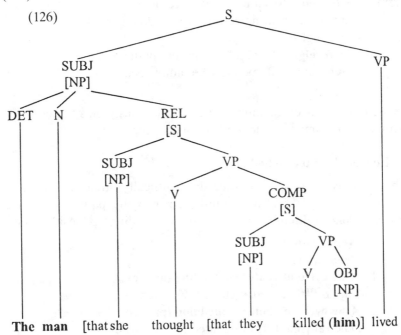

The acceptability of structures such as (126) with the anaphoric pronoun suggests that speakers find these structures hard to process without the pronoun, presumably because here as well the co-reference relations are stretched across an intervening clause. And the intervening clause may be of other types as well, as in:[33]

(127) "...you address **someone** [who you don't know [who **they** are...]]"

One may argue that the constraints on coreference relations in relativization involve the **temporal distance** between the head noun and its co-referent, rather than a constraint on clause adjacency or crossing more than one clausal boundary. But at least some facts seem to suggest that an intervening clause — rather than an intervening string of words — is at issue. To illustrate this, compare in (128a) and (128b) below. The phonological distance between the head noun 'foreign official' and the REL-pronoun 'who' in the extraposed REL-clause is roughly equal in the two examples. However, the intervening material includes a clause — V-complement — in the unacceptable (128b), but it is not a clause in the acceptable (128a):

(128) a. **A foreign official** came into a congressional
committee hearing yesterday **who** didn't speak
any English.

b. *__A foreign official__ told us yesterday that the
situation was desperate **who** didn't speak any
English.

The clausehood status of the intervening material thus seems to play a role in determining the limits of tolerated syntactic complexity.

9.8.3. Repeated center embedding

The increase in speech-processing difficulty that accompanies increased embedding can also be illustrated with the pattern known as **center embedding** ('self embedding', 'nested embedding'). Consider first:

(129) a. **Main clause**:
The rat died.

b. **One cycle of center embedding (active)**:
The rat [that the cat chased [Ø]] died.

c. **One cycle of center embedding (passive)**:
The rat [that [Ø] was chased by the cat] died

d. **Two cycles of center embedding (active)**:
*The rat [that the cat [that the dog hated [Ø]]
chased [Ø]] died

e. **Two cycles of center embedding (passive)**:
The rat [that [Ø] was chased by the cat
[that [Ø] was hated by the dog]] died

The simple main clause (129a) is unproblematic. With one cycle of center embedding, as in (129b), processing is still possible, although the alternative passive construction in (129c) is probably easier to process. With one more embedding cycle, as in (129d), the construction seems to exceed the tolerance of most speakers. But converting (129d) away from center embedding by passivization, as in (129e), again makes the complexity tolerable.

There are two alternative explanations for why the center embedding in (129d) is hard to process. The first notes the peculiar surface pattern in (129d), schematically given as:

(130) **SUBJ** [*SUBJ* [SUBJ VP] *VP*] **VP**

This pattern separates the subject of each clause (except the innermost one) from its predicate (VP) by a whole intervening clause. The normal processing strategy is keyed to subjects being adjacent to their predicates. The validity of this explanation suffers from a fatal flaw: In the once-embedded (129b), the very same separation between subject and its proper VP already exists, seemingly without creating any processing difficulty.

An alternative explanation invokes the constraint we have noted repeatedly above — the proscription on co-reference relations in relativization stretching across an **intervening clause**. In the twice center-embedded (129d), the head noun 'cat' is separated from the location of its co-referent inside the REL-clause by precisely such an intervening clause. In the once center-embedded (129b), on the other hand, no such separation exists. And neither does such separation exist in the twice-embedded (129e) with passive structures. Our second explanation thus seems to account for a wider range of facts in a more general way, without making unsupported predictions.[34]

9.9. NON-FINITE RELATIVE CLAUSES

9.9.1. Preamble

The REL-clauses discussed above were, without exception, **finite** clauses, in the sense defined in chapter 6. Their finite status can be gauged from three facets of their morpho-syntactic structure:

    (a) The verbs in all these REL-clauses are marked with the normal tense-aspect-modality found in simple main clauses.

    (b) The verbs in such REL-clauses show the same pattern of subject-verb agreement as they would in simple main clauses.

    (c) When the subject or object are present, i.e. not missing due to co-reference, they are marked morphologically and syntactically the same way they would be in simple main clauses.

In this section we discuss another type of subordinate — embedded — construction that seems to fall under at least the semantic portion (3a) of our general definition of REL-clauses. To begin with, such clauses are adjacent to what seems to be a head-noun within a main clause. Further, one of the REL-clause's participants is co-referential with that head noun. In terms of morpho-syntactic structure, however, **non-finite REL-clauses** deviate from finite REL-clauses.

9.9.2. Complement-like structure

As examples of non-finite REL-clauses, consider first:

(131) a. She was looking for **someone** to stay at her house.
　　　 b. We found **someone** to fix the roof.
　　　 c. I need **someone** to come over tomorrow and...
　　　 d. She wanted **someone** to come over right away.
　　　 e. She had **nobody** to do it with.

Examples (131) display the following semantic and syntactic characteristics of non-implicative manipulative-verb complement constructions:[35]

(132) **Semantic and syntactic properties**:
　　　 (a) The main verb is transitive, and has an object that is either non-referring or unspecified.
　　　 (b) The verb in the subordinate clause is marked by the infinitive form.
　　　 (c) The subject of the subordinate clause is zero-marked.
　　　 (d) The subject of the subordinate clause is co-referent with the object of the main clause.

Because the object of the main clause is adjacent to the subordinate clause, however, the co-reference condition (132d) also matches the co-reference condition on REL-clauses — provided the object is interpreted as a head noun.

9.9.3. REL-clause-like meaning

When one is called upon to paraphrase constructions such as (131), both a V-complement paraphrase and a REL-clause paraphrase turn out to be plausible, at least for some of the examples. As an illustration of this possibility, consider the two possible paraphrases of (131a), repeated as (133a):

(133) a. **Non-finite REL-clause version**:
   She was looking for someone **to stay at her house**

b. **V-complement paraphrase**:
   She was looking for someone
   so that they would stay at her house.

c. **REL-clause paraphrase**:
   She was looking for someone
   who would stay at her house.

For other examples in (131), however, only the REL-clause interpretation is plausible. One such example is (131d) above, repeated as (134a):

(134) a. **Non-finite REL-clause**:
   She wanted someone **to come over right away**.

b. **V-complement paraphrase**:
   *She wanted someone
   so that they would come over right away.

c. **REL-clause paraphrase**:
   She wanted someone
   who would come over right away.

And similarly for (131e), reproduced in (135a):

(135) a. **Non-finite REL-clause**
   She had **nobody to do it with**.

b. **V-complement paraphrase**:
   *She had nobody **so that they would do it**.

c. **REL-clause complement**:
   She had nobody **who she could do it with**.

Likewise for (131b), reproduced as (136a):

(136) a. **Non-finite REL-clause**:
   We found someone **to fix the roof**.

b. **V-complement paraphrase**:
   ?We found someone **so that they would do it**.

c. **REL-clause paraphrase**:
   We found someone **who would fix the roof**.

Non-finite REL-clauses seem to be **syntactic hybrids**: They display much of the morpho-syntactic structure of verb complements, but they also seem to share some of the meaning structure of REL-clauses. As it turns out, the situation is more complicated.

9.9.4. Problems of co-reference[36]

In constructing examples (131), two factors were manipulated deliberately in order to direct the co-reference relationship into one that would
hold between the object of the main clause and the zero-marked subject of
the subordinate clause:

   (a) The verbs in the subordinate clauses were either kept
       intransitive, or had an object whose semantical properties
       barred co-reference with either the subject or the object
       of the main clause.

   (b) The verbs in the subordinate clauses were selected so co-
       reference between the subject of the subordinate clause
       and the subject of the main clause would be semantically
       implausible.

But the hybrid non-finite subordinate clauses we deal with here do not of
themselves demand such stringent co-reference conditions. And when these
restrictions are removed, a vastly more complex co-reference situation is
revealed.

Consider first:

   (137) a. She was looking for someone to teach.
         b. She was looking for someone to teach French.
         c. She was looking for someone to teach French **to**.
         d. She was looking for someone to teach **her** French.

In (137d), the main-clause subject 'she' is co-referent with the subordinate-
clause object 'her' — in the absence of other visible candidates. The
remaining argument of the subordinate clause — its zero-marked subject —
could still presumably be coreferent with 'she'. However, if that were the
case, the anaphoric object pronoun should have been the reflexive 'herself'.
That is:

   (138) *She is looking for someone to teach **herself** French

But (138) is implausible because 'someone' cannot be coreferent with 'her',
but only with the zero-marked subject of the subordinate clause.[37] However, that subject is already pre-empted as the co-referent of 'she' — given
the reflexive pronoun. So, with the reflexive interpretation ruled out, a
combination of non-arbitrary semantic and syntactic considerations completely dictates the choice of co-reference in (137d).

Consider next (137c). The stranded preposition 'to' is a clear REL-clause recoverability device, tagging the head noun as co-referent with the zero-marked indirect object in the subordinate clause. The only adjacent head noun available — assuming a REL-clause configuration — is 'someone'. Again, the non-reflexive form rules out co-reference between 'someone' and 'she'. So only 'she' could be co-referent with the zero-marked subject in the subordinate clause. And the only subordinate clause slot left open for co-reference with 'she' is the subject slot. Once again, non-arbitrary semantic and syntactic considerations combine to fully determine the assignment of co-reference.

Consider next (137a). Here both the subject and object in the subordinate clause are zero-marked, and are presumably equally open to an arbitrary assignment of co-reference. But an **equi-case** constraint now seems to prevail: The subordinate clause subject must be coreferent with the main-clause object. But why?

Before explaining why, let us formulate the constraint more precisely as a **default equi-subject** constraint:

(139) **Default equi-subject constraint**:

"If

(a) both the subject and object in the subordinate clause are zero-marked, and are open for co-reference to either the subject or object of the main clause;

and if

(b) no semantic, syntactic or pragmatic factors exist to bias the co-reference one way or another; then an equi-subject co-reference strategy holds.

That is:

(c) The zero-marked subject will be interpreted as co-referent with the main-clause subject; and

(d) The zero-marked object will, by default, be interpreted with whatever other case-role that is available in the main clause".

In formulating (139), we chose to interpret the **equi-subject condition** (139c) as the main component of the general constraint, and to view the **equi-object condition** (139d) as the mere consequence of the equi-subject constraint. The reason for such a choice will be made apparent further below.

Consider next:

(140) a. John was looking for someone to marry **him**
      b. John was looking for someone to marry

In (140a), the object pronoun 'him' could only be co-referent with the main-clause subject 'John', for a combination of reasons:
   (a) The masculine gender of 'him'.
   (b) The cultural-pragmatic constraints against same-sex marriage.
   (c) The cultural-semantic constraint against self-marriage.
The only co-reference relation left open for the zero-marked subject of the subordinate clause in (140a) is then with the main-clause object 'someone'. And so reasons (a),(b),(c) constitute the substance of escape-clause (139b), contravening the default equi-subject condition (139c). In (140b), on the other hand, no semantic, syntactic or pragmatic factors constrain the assignment of co-reference one way or another. With no motivation in sight to specify otherwise, the default equi-subject condition (139c) decides the matter. Consider next:[38]

(141) a. John needs someone to work for
      b. John needs someone to work for **him**

This example conforms in all details to (140), and abides by exactly the same procedure of assigning co-reference.

In the next few examples, the object of the main clause is referring:

(142) a. I have orders to deliver
      b. I have bread to deliver

Example (142a) is — at least potentially — ambiguous, accommodating the readings of either (143a) or (143b) below:

(143) a. **V-complement interpretation**:
          Someone ordered me to deliver something.
      b. **REL-clause interpretation**:
          I have orders that must be delivered by me.

The ambiguity of (142a) hinges on 'orders' being either a simple object noun or a nominalized verb. When the nominalized-verb interpretation of 'orders' is chosen, as in (143a), the subordinate clause is taken to be the verbal complement of 'order'. When the noun interpretation of 'orders' is chosen, as in (143b), the subordinate clause is taken to be a REL-clause modifying a head noun. But one way or another, neither the nominalized 'orders' nor the noun 'orders' can be the subject of 'deliver', which requires a human-agent subject. So in either interpretation, the only argument in the main clause that is available for co-reference with the zero-marked subject of 'deliver' is the subject 'I'. Once again, non-arbitrary semantic and syntactic considerations decide the assignment of co-reference. Superficially, the equi-subject condition (139c) is obeyed. But the issue is settled by condition (139b), without invoking condition (139c).

Consider next the unambiguous example (142b). The main-clause object 'bread' could not be a nominalized verb. Further, 'bread' cannot be the subject of 'deliver', only its object. Therefore only the main-clause subject 'I' is available for co-reference with the zero-marked subject of 'deliver'. Once again, co-reference is assigned by non-arbitrary semantic and syntactic considerations (139b), making condition (139c) moot.

Consider finally:

(144) a. We received instructions to distribute.
      a. We received books to distribute.

The principles that govern co-reference assignment in (144a,b) completely parallel those in (142a,b). Again, (144a) is ambiguous. Again, (144b) is unambiguous; again, independent semantic and syntactic factors in (144b) conform superficially to the equi-subject condition (139c). But again, non-arbitrary semantic factors determine the assignment of co-reference in both cases, and make it unnecessary to invoke the default condition.

9.9.5. Why the equi-subject condition?

We return now to our equi-subject principle (139c). What it says in simple language is this:

> "If no exceptional clues are present to stir the assignment of co-reference otherwise, the natural tendency in language would be to assign the co-reference of a zero-marked subject to the subject of the preceding clause. In other words, the natural ('default') choice in language is to assume **subject continuity**".

The bias toward subject continuity in discourse is a well recognized phenomenon. The thematic continuity of a natural text is manifest most conspicuously by the **continuity of the topical referent** across a chain of clauses. As noted in earlier chapters,[39] the grammatical subject tends to be the most topical clause participant, the one that is most likely to be talked about and therefore to recur in discourse.[40] Our equi-subject principle (139c) is one more reflection of a general strategy of constructing coherent discourse.

The equi-subject principle (139c) of assigning co-reference to zero-marked NPs is independently attested in many constructions in English. Consider for example a simple clausal conjunction,[41] as in:

(145) **Mary** called Sally and then [Ø] went to see Joe.

The zero-marked subject of 'went' in (145) could only be co-referent with the preceding clause's subject ('Mary'), not with its object ('Sally'). What is more, the zero-marked anaphoric referent in the conjoined (second) clause could be its subject, but never its object. For this reason (146a) below is not an appropriate way of conjoining two clauses coherently:

(146) a. *Mary called Sally and then Joe went to see [Ø].
     b. Mary called Sally and then Joe went to see **her**.
     c. Mary called Sally and then Joe came to see **her**.

In contrast, (146b) is grammatical and coherent. It is not clear whether 'her' in (146b) is biased toward co-reference with 'Mary' rather than with 'Sally'. If a bias exists, it is probably due to pragmatic considerations. And the bias may be different in (146c).[42]

Finally the equi-subject principle also seems to govern the assignment of co-reference in the case of participial ADV-clauses, as in:[43]

(147) a. [Ø] Throwing caution to the wind, **John** called Mary.
     b. **Mary** called Joe, [Ø] having first taken a long nap.

The equi-subject principle governing co-reference assignment is not an arbitrary grammatical convention. Rather, it is a well-known strategy used to establish discourse coherence. By pointing out its functional motivation, one does not necessarily make such a grammatical convention less 'grammatical'. Rather, one simply points out to the non-arbitrary motivation for — much of — grammar.[44]

NOTES

1) See chapter 5 and chapter 13.

2) Intonation is probably the most reliable criterion for deciding whether a clause is embedded within another clause. A unified intonation contour over two verbal clauses is a strong indication that they are joined together into a single complex clause. Other grammatical indicators of embedding tend to correlate with intonation.

3) Taken as a mental model, the transformational terminology may suggest actual mental operations, with a similar input-output relation during speech production, and a converse relation during speech perception. The validity of such a model has yet to be demonstrated empirically.

4) See chapter 1, section 1.4.

5) As we shall see below, the sense of 'presupposition' that is relevant here is considerably weaker than the logical definition of presupposition.

6) The reason examples (7a,b,c) were not replicated here is because each one involves information to which either the speaker ('I') or the hearer ('you') has *privileged access*. The rules of evidence governing the epistemic status of propositions automatically shield such information from challenge. For discussion of this, see Givón (1984a, chapter 7).

7) For discussion of this structure-building framework from a cognitive perspective, see Gernsbacher (1990).

8) For the general framework within which this interpretation is anchored, see again chapter 5, as well as Givón (1990, chapter 20).

9) Grounding via a RRC is probably superfluous for unique generic definites such as (15c). They depict unique referents.

10) Cf. example (15c) above.

11) I owe this example to Dwight Bolinger (in personal communication).

12) This is an example of the past-marked *subjunctive* form in English. The use of the past-tense under an irrealis scope creates a less probable hypothetical situation. See further discussion of the subjunctive in conditional ADV-clauses, chapter 13.

13) For gradation of referential intent, see chapter 5, section 5.2.6.

14) For headless REL-clauses, see section 9.5., below.

15) The past-habitual use of 'would' here of course makes a referring interpretation of the head noun possible, since it allows 'the man' to be a referring subject of the REL-clause.

16) Section 5.4.

17) For various topicalizing constructions, see chapters 10 and 11. As noted in chapter 5 (section 5.10.), reference in language involves primarily the pragmatics of topicality, rather than the logic ('semantics') of unique reference.

18) Adopting such a transformational description — or metaphor — following Chomsky (1965) is a matter of convenience, and makes no compelling claims about the mental reality of such a process.

19) For interrogative speech-acts and the use of interrogative pronouns, see chapter 12.

20) It is not an accident that the head nouns in these constructions are optional, given that they don't add much more case-role information than is already given in the REL-pronoun. Such REL-clause are easily be rendered *headless*; see section 9.5. below.

21) Elmore Leonard, **Get Shorty**, NY: Dell (1990).

22) The choice between variants may again be a matter of dialect, register, style or individual preference. One suspects that more systematic communicative factors may also condition the choice, but for the moment it is not clear what they are.

23) The term 'deep structure' is used here in Chomsky's (1965) sense of 'underlying' semantic configuration.

24) See sections 9.3.5., 9.3.6. above.

25) Or 'which', under certain conditions; see further below.

26) This may of course be the consequence of the context within which such headless expressions can be used — embedded WH-questions. See chapter 12.

27) Because of the strong correlation between the non-fact modality and the non-referring interpretation of nominal referents, the test environments below deliberately bias the unstressed examples toward a realis mode, and the stressed ones toward irrealis mode.

28) Bolinger (in personal communication, citing the observed behavior of a prominent linguist during a 1977 lecture).

29) See discussion in chapter 7, section 7.5.3.

30) Other large post-nominal modifiers, such as possessive phrases and noun complements, fall in this class.

31) In a more formal system, one would need to worry about whether to represent the two REL-clauses as either a coordinated-restricted or a subordinated-restricted configuration. While this is a potentially-useful logical distinction, we will not deal with it further here. The distinction may be illustrated in the following examples, respectively:

    (a) The man [who came yesterday] [(and) who left early]...
    (b) The man [[who came yesterday] who left early]...

The subordinate-restricted structure (b) is presumably used in a context when several men may have come yesterday, but only one left early. In using such a configuration, the first REL-clause restricts the domain of the head noun 'man', the second the domain of the already-restricted NP 'the man who came yesterday'. In the coordinate-restricted structure (a), each REL-clause modifies only the head noun, suggesting a context whereby only one man came yesterday and only that man left early.

32) In addition, the second REL-clause in (120) is ambiguous, and may be interpreted as either 'The man bit the dog' or 'The dog bit the man'.

33) Spontaneous contribution by a graduate student in a seminar discussion.

34) See Chomsky (1965), where this construction is used to illustrate the difference between 'performance' (cognitive complexity) and 'competence' (grammaticality).

35) See chapter 7.

36) I am indebted to Derek Bickerton for drawing my attention to the co-reference problems of these hybrid constructions. His conclusion, derived from Chomsky's work, was that no function-based explanation existed that would make sense of the seeming chaos of co-reference assignment decisions. My own conclusion is that indeed no simple, single-factor functional explanation exists. Rather, a number of semantic, syntactic and pragmatic factors collaborate in guiding the language user toward a preferred co-reference assignment. This represents a paradigm case of how complex and interactive the use of language in communication is, and why one should not insist *apriori* that functional accounts of language behavior be simple and invoke only a single factor. As in biologically-based behavior elsewhere, complex phenomena are seldom accounted for by simple, single-cause explanations.

37) Not to mention that a double-reflexive situation would have obtained then, one that would need to be coded as the semantically odd: '*She was looking for herself to teach herself French'.

38) This was Bickerton's original example.

39) See in particular chapters 3, 5 and 8.

40) For a cross-linguistic, quantified documentation of this, see Givón (ed., 1983a).

41) For conjoined clauses, see chapter 13.

42) The pragmatics of perspective and deictic point-of-reference may intervene here. 'Mary' is the subject of the first clause, and her perspective is more likely to determine the selection of reference point for the second clause, all other things being equal. With the verb 'go' carrying the inference of "motion away from the reference point", and with 'Joe' being the subject of 'go', the context seems to weaken Mary's claim on the point of reference. 'Come', on the other hand, carries the inference of "motion toward the reference point". The context now makes it more plausible for Mary's location to be the reference point for Joe's motion. But the factors that control the assignment of reference-point in motion clauses are complex and subtle.

43) For participial ADV-clauses, see chapter 13.

44) And by showing that most grammatical rules are functionally motivated, one does not necessarily need to preclude the possibility that some are more arbitrary. There are perfectly normal biological mechanisms that contribute to less-than-perfect structure-function pairing.

10 | CONTRASTIVE FOCUS CONSTRUCTIONS

10.1 INTRODUCTION

The sense of the term 'focus' we deal with here is fairly narrow, having to do with the notions of **contrast** or **emphasis**. Another usage of the term 'focus' does exist, i.e. the **focus of assertion** ('focus of new information') in the clause.[1] While this second notion is indeed important, it will not be dealt with directly here — except for noting its logical relationship with contrastive focus.

The logical relationship between contrastive focus and assertion focus can be given as a one-way conditional implication:

(1) "If contrastive focus, then also assertion focus"
      (but not necessarily vice versa)

The conditional expression in (1) means that contrasted information is always under assertion focus, but items under assertion focus may or may not be contrasted. A similar partial inclusion relation also exists between contrastive focus and **topicality** ('referential importance').[2] That is:

(2) "If contrastive, then topical"
      (but not necessarily vice versa).

The conditional expression in (2) means that contrasted elements are also topical, but topical elements may or may not be under contrastive focus.

The difference between 'contrast' and 'topicality' may be put in the following terms: Importance tends to involve the **speaker's** evaluation of the status of the information. Contrast, on the other hand, tends to also involve the speaker's evaluation of the **hearer's** attitude toward the information.[3]

10.2. FUNCTIONAL ASPECTS OF CONTRASTIVE FOCUS

10.2.1. Predictability, expectation and contrast

The grammatical notion 'contrast' depends on the more general cognitive dimension of informational **predictability** or its converse, **counter-expectancy**. Verbal clauses often carry several chunks of information, where each 'chunk' is usually a word. Each word in the clause then carries its own specific level of predictability.

One dimension of informational predictability is **identifiability**. Some chunks of information are considered by the speaker as identifiable to the hearer, i.e. (roughly) **definite**.[4] Such chunks are in an obvious sense more predictable. Other chunks of information are not identifiable, i.e. (roughly) **indefinite**.[5] Such chunks are obviously less predictable. But informational predictability does not depend merely on identifiability or definiteness. Rather, it depends on the communicative context ('perspective') within which the information is transacted. In the appropriate context, a chunk of identifiable information can be unpredictable and contrastive. Likewise, in the appropriate context a chunk of non-identifiable new information can be predictable and non-contrastive.

We may illustrate the dissociation of notions of identifiability ('definiteness') and predictability ('contrast') with a simple-minded example. Consider:

(3)   a. Joe lent me a bike.
      b. It was **Joe** who lent me a bike.
          (> You are right, someone lent me a bike.
          But it wasn't Mary, it was **Joe**).
      c. It was **a bike** that Joe lent me.
          (> You are right, Joe lent me something.
          But it wasn't a car, it was **a bike**).

Either the definite (identifiable) subject of (3a) or its indefinite (non-identifiable) object may be placed in contrastive focus, as in (3b), (3c), respectively. Their un-predictability in either case does not arise from their status as identifiable (3b) or un-identifiable (3c). Rather, it arises from expectations established in the local discourse context (suggested in parentheses in (3b,c)). That is, the un-predictability arises from the speaker's assessment of what the hearer's expectations are in the particular context. Definiteness and identifiability *per se*, it seems, are not the decisive factors in placing chunks of information under contrastive focus.

Similarly, in (3b) the indefinite 'a bike' falls under the scope of the **presupposition**, while in (3c) it is the definite 'Joe' that falls under presupposition scope. Clearly, definiteness ('identifiability') is not only independent of contrast, but also of presupposition.

10.2.2. Identifiability vs. presupposition

There are good reasons for believing that the distinction between definite and indefinite is not interchangeable with the distinction between 'presupposed' and 'asserted'. To begin with, their domain of applicability is rather different: Definiteness ('identifiability') pertains primarily to nominals ('nouns phrases'); presupposition pertains primarily to propositions (or their fragments). We have already demonstrated in (3) above how definiteness is independent of both contrast and presupposition. A simple example may illustrate how it is also independent of assertion scope. That is, either definite or indefinite referents may fall under the scope of assertion. Consider:

(4) a. CONTEXT: Who did you give the book to?
     b. RESPONSE: I gave it **to Mary**
     c. CONTEXT: What did you give Mary?
     d. RESPONSE: I gave her **a book**

The interrogative contexts (4a) and (4c) establish the propriety of either the definite proper name in (4b) or the indefinite noun in (4d), respectively, falling under the scope of assertion.

10.2.3. Assertion scope vs. contrastive focus

Most main clauses in human discourse tend to have one chunk of new information. The rest — perhaps the bulk — of the information in the clause is not under the focus of assertion, and thus is not new information. As suggested in (1) above, the contrasted element in the clause is also under assertion focus (but not vice versa). One may say that contrastive focus automatically "attracts the focus of assertion".

10.2.4. Normative expectations vs. contrast

When the asserted information is not contrastive, we tend to consider the clause pattern neutral. This intuitive notion of information that is 'neutrally asserted' bears some scrutiny. Broadly speaking, any asserted information is transacted by the speaker in the context of some expectations about what the hearer knows or doesn't know. These expectations presumably range somewhere between two extreme points:

(5)   **Extreme limits of the speaker's expectations about the hearer's knowledge**:
    a. **Ignorance**: The hearer does not know the information.
    b. **Contrary belief**: The hearer holds contrary beliefs.

Between the two extreme limits there exist, at least in principle, a large number of intermediates, all having to do either with the speaker's assessment of the hearer's degree of ignorance or strength of contrary belief. The two extreme points may be represented by two conventional contexts — ignorance by an information question, and contrary belief by a contrary assertion:

(6)   a. **Ignorance (non-contrastive response)**:
      CONTEXT: **When** did she leave?
      RESPONSE: She left **at eight**.
    b. **Contrary belief (contrastive response)**:
      CONTEXT: She left **at seven**.
      RESPONSE: No, she left **at EIGHT**.

It is fairly clear that the extreme context of overtly expressed contrary belief (6b) precipitates the placing of the relevant chunk of information under contrastive focus, coded here by **contrastive stress**. It is not as clear that the extreme context (6a) — total ignorance — should be designated 'neutral' (or 'norm') by fiat. To so designate it, one must first demonstrate a reliable association between the neutral norm and higher text frequency. Without such an association, the notion of norm is vacuous. Further, it is doubtful that information in connected discourse is ever transacted in the context of total ignorance. The accretion of new information in discourse is a gradual process, characterized by two important flow constraints:

(7)   **Constraints on information flow in discourse**:
    a. The amount of new information added in each clause is relatively small, perhaps on the average **one chunk per clause**.
    b. The amount of background information in each clause is relatively large, perhaps on the average **two to three chunks per clause**.

But what is the reason for including so much old information in the clause? The answer may be:

(8)   **Function of old information in the clause**:
      The function of the chunks of old information in the clause is to establish **coherence** for the new information; that is, to ground it to the existing — already stored — old information.

10.3.   CONTRASTIVE GRAMMATICAL DEVICES

English has a variety of grammatical devices that signal contrast. While functionally related, these devices are not interchangeable. We will discuss both their functional and structural differences.

10.3.1. Devices with strong contrastive stress

One may rank-order the major contrastive devices in English according to their contrastive strength. At the very top of the contrastive scale we find two devices, both characterized by strong **contrastive stress** on the focused constituent — **stress-focus** and **cleft**. As illustrations consider:

(9)   **Neutral**:   contrasted element
      Joe will milk the goat   (none)

(10) **Stress-focus**:
      a. **JOE** will milk the goat   (subject)
      b. Joe **WILL** milk the goat   (auxiliary)
      c. Joe will **MILK** the goat   (verb)
      d. Joe will milk **THE GOAT**   (object)

(11) **Cleft**:
      a. It's **JOE** who will milk the goat   (subject)
      b. It's **THE GOAT** that Joe will milk   (object)

Some people also count another construction, the **pseudo-cleft**, as a contrastive device. But while clefted constituents must be contrastive, pseudo-clefted ones may or may not be contrastive. That is:

(12) **Contrastive pseudo-cleft**:
    a. The one who will milk the goat is **JOE**   (subject)
    b. What Joe will do to the goat is **MILK** it   (verb)
    c. What Joe will do is **MILK THE GOAT**   (VP)
    d. What Joe will milk is **THE GOAT**   (object)
Non-contrastive pseudo-cleft:
    a. The one who will kill the goat is *Joe*   (subject)
    b. What Joe will do to the goat is *milk* it   (verb)
    c. What Joe will do is *milk the goat*   (VP)
    d. What Joe will milk is *the goat*   (object)

The pseudo-cleft is thus a contrastive device only when associated with stress-focus, while the cleft construction is always a contrastive device, and is always associated with contrastive stress. The pseudo-cleft clause, regardless of the presence or absence of contrastive stress, can be described as having

    (a) a headless REL-clause functioning as its subject; and

    (b) a nominal predicate.

Such a structure can be diagrammed as (cf. (12d)):

(13)

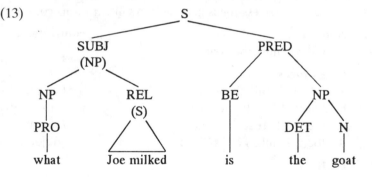

The predicate noun in the pseudo-cleft clause may then be optionally stress-focused.

    Stress-focus in English, as in (10), is the least restrictive in its application. It may be placed not only on nouns but also on verbs, not only on lexical but also on grammatical morphemes. In fact, it may also apply to bound morphemes, as in:

    (14) I didn't say **IN**duction, I said **DE**duction!

The cleft construction is the most restrictive of the strong stress constructions, and applies primarily to nouns. The contrastive pseudo-cleft seems to apply more permissively than cleft, but not quite as permissively as the simple stress-focus.

Dwight Bolinger (in personal communication) points out one apparent exception to the obligatory stressing of clefted constituents. The exception crops up in the second of two thematically linked cleft clauses that appear in a rapid exchange. In such a context, the second cleft contradicts assumptions that were expressed, but not as the contrasted focus, in the first cleft:

(15) a. A: -It's always **ME** you're picking on.
          B: -No, it's you I **ADMIRE**!
     b. A: -It's **JOHN** who left first.
          B: -No, it's John who left **LAST**!

Speaker B's responses above switch the contrastive focus from the object to the verb in (15a), and from the subject to the adverb in (15b). The B responses in (15) are not used as normal cleft-focus devices, since the clefted constituents are not stressed. Rather, these cleft-like clauses are used as **syntactic echoes** of speaker A's immediately preceding contribution. Speaker B uses this device to shift the contrastive focus to another element — which is now marked by stress-focus alone. The contrasts made by speaker B in (15) could have easily been rendered without any clefting, as in, respectively:

(16) a. -Nonsense. I don't **pick** on you, I **ADMIRE** you!
     b. -On the contrary. John didn't leave **first**,
          he left **LAST**!

Strong contrastive-stress devices always involve a strong assumption of the hearer's **contrary belief**. The basis upon which the speaker makes such an assumption may vary. It may be due to the hearer's overt assertions (as in (6b)). It may also be due to the speaker deliberately inducing contrary expectations in the hearer. As illustration of that, consider:

(17) **Contrastive focus due to speaker-generated expectations**:
     CONTEXT: I went through the whole family — mom,
               dad, my three brothers, my sister, the lot —
               you'd think someone would offer to help,
               but heck, they all refused....
     CONTINUATION: ...It was **MY FRIEND MARV** who
                       finally stepped in and...

In ticking off the list of family members that declined to help, the speaker sets up strong expectation of not receiving help, not even from family. On that **normative background**, the rescue by non-family is a contrasted **counter-norm**.

10.3.2. The Y-movement construction

The so-called **Y-movement** construction[6] is also referred to as **contrastive topicalization**. Much like the cleft construction, Y-movement is restricted most commonly to nominal or adverbial elements of the clause. Syntactically, this construction involves **fronting** the contrasted topical element, i.e. placing it at the clause-initial position. This is true only trivially for the subject NP, which tends to occupy the clause-initial position to begin with. The fronted element in the Y-movement clause is stressed, although to a lesser degree than the focused constituent in cleft and other strong contrastive-stress devices.

As a typical example of Y-movement, taken here from quoted spoken English, consider:

(18)   "...After buying a copy of **The Racing Times** at a Manhattan newsstand, Ed Piesman, a dentist and an avid horseracing fan, said he preferred the new paper to the venerable **Daily Racing Form** because "the columnists are much better" and some of the statistics "are much much better". **But** the news dealer who sold him the paper said people like Dr. Piesman are few. "**The Racing Time, I sell two a day**, maybe five when there is a big race", said Ashok Patel, whose stand at 72nd Street and Broadway is adjacent to an off-track betting parlor. "**The Daily Racing Form, I sell 40 or 50 a day**"..."
>   The New York Times
>   Daily Business Section,
>   June 3, 1991, p. C1

Unlike strong contrastive-stress devices, the context that motivates contrary expectations in Y-movement is typically set up by the speaker himself/herself. In passage (18) above, the first portion sets up these contrary expectations. The contrastive conjunction 'but' then marks the transition to the second portion, where those expectations are contrasted, and where both contrasted topics reappear in Y-movement clauses.

To illustrate the contextual difference between Y-movement and cleft-focus, consider (19) below, where the context (19a) is compatible with Y-movement continuation but not with cleft continuation:

(19) a. CONTEXT: She has two brothers, Tom and Jerry.
                   She likes **Tom** a lot.
       b. CONTINUATION:
           (i) **Y-movement**: ...**Jerry** she can't stand.
           (ii) **Cleft**:   ...?It's **JERRY** that she can't stand.

The speaker-generated expectations that serve as context for Y-movement are most typically created by listing various members of a group (type, genus), whose members are expected to display similar behavior or receive similar treatment. The contrast then arises from breaking these expectations.

The incompatibility of the cleft continuation in (19b) with the context (19a) suggests that in the use of Y-movement, the contrast does not involve the stronger condition — the speaker's assumption of the hearer's **strong contrary belief** — that was characteristic of cleft and stress-focus. If one were to set up such a stronger context, as in (20a) below, the acceptability of the two constructions would be reversed:

(20) a. CONTEXT: She can't stand Tom.
       b. CONTINUATION:
           (i) **Cleft**:   No, it's **JERRY** that she can't stand.
           (ii) **Y-movement**: ?**Jerry** she can't stand.

10.4. THE DISCOURSE-PRAGMATICS OF CONTRAST

10.4.1. Reference and topicality

So far we have considered primarily the functional dimension of **contrast**. But as noted earlier, most contrastive devices also involve the dimension of **topicality**. That is, they also partake in the grammar of **referential coherence**. In this section we will briefly consider the topicality and reference properties of two contrastive devices — cleft (or stress-focus) and Y-movement.

By reference properties of a noun phrase we mean here only semantic referentiality;[7] that is, whether the referent does or does not refer to some entity established verbally in the universe of discourse. As noted earlier, the semantics of reference is a narrower sub-case of the pragmatics of topicality. The two phenomena are thus not logically equivalent, although they display a strong statistical association.[8] By the 'pragmatics' of topicality we mean primarily two properties of the referent, one anaphoric, the other cataphoric:

  (a) **Referential accessibility** (anaphoric)
  (b) **Thematic importance** (cataphoric)

Briefly, referential accessibility has to do with the speaker's judgement about how accessible a referent is to the hearer, given the preceding ('anaphoric') discourse context. In choosing appropriate grammatical devices to code the referent, the speaker transmits to the hearer some information concerning the storage location of the referent in episodic memory, perhaps even the most likely path of search and retrieval.

Thematic importance pertains primarily to the speaker's sense of how important the referent is going to be in the upcoming ('cataphoric') discourse. In choosing an appropriate grammatical device to code a cataphorically-important referent, the speaker instructs the hearer to pay more attention to such a referent, and perhaps also to organize the thematic structure of the unfolding discourse around that referent.

10.4.2. Contrast and semantic referentiality

Both cleft-focus and Y-movement tend to apply primarily to highly topical — anaphorically accessible, thematically important — referents. The contrasted nominal in these constructions tends to be either referring-definite or generic, but not referring-indefinite. Pragmatically thus, these constructions are not used to introduce new topical participants into the discourse. As an illustration consider first cleft-focus:

  (21) a. **Generic**:
           It's **POTATOES** I like (not **TOMATOES**)!
        b. **REF-definite**:
           It's **the MAN** I saw (not **the WOMAN**)!
        c. **REF-indefinite**:
           *It's **a MAN** I saw (not **a WOMAN**)!

Example (21c) may of course be acceptable — but only if the indefinite NP is interpreted as **non-referring**. To corroborate this, one may substitute the referring-indefinite unstressed article 'this' for 'a':[9]

  (22) *It's **this MAN** I like (not **this WOMAN**)

Essentially the same restriction applies to Y-movement:

(23) a. **Generic**:
(I don't like tomatoes), **potatoes** I like.
b. **REF-definite**:
(I don't like him), **her** I adore.
c. **REF-indefinite**:
*(I saw a man sitting there,) **a woman** I didn't see.

10.4.3. The anaphoric antecedence of contrastive topics

We noted above that Y-moved or clefted referents tend to be topical or thematically important. That is, they are likely to recur as topics in the subsequent discourse. The restriction on REF-indefinites (cf. (21), (22), (23)) also suggests that the contrasted referents in both constructions are anaphorically accessible. That is, that they have been topical in the preceding discourse. This suggestion has been corroborated, at least for the Y-movement construction, by discourse distributional studies.[10] Such studies have shown that the antecedent of a Y-moved referent is usually found 2-3 clauses back in the preceding discourse. Anaphoric antecedence in either the directly-preceding clause or across a larger gap is not typical for Y-moved referents. The typical anaphoric antecedence of Y-moved referents may be illustrated in examples (24) below, where (24a) represents the typical 2-3 clause distance, while both the long-distance in (24b) and the one-clause distance in (24c) are odd:

(24) a. **2-3 clause anaphoric distance**:
CONTEXT: **A man** and **a woman** came in, They looked a bit disoriented. We talked to **the woman** first.
CONTINUATION: **The man** we ignored.

b. **Larger anaphoric distance**:
CONTEXT: **A man** and **a woman** came in. They looked a bit disoriented. We talked to **the woman** first. She was more than a trifle irritated, having come all the way across the country just to find out that it was all a mistake and that they had to turn around now and go back where they came from.
CONTINUATION: ?**The man** we ignored.

c. **1-clause anaphoric distance**:
CONTEXT: **A man** and **a woman** came in.
CONTINUATION: ?**The woman** we ignored.
                       ?**Her** we ignored.

Part of the reason why the one-clause anaphoric distance in (24c) is odd is that although a potentially contrasting referent ('a man') is there, no basis has been given for contrasting the behavior of the Y-moved referent ('a woman') with that first referent. The 2-3 clause anaphoric distance that characterizes Y-moved constituents is typically the text-span used to establish the grounds for contrast.

10.4.4. Explicit vs. implicit anaphoric antecedence

As noted above, Y-moved referents may be either referential or generic. But the anaphoric antecedent of a Y-moved nominal need not be explicit. Consider for example:

(25) **Explicit referring antecedent; referring Y-moved topic**:
CONTEXT: ...Later on **a man** came in, and after a
                      while **a woman** followed.
CONTINUATION: To **the man** they offered tea; to
                           the woman they offered coffee.

(26) **Implicit generic antecedent; referring Y-moved topic**:
CONTEXT: ...Next they offered us **lunch**. I finished
                      my sandwich right away.
CONTINUATION: The **salad** I didn't touch.

(27) **Explicit generic antecedent; generic Y-moved topic**:
CONTEXT: Speaking of **vegetables**, I love **tomatoes**.
CONTINUATION: **Potatoes** I hate.

(28) **Implicit generic antecedent, generic Y-moved topic**:
CONTEXT: ...I was rather **hungry**, and sure, I do
                      love **tomatoes**.
CONTINUATION: But **potatoes** I could never stand.

The explicitness of a generic antecedent may be a matter of degree. For example, 'vegetables' in (27) is the fairly well acknowledged genus of both 'tomatoes' and 'potatoes'. In (26), on the other hand, 'lunch' is a slightly less explicit antecedent of 'my sandwich' and 'the salad'. And in (28), likewise, 'hungry' is perhaps an even less explicit antecedent of 'tomatoes' and 'potatoes'.

In principle, implicit generic antecedence can trail off into extreme subtlety. This fact is not specific to Y-movement, but rather is general to all anaphoric reference. For example:

(29) CONTEXT: She went into **a restaurant**, sat down and waited.
      CONTINUATIONS:
      a. Eventually **a waiter** came over.
      b. **No waiter** was anywhere to be seen.
      c. She could have used **some food**, she thought.
      d. She was **hungry**.
      e. She needed **a warm place** to hide.
      f. She didn't have **too much money** on her.
      g. It was nice to hear **some human voices**.

The culturally-shared **conventional frame** 'restaurant' naturally evokes any of the referents in (30a-g) above, though some of them presumably to a stronger degree. The systematic implicit evocation of subsequent reference indeed involves highly conventional frames, whereby the larger frame serves as the anaphoric antecedent to its component parts, as in:

(30) a. My boy missed **school** today,
          he was late for **the bus**.
      b. He showed us **this gorgeous house**,
          but **the living room** was too small.
      c. She went into a **restaurant**
          and asked **the waiter** for **the menu**.

A similar anaphoric evocation involves physical **whole-part** relations, as in:

(31) a. She grabbed **the fish** and chopped off **its head**.
      f. **The table** is missing **a leg**.
      c. **The house** was a mess, **the roof** leaked.

Another explicit relation that licenses anaphoric evocation is that of human kinship, as in:

(32) a. **John** just got a job working for **his father**.
      b. **Mary** is upset, **her kids** keep flunking highschool
      c. **My wife** called and said...

In (32c), the anaphoric referent 'my wife' is legitimized by two general conventions:

(a) **The communicative contract**:
     The speaker refers to him/herself by the pronoun 'I'.
(b) **Culturally-shared conventional knowledge**:
     A male person may have a wife, and only one wife.

10.4.5. Anaphoric antecedence and paragraph boundary

The antecedents of Y-moved referents must not only appear at a short referential distance, but also typically not across a paragraph boundary. Consider for example:

(33)   CONTEXT: So **the woman** did all the weeding
                         in the garden, while **the man** loafed.
       CONTINUATION AS A NEW PARAGRAPH:
       a.   The following spring, we saw **the woman**...
       b.   *The following spring, **the woman** we saw...

As noted above, cleft-focused referents also tend to be highly accessible anaphorically. Much like Y-movement, clefting is not a paragraph-initial device. To illustrate this, compare the following openings:

(34)   a.   **Non-contrastive pseudo-cleft**:
            What we're going to talk about today is love.
       b.   **Cleft**:
            *It's **LOVE** that we're going to talk about today.
       c.   **Contrastive pseudo-cleft**:
            *What we're going to talk about today is **LOVE**.

The generic topic 'love' in (34a) is unstressed; it is not under contrastive focus, only under the focus of assertion. In both the cleft-focus (34b) and the contrastive pseudo-cleft (34c) 'love' carries contrastive stress. The oddity of (34b,c) suggests that the use of a strong contrastive device requires a certain buildup of **contrary expectations** within the current thematic paragraph. These expectations may be supplied overtly by the hearer, in his/her directly-preceding contribution. But they may also be set up by the speaker in the directly-preceding discourse. It may well be that a paragraph boundary may obliterate the buildup of background expectations.

The use of cleft and other strong-contrast devices in discourse has not been investigated in sufficient depth, so that the last word on the subject is not yet in. In the following example, taken from a detective novel, a cleft construction is used across a chapter boundary, approximately one page away from any plausible anaphoric antecedent:[11]

(35) "...The room itself is fifteen by fifteen square, out-
      fitted as livingroom, bedroom, kitchen, bathroom,
      closet and laundry facility. Originally this was
      Henry's garage...[p. 14]
      Then too, Rosie's cooking is inventive, a sort of
      devil-may-care cuisine, with a Hungarian twist. **It is
      with Rosie that Henry Pitt barters baked goods**, so
      I can get to eat his breads and pies as a dividend..."
      [mid p.15; new chapter]

10.5. FOCUS ATTRACTION, ASSERTION SCOPE AND CONTRASTIVE FOCUS

10.5.1. Preamble

In this section we consider the interaction of negation and yes/no question with both contrastive focus and assertion focus. One by-product of the
discussion would be to re-confirm the earlier suggestion concerning the
one-way conditional association between the two notions of focus. That is,
that contrastive focus implies assertion focus, but not vice versa. We will
consider first the behavior of optional clausal constituents.

As noted earlier,[12] optional constituents of the clause, in particular
optional case-roles and adverbials, tend to attract the focus of assertion.
That is, when they are present in the clause, the scope of assertion tends to
narrow down to the optional element alone, excluding all other clausal elements. Typically, in a clause that does not have such optional elements, the
verb tends to fall under the scope of assertion. But when an optional element is present, the verb tends to be excluded from the scope of assertion.
The attraction of assertion focus to an optional clausal constituent is, in all
likelihood, another reflection of the processing principle of "one chunk of
new information per clause". In the case of optional constituents, this principle seems to be coupled with the following pragmatic inference concerning the information-processing norm:

(36) "If an optional element is mentioned in a clause,
      it is itself the focus of asserted information".

The best way to demonstrate the attraction of the focus of assertion to optional constituents is by means of negation. This is so because negation tends to apply only to the clausal element that is the focus of the assertion.

10.5.2. Negation and focus attraction

Consider the negation of a clause that has only obligatory constituents, say the subject, verb and object. Both are obligatory with a transitive verb:

(37)   Joe didn't kill the goat
            (> the goat was not killed)
            (> the event 'Joe killed the goat' did not occur)

When uttered with no contrastive stress on any of its lexical constituents, the normal inference drawn from (37) is that the event — killing the goat — did not take place at all. In other words, the entire verb phrase is under the scope of negated assertion. Consider now the same clause with an optional constituent.

(38)   a.   Joe didn't kill the goat **deliberately**
                  (> He killed it by accident)
         b.   Joe didn't kill the goat **on Sunday**
                  (> He killed it some other time)
         c.   Joe didn't kill the goat **in anger**
                  (> He killed it in cold blood)
         d.   Joe didn't kill the goat **in the barn**
                  (> He killed it somewhere else)
         e.   Joe didn't kill the goat **for Mary**
                  (> He killed it for someone else)

In the presence of an optional constituent, so it seems, the normative inference changes; the scope of the negated assertion narrows down, excluding everything except the optional constituent.

As noted in chapter 4, negation is itself a **contrary speech-act**. In the absence of optional constituents, the negative contrastive focus has a wider scope. In the presence of an optional constituent, a contrastive interpretation of any other clausal element is odd. Compare, for example, (38) above with (39) below:

(39) a. Joe didn't kill the goat **DELIBERATELY**
          (> but rather **accidentally**)
      b. ?**JOE** didn't kill the goat deliberately
          (> **someone else** did it deliberately)
      c. ?Joe didn't **KILL** the goat deliberately
          (> he **fed** it deliberately)
      d. ?Joe didn't kill **the GOAT** deliberately
          (> he killed **the cow** deliberately)
      e. ?Joe didn't kill **the GOAT** for Mary
          (> he killed **the cow** for Mary)

The value of the question mark on examples (39b,c,d,e) is not to suggest that such examples are absolutely unacceptable, but rather that they are less preferred. This amounts to the prediction, yet to be tested, that examples such as (39b,c,d,e) will be rare in text as compared to examples such as (38b,c,d,e).

Clausal constituent may be in negative-contrastive focus. Thus compare:

(40) a. **JOE** didn't kill the goat
          (> **someone else** did)
      b. Joe didn't **KILL** the goat
          (> he only **kicked** it)
      c. Joe didn't kill **the GOAT**
          (> he killed **the cow**)

10.5.3. Yes/no question and focus attraction

A similar narrowing of scope — and attraction of the information focus — occurs in yes/no questions. When the clause has only obligatory constituents, the scope of a yes/no question is wide open, and certainly can take the entire VP or even include the subject. Thus:

(41) Did Joe kill the goat?
          (> Was the goat killed?)
          (> Did the event 'Joe killed the goat' occur?)

Once an optional constituent is present, it attracts the focus of the yes/no question. Thus compare:

(42) a. Did Joe kill the goat **deliberately**?
          (> or did he do it **accidentally**?)
      b. Did Joe kill the goat **on Sunday**?
          (> or did he do it **on Monday**?)
      c. Did Joe kill the goat **in anger**?
          (> or did he do it **in cold blood**?)
      d. Did Joe kill the goat **in the barn**?
          (> or did he do it **on the lawn**?)
      e. Did Joe kill the goat **for Mary**?
          (> or did he do it **for Sue**?)

As in the case of negation, when an optional constituent is present in the yes-no question, contrastive stress-focus is more naturally placed on that constituent, rather than on any obligatory clausal constituent. Thus compare:

(43) a. Did Joe kill the goat **on PURPOSE**?
          (> or did he do it **accidentally**?)
      b. ?Did **JOE** kill the goat on purpose?
          (> or did **someone else** do it on purpose?)
      c. ?Did Joe **KILL** the goat on purpose?
          (> or did he **feed** it on purpose?)
      d. ?Did Joe kill **the GOAT** on purpose?
          (> or did he kill **the cow** on purpose?)

As in the case of negation, when a clause without an optional element is questioned, contrastive focus may apply to any constituent:

(44) a. Did **JOE** kill the goat?
          (or did **someone else**?)
      b. Did Joe **KILL** the goat?
          (or did he only **kick** it?)
      c. Did Joe kill **the GOAT**?
          (or did he kill **the cow**?)

The systematic focus-attracting behavior of both negation and the yes/no question further illuminates the existence of a one-way conditional association between contrastive focus and the focus of assertion. Optional constituents attract the focus of assertion. Since contrastive focus is obligatorily also the focus of assertion (but not vice versa), optional constituents that attract the contrastive focus automatically also attract the focus of assertion.[13]

10.6. OTHER FOCUS-ATTRACTING GRAMMATICAL DEVICES

In the preceding section we saw how optional clausal constituents attract both the focus of assertion and contrastive focus. Other grammatical elements display similar behavior. In this section we will briefly consider some of those.

10.6.1. WH-questions

There are strong syntactic connections between contrastive focus and WH-questions.[14] Not surprisingly, the connections are also functional. Much like strong contrastive focus, WH-questions involve a proposition or clause that is almost entirely presupposed, except for one element. In the declarative contrastive clauses, that element is placed under contrastive focus, and thus automatically also under the focus of assertion. In WH-questions, that element is queried, and is automatically under the information scope, analogous — in this case — to the scope of interrogation. For this reason, placing contrastive stress on any other constituent in the WH-questions tends to be odd. For example:

(45) a. **WHO** killed the goat?
      b. ?Who killed **the GOAT**?
      c. ?Who **KILLED** the goat?
      d. **WHAT** did Joe kill?
      e. ?What did **JOE** kill?
      f. ?What did Joe **KILL**?

Again, the restriction in (45) is far from absolute. Thus Dwight Bolinger (in personal communication) notes examples such as:

(46) A: Jerry threw mud at his sister and broke a window
         and left the kitchen sink all icky.
      B: Oh yeah? And what did **YOU** do?

And one could easily build a context for (45e):

(47) Marvin killed a rat. Now, what did **JOE** kill?

Set expressions such as (48a,b) below also exist (John Haiman, in personal communication):

(48) a. What's **the MATTER** with you?
      b. Now what's the matter **with HER**?

While such uses indeed exist, perhaps they do not represent the more common norm.

10.6.2. Contrastive quantifiers

Some noun modifiers seem to attract contrastive focus almost obligatorily. These are quantifiers such as 'even', 'all', 'every', 'other', 'first', 'only', 'self', 'really' or 'just'. There are some grounds for believing, that these modifiers do not attract the stronger contrastive focus, as in cleft, but rather the weaker one, as in Y-movement. As noted earlier above, Y-movement usually involves the building up, by the speaker, of contrastive expectations within the immediately-preceding discourse environment. There seems to be a strong distribution association in text between contrastive quantifiers and Y-movement. This association suggests that these quantifiers indeed involve speaker-generated contrastive expectations whose anaphoric antecedence is found within short anaphoric range that is typical of Y-moved contrastive topics. Typical examples of this type are:[15]

(49) a. CONTEXT: We didn't want to kill Mom's cat...
         CONTRAST: ...so we killed **another one**...
      b. CONTEXT: It was going to be hard to kill the cat...
         CONTRAST: ...we hit and killed it with **only one strike**...
      c. CONTEXT: It was a complex, multi-factored subject...
         CONTRAST: ...if you understood it **only with logic** it would**n't** have been any good...
      d. CONTEXT: One respects one's mate's privacy in a crowded apartment...
         CONTRAST: ...he suddenly barged into the room **without even a knock**...
      e. CONTEXT: It was a tough subject to master...
         CONTRAST: ...you had to **really** learn the stuff...
      f. CONTEXT: The ticket was for someone else...
         CONTRAST: ...we paid the money **ourselves first**, then gave the tickets to him...
      g. CONTEXT: They came home after work expecting to find some food...
         CONTRAST: ...and there were **no** dates left...

10.6.3. Restrictive modifiers

The discussion thus far suggests that there exist at least three levels of contrastive strength:

(50) **Levels of contrast**:
   a. Weakest = neutral
   b. Intermediate = Y-movement
   b. Strongest = stress-focus, cleft-focus

One could demonstrate the existence of at least one more level, above the neutral but probably below Y-movement. This is possible when one notes the difference between restrictive and non-restrictive modifiers.

Restrictive modifiers[16] narrow the domain of referent nouns, while non-restrictive ones do not. Further, restrictive modifiers may be either stressed or unstressed, while non-restrictive modifiers are typically unstressed. When an adjective is unstressed, both a restrictive (R) and non-restrictive (NR) interpretation is possible:

(51) **Unstressed**:
   The tall man left.
   a. **R-interpretation**:
   Of the men there, only one was tall, and only he left.
   b. **NR-interpretation**:
   There was only one man there, a tall one, and he left.

When the adjective is stressed, only the non-restrictive interpretation remains viable:

(52) **Stressed**:
   The **tall** man left.
   a. **R-interpretation**:
   Of the men there, only one was tall,
   and only **that man** left.
   b. **NR-interpretation**:
   *There was only one man there, a tall one, and he left.

What these facts suggest is that there is a one-way conditional association between contrastive focus and restrictive modification:

(53) **Conditional association between contrast and restriction**:
   "If contrastive, then also restrictive"
   (but not necessarily vice versa).

This one-way conditional association is probably not spurious. In all likelihood it arises from the fact that restrictive modifiers involve a certain — though low — level of surprise or counter-expectancy. Their counter-expectancy level, however, is probably lower than that of Y-movement.

10.7. STRONG CONTRASTIVE FOCUS AND RELATIVIZATION

The structural connection between relativization and some focus constructions — particularly cleft and pseudo-cleft — is fairly transparent. A cleft combines a presupposed clause and a focused element. That presupposed clause shares with REL-clauses the pragmatic property of presupposition (or backgroundedness). As Schachter (1971) has noted, it also shares many of the syntactic properties of REL-clauses. Thus compare:

(54) a. The man [who killed the goat]   (subject REL)
      b. It's **Joe** [who killed the goat]   (subject cleft)
      c. The goat [that Joe killed]   (DO REL)
      d. It's **the goat** [that Joe killed]   (DO cleft)
      e. The woman [(that) he gave the book to] (IO REL)
      f. It's **Mary** [(that) he gave the book to   (IO cleft)

The parallel in grammatical structure between cleft constructions and REL-clauses is not absolute, however. Thus, for example, indirect object REL-clauses allow several variants:

(55) a. **Zero subordinator**:
          The woman I gave the book **to**...
      b. **The subordinator 'that'**:
          The woman **that** I gave the book **to**...
      c. **The subordinator 'who(m)'**:
          The woman **who(m)** I gave the book **to**...
      d. **Fronted preposition**:
          The woman **to whom** I gave the book...

The range of options seems to narrow down in cleft constructions, so that some of them seem less natural there. Thus compare:[17]

(56) a. **Zero subordinator**:
          It's **MARY** I gave the book **to**.
      b. **The subordinator 'that'**:
          It's **MARY** that I gave the book *to*.
      c. **The subordinator 'who(m)'**:
          ?It's **MARY** who(m) I gave the book *to*.
      d. **Fronting of the preposition**:
          ?It's **MARY** to whom I gave the book.

10.8. RESTRICTIONS ON CLEFTING

Contrastive stress can apply to any constituents of the clause, including many grammatical morphemes as long as they are written as independent words. On occasion, contrastive stress may even be placed on derivational morphemes. Clefting, on the other hand, is much more restricted. This may be due in part to morphotactic considerations — clefting (or pseudo-clefting) can only apply to free lexical words. The restrictions may also be syntactically motivated — the clefted constituents occupies a **nominal predicate** slot following the copula 'be', so that one would expect that other words, such as verbs, adverbs, auxiliaries or even adjectives, will be harder to place in such a slot. The restrictions may be in part discourse-pragmatic. As noted earlier, the clefted constituent tends to be **anaphorically topical**. Verbs, adverbs, auxiliaries and adjectives are less likely to be topical in the clause, but rather are more likely to be part of the asserted information. To illustrate these restrictions, consider:

(57) a. **Subject**:
          It's **JOE** who killed the goat
      b. **Direct object**:
          It's **the GOAT** that Joe killed
      c. **Indirect object**:
          It's **MARY** that he gave his ring to
      d. **Nominal adverb of time**:
          It's **YESTERDAY** that he did it
      e. **Prepositional adverb of purpose**:
          ?It's **on PURPOSE** that he did it
      f. **Suffixed adverb of purpose**:
          ?It's **DELIBERATELY** that he did it

   g. **Manner adverb**:
      ?It's **HARD** that she worked
   h. **Adjective**:
      *It's **TALL** that Joe is
   i. **Verb**:
      *It's **KILLING** that Joe did to the goat
   j. **Verb phrase**:
      ?It's **KILLING THE GOAT** that he did

10.9. SOME COGNITIVE CONSIDERATIONS

10.9.1. Attention and contrastive stress

The grammatical common denominator of all contrastive focus devices is contrastive stress, i.e. the assignment of a perceptually prominent intonation to the focused constituent. Whether other coding devices are present or not, stress is always there. The use of contrastive stress may be viewed as an instance of the **code quantity principle**:

  (58) **The code quantity principle**:
       "The less **predictable** the information is, or the
       more **important**, the more prominent or larger
       coding it will receive".

Contrasted constituents tend to be both thematically important ('topical') and counter-expected ('unpredictable'). They thus qualify for more prominent coding — more prominent stress — on both counts.

As Bolinger (1985) has noted, intonation is probably the most consistently and transparently iconic coding element in language. Its roots reach back to the pre-human gestural system. Its iconic motivation is transparent:

  (59) **Code-quantity, attention and memory**:
      a. More prominent, more distinct signals attract more
          attention.
      b. Information that attracts more attention is stored
          and retrieved more efficiently in **memory**.

10.9.2. Attention and word-order

The use of word-order in the coding of contrastive focus is almost as wide-spread as the use of stress. Of the three contrastive devices we surveyed — stress-focus, cleft and Y-movement — two also involve **fronting** or **clause-initial placement** of the focused constituent. The association of fronting with contrastive focus may be given as a sub-instance of the principle that governs the pragmatics of word-order:

(60) **The pre-posed order principle**:
      "More **important** information is more likely to be placed earlier in the clause".

The cognitive basis of principle (60) is well grounded in the psychology of attention and memory. It may be summed up as:[18]

(61) **Word-order, attention and memory**:
      a. The earlier a chunk of information is placed within its relevant unit, the more **attention** it attracts.
      b. Information that attracts more attention is **memorized**, stored and retrieved more efficiently.

The coding of contrasted constituents in English, always with prominent stress and often with fronted word-order, thus reflects universal cognitively-based principles.

NOTES

1) Chafe (1976) has suggested that the two notions of focus are related in the following way: Focus of assertion is a 'single focus', while contrastive focus is a 'double focus'. While terminologically plausible, the theoretical justification for this approach remains to be argued.

2) See chapter 11. We have already noted (chapter 3) that clauses tend to be organized in such a way that one noun phrase is the main topic.

3) The difference is probably a matter of degree, since in principle the speaker always makes some anticipatory assumptions about the hearer's attitude toward the information.

4) See chapter 5. Definiteness, however, pertains only to noun phrases ('referents'). The corresponding notion for verbal propositions is 'presupposition', 'background information' or 'old information' (see chapter 4).

5) See again chapter 5, where indefiniteness pertains to noun phrases. The corresponding notion for verbal propositions is 'asserted information' or 'new information' (see again chapter 4).

6) The name "Y-movement" is a historical accident apocryphally attributed to Paul Postal. It may have been conferred under the misguided assumption that such a device was more characteristic of Yiddish ('Y') than of English. It is perhaps true that Y-movement is more frequent in spoken than in written English, and that the Yiddish-flavored usage that gave rise to the name was indeed a spoken register, and was then compared to written English.

7) See chapter 5.

8) In terms of probabilistic tendencies in human-oriented narrative text, the association tends to be more like a one-way conditional association: "If pragmatically topical, then semantically referential" (but not necessarily vice versa). Logically, however, the association is weaker, since one can have both types of dissociation: (a) the more common case, nominals that are semantically referring but pragmatically non-topical; and (b) the less common case, nominals that are pragmatically topical but semantically non-referring. For a more extensive discussion of this, see Givón (1989, ch. 5).

9) If 'this' in (23) is stressed it becomes a definite determiner (demonstrative), in which case it is compatible with the cleft context.

10) See Fox (1983), in a study of Biblical Hebrew, and Sun and Givón (1985), in a study of Mandarin Chinese. Both languages are rigid VO languages, like English.

11) Sue Grafton, **A is for Alibi**, NY: Bantam (1982). In the English spoken in Ireland (Hiberno-English), the frequency of clefting is so high that it is unlikely to be used as a contrastive device. Odlin (1992) has documented many non-contrastive uses of the cleft construction in both Hiberno English and British English. He notes that the frequency of clefts in text is highest in the areas of Ireland where the use of Gaelic has remained most entrenched, and suggests a correlation between the high frequency of clefts in Hiberno-English and Gaelic. Whether non-contrastive uses of cleft are developing independently in American English remains to be seen.

12) See chapter 4, section 4.7.7.

13) More precisely, not only the focus of assertion is at issue, but rather the focus of whatever speech-act that is involved, in this case also negation (chapter 4) and yes/no question (chapter 12).

14) For WH-questions see chapter 12.

15) These examples were translated from transcripts of Mandarin Chinese conversations, where such focus-attracting operators were shown to have a strong association with the use of Y-movement, i.e. the OV word-order (Sun and Givón, 1985).

16) See chapters 6, 9.

17) John Haiman (in personal communication) feels that examples (57c,d) are just as natural as (75a,b).

18) See Gernsbacher (1990, ch. 2).

11 | TOPICALIZING CONSTRUCTIONS

11.1. INTRODUCTION

Many aspects of the topicality of nominal referents have already been discussed in earlier chapters.[1] This extensive coverage of what seems to be a single topic — the grammar of **referential coherence** — is not an accident. Marking the topicality status of the nominal participants in state/event clauses and ultimately in discourse is one of the two main foci in the organization of grammar.[2] If the topic-coding constructions covered in this chapter share a common theme, it is the pragmatic use of word-order. This is not always apparent, since other grammatical code-elements — such as morphology and intonation — may be also involved. But the common denominator remains the pragmatic use of **word-order**,[3] even in a language as rigidly ordered as English. The topic-coding devices covered in this chapter are:

(a) Existential-presentative constructions
(b) Left dislocation
(c) Right dislocation
(d) Dative-shifting
(e) Raising

Two natural members of this set, cleft-focus and Y-movement, have already been covered in the preceding chapter.

11.2. FUNCTIONAL ASPECTS OF TOPICALITY

Topicality is a property of the **nominal participants** ('referents', NPs) in clauses. Propositional information about states or events, coded as clauses, tends to be about some participant(s) in the state/event. Such participants, most commonly the subjects, direct-objects or indirect-objects, are thus topical by virtue of the information being "about them". Typically, they are nouns or noun phrases — **entities** — rather than verbs ('events') or adjectives ('states'). When a whole event or state is topical, it is almost always **nominalized**, and then made the subject or object of another clause. That is, they are made to look, morphosyntactically, like noun phrases.[4] Thus in (1) below, roughly the same event is coded from two different perspectives. In (1a), the agent is topical, and thus occupies the subject position. In (1b), the whole event clause is topical, and is thus nominalized and made the subject:

> (1) a. **Topical agent**:
>   **He** surprised Sylvia by showing up with flowers.
>   b. **Topical event**:
>   **His showing up with flowers** surprised Sylvia.

While being grammatically manifest at the clause level, topicality is not functionally a clause-level phenomenon, but rather a discourse phenomenon. This simple fact has often been masked by a common practice — extracting a well-coded clause out of its discourse context, then noting how its subject is more topical than its direct object, and the direct object more topical than the indirect object, etc. But the isolated clause that one studies this way is an artifact. What makes a clausal participant topical is not its status as the grammatical subject, object or "marked topic" in a self-contained clause. Rather, a participant is coded by various topic-marking means because it is topical **across a multi-clause span**. That is, because it is important, recurrent, or being talked about in the **discourse**.[5]

11.2.1. Referential accessibility and thematic importance

As noted earlier, the topicality of clausal arguments in connected discourse involves two distinct aspects of referential coherence, one anaphoric, the other cataphoric:

> (a) **Anaphoric**: The referent's accessibility
> (b) **Cataphoric**: The referent's thematic importance

By 'anaphoric' we mean accessibility or identifiability of the referent somewhere in the hearer's **previously stored knowledge**. By 'cataphoric' we mean the assignment of the referent's **importance** in the (yet-to-be-produced) **subsequent discourse**. Three bodies of stored knowledge are particularly relevant to anaphoric referential coherence:

> (a) The speaker's mental model of the speech situation
> (b) The speaker's mental model of culturally-shared knowledge
> (c) The speaker's episodic memory of the current discourse

Anaphoric grammatical devices clue the hearer about searching for the referent, in particular:

(i) In which existing mental model should one search for the referent?

(ii) How should one locate the referent within the relevant mental model?

Cataphoric grammatical devices clue the hearer about how important the referent will be in the upcoming discourse. Unimportant referents are filed as pieces of in-coming new information. Important referents are integrated as **important thematic nodes** in the unfolding skeletal structure of the upcoming discourse. The grammar of referential coherence thus involves both aspects of topicality, with different grammatical devices skewed more toward one or the other. As we have seen in chapter 10, many devices involve both aspects of topicality. This is true, for example, of both Y-movement and cleft-focus.

11.3. THE VARIETY OF TOPICALIZING CONSTRUCTIONS

11.3.1. Preamble

The constructions discussed in this chapter tend to code less accessible — discontinuous — topics. This is already obvious from the fact that a referent is coded as full NP.[6] The low accessibility of the referent may be due to the topic being **newly introduced** into the discourse. It may be due to the topic being **re-introduced** into the discourse after a considerable **gap of absence**. Or it may be due to **referential competition**, often associated with contrast (see chapter 10). One way or another, topicalizing constructions are not an isolated area of the grammar. They interact with other topic-coding devices.

11.3.2. Indefinite-subject constructions

Indefinite subject constructions are typically used to introduce new referents into the discourse, referents that are thematically important and thus tend to persist in the subsequent text. This can be illustrated by comparing the topic persistence of indefinite referents that are introduced by various grammatical devices. As noted earlier (chapter 10), the **text-frequency** of a referent is a fairly reliable indicator of its thematic importance.

The use of this indicator is founded on the following common-sensical assumption:

(2)   **Text-frequency and thematic importance**:
       "Thematically important referents are likely to be talked
       about more frequently — persistently — in the discourse".

11.3.2.1. Indefinite articles in spoken English

Morphologically, singular indefinite (newly introduced) referents in informal spoken American English are marked by either one of two indefinite articles, *this* or *a(n)*. Further, indefinites marked by these articles may be introduced into the discourse in either the subject or object position. The four possible combinations of these two binary contrasts are:[7]

(3)   a. **Subject with 'this'**:
           '...there's *this guy*...'
       b. **Subject with 'a'**:
           '...and there was *a fly to first base*...'
       c. **Object with 'this'**:
           '...he saw *this great bear*...'
       d. **Object with 'a'**:
           '...he saw this monkey holding *a candy bar*...'

The average topic persistence (TP) figures for the four coding possibilities in (3) are given in (4) below. The figure signifies the average number of times the referent recurs within the next 10 clauses following its first introduction into the discourse, i.e. as an indefinite marked either as (3a,b,c,d).

(4)   **Average persistence of indefinite referents
       in spoken English, introduced as subject or
       object, with the article 'this' or 'a'**
       (Wright and Givón, 1987)

referent-coding device	mean persistence in # of clauses out of the next 10 clauses
subject + 'this'	6.95
object + 'this'	2.40
subject + 'a'	1.54
object + 'a'	0.56

The persistence of *this*-marked indefinite referents introduced as subjects — 6.95 subsequent mentions per 10 clauses — is much greater than of *this*-marked indefinites introduced as objects (2.40 mentions per 10 clauses). And the same is true, albeit less dramatically, for *a(n)*-marked indefinites. The comparison in (4) also recapitulates the contrast between the indefinite articles *this* and *a(n)*.[8]

The same study also compared the percent of indefinite subjects and indefinite objects that were highly persistent in the text, with high persistence defined as more than 2 mentions in the 10 clauses following first introduction as an indefinite. The results are summarized in (5) below.

(5)   **Distribution of the high-persistence (TP > 2) and low-persistence (TP 0-2) tokens within the four grammatical categories**

| | marked by 'this' | | | | | | marked by 'a(n)' | | | | | |
| | SUBJECT | | NON-SUBJ | | TOTAL | | SUBJECT | | NON-SUBJ | | TOTAL | |
TP	N	%	N	%	N	%	N	%	N	%	N	%
0-2	4	14.2	10	**66.6**	14	32.5	10	**76.9**	89	**94.6**	99	**92.5**
>2	24	**85.8**	5	33.4	29	**67.5**	3.	23.1	5	5.4	8	7.5
total:	28		15		43		13		94		107	

Of the entire population of indefinite referents introduced as subjects, 67% were important (persistence of 2 or more per 10 succeeding clauses) and 33% unimportant (persistence of below 2 per 10 succeeding clauses). In contrast, of the indefinites introduced as objects, 94% were unimportant and only 6% important. Finally, the bulk of *this*-marked indefinites — 28 out of 43 or 65.1% — occupied the subject position. In contrast, the bulk of *a(n)*-marked indefinites — 94 out of 107 or 87.8% — occupied the object position.

As illustration of the difference between *this* and *a(n)* as indefinite articles, consider again the passage from an old Dear Abby column:[9]

(6)   "Dear Abby: There's **this guy** I've been going with for near
       three years. Well, the problem is that *he* hits me. *He*
       started last year. *He* has done it only four or five times, but
       each time it was worse than before. Every time *he* hits me
       it was because *he* thought I was flirting (I wasn't). Last
       time *he* accused me of coming on to **a friend** of *his*. First *he*
       called me a lot of dirty names, then *he* punched my face so
       bad it left me with a black eye and black-and-blue bruises
       over half of my face. It was very noticeable, so I told my
       folks that the car I was riding in stopped suddenly and my
       face hit the windshield. Abby, *he*'s 19 and I'm 17, and
       already I feel like **an old married lady** who lets her husband
       push her around. I haven't spoken to *him* since this hap-
       pened. *He* keeps bugging me to give *him* one more chance.
       I think I've given *him* enough chances. Should I keep
       avoiding *him* or what?
                Black and Blue".

Of the three third-person indefinite referents introduced in this text,[10] the
one that is clearly most topical — and persists through the entire text — is
introduced with the indefinite article *this*. The two others do not persist.
One of them is semantically referring ('a friend of his'); the other is non-
referring (the attributive 'an old lady'). Both are marked with the indefinite
article *a(n)*.

11.3.2.2. The existential-presentative clause

As noted above, there is a strong statistical association in colloquial
English between the indefinite article *this* and the subject position, in particular with the subject of the **existential-presentative clause** (henceforth
EPC). The association is due to the fact that the EPC is used to introduce
thematically-important new referents into the discourse. In the space below
we will review the most salient syntactic features that characterize the EPC
in English.

a.   Verb type

The most common existential verb in English is 'be', or its less colloquial counterpart 'exist'. But other verbs of being on or emergence onto
the scene may also be used, most typically locational verbs such as 'sit',
'stand', 'lie', 'live', 'stay' or 'remain', as well as entrance verbs such as
'come', 'arrive', 'appear' or 'approach'. Thus consider:

(7) a. There **is** a man here who wants to see you
      b. There **exists** one person who could answer this
      c. There once **lived** a king in a faraway land...
      d. There **stood** one man there who...
      e. There **remains** one issue we need to resolve
      f. There **comes** a time in one's life when...
      g. A minute later there **arrived** three guys who...

b. Loss of verb agreement

In formal written English, the indefinite subject of the EPC retains control of singular vs. plural verb agreement:

(8) a. **Singular**: There **is** a man looking for you
      b. **Plural**: There **are** some men looking for you

In informal speech, however, there is a strong tendency to use the contracted singular form of 'be' — *there's* — for both singular and plural subjects, as in:

(9) a. **There's** a guy in there lookin' for ya...
      c. **There's** two guys in there lookin' for ya...

c. Inverted word-order

The normal word-order in simple clauses in English is S-V-O. But the referring-indefinite subject in EPCs follows the existential verb:

(10) a. **Normal S-V-O order (DEF subject)**:
          The bookshelf is near the wall
      b. **LOC-V-S order (INDEF subject)**:
          There's a bookshelf near the wall
      c. **Normal S-V-O order (DEF subject)**:
          The man is there, waiting for you
      d. **LOC-V-S order (INDEF subject)**:
          There's a man waiting for you
      e. **Normal S-V-O order (DEF subject)**:
          So all of a sudden that woman walks in and...
      f. **LOC-V-S order (INDEF subject)**:
          So all of a sudden in walks this woman and...

d. An attached predication

There is an extremely high tendency, at the level of 99% in written English text, for EPCs to include another predicate — often a full clause — under the same intonation contour. In written English the tight connection between the EPC and that extra predication is indicated by lack of comma separating that extra predication from the EPC. The extra predication is typically a REL-clause, an adjective, a LOC-prepositional phrase, a noun complement, a possessive modifier or an associative phrase. Typical examples are:[11]

(11) a. **REL-clause**:
         ...there were big wrought-iron planters **placed along the sea-wall**...
      b. **Adjective**:
         ...There was a **sudden** explosion...
      c. **LOC-phrase**:
         ...there were about thirty **in the two countries**...
      d. **N-complement**:
         ...there was still doubt **about the nature of**...
      e. **Possessive phrase**:
         ...there was the sound **of rushing water**...
      f. **Associative phrase**:
         ...there was a large park **with gardens and shade trees**...

As noted by Fox and Thompson (1990), the extra predication that commonly appears with EPCs, in particular REL-clauses, is used to establish the **relevance**, **coherence**, or **grounding** of the newly introduced referent — at the particular text point when the new referent is introduced. The new referent has no anaphoric grounding in the preceding text. The extra predication attached to the EPC thus gives it **cataphoric grounding**.[12]

11.3.2.3. The fronted-locative clause

In written English, there is a variant of the EPC that requires no use of the fronted 'there'. Rather, a fronted locative phrase is used instead, and the subject is placed after the verb, as in EPCs. The verbs in such clauses are of the same general type as in EPCs — location, being, or emergence onto the scene. But the subject may be either definite or indefinite. Typical examples are:

(12) a. And right there near the bar **stood** a giant biker...
      b. Right in front of us **towered** the cliffs...
      c. At the table **sat** three judges wearing dark robes...
      d. And right there on the ground **lay** my friend John...
      e. On top of the house **was** a small zoo...

Fronted-locative clauses are used to introduce **unexpected** important participants into the discourse.[13] The fronted-locative clause of English shares some of the characteristics of *there*-marked EPCs, such as the inverted word-order (VS), the locative verbs, perhaps others.

11.3.2.4. Simple REF-indefinite-subject clause

The same presentative function performed by EPCs in English may also be achieved by using an indefinite subject in the normal SV word-order, but with an appropriate presentative verb. Typically, an extra predication is associated with such presentative clause, under the same intonational contour:

(13) a. An **immense** man came in yesterday and...
      b. Two guys **with no clothes on** stepped in and...
      c. A brief message **about the incident** flashed on the screen...
      d. Someone **who couldn't figure out what was going on** finally raised his hand and...
      e. A woman **I last saw in 1973** called yesterday and...

It is not clear how these constructions differ functionally from EPCs. As in EPCs, the extra predication supplies the **cataphoric grounding** of the new referent, establishing its coherence in or relevance to the discourse context.

11.3.3. Left dislocation

> Me, I'm fat 'n ugly,
> I sit 'n knit all day,
> I make baby blankets.
> But my ol' man, he rides with the Angels.
>   [Heard in a waiting room,
>   LA County General Hospital,
>   ca. 1970]

11.3.3.1. Functional aspects

Left dislocation is used to mark important referents — most commonly definite or generic — that are brought back into the discourse after a considerable **gap of absence**. That such referents are anaphorically accessible is suggested by the fact that they may be either definite or generic, but never referring-indefinite. In other words, L-dislocation is not used to introduce new referents into the discourse. This restriction on referring-indefinites parallels the one seen in cleft-focus and Y-movement.[14] Thus consider:

(14)　a.　**Definite**:
　　　　　John, I saw **him** there yesterday.
　　　b.　**Generic**:
　　　　　Politicians, I've never met **one** I could trust.
　　　c.　**REF-indefinite**:
　　　　　*__*A politician__, I saw **him** there yesterday.

L-dislocation is confined almost exclusively to the spoken-informal register of English, although its functional equivalents are also found in written English. Typically, the **anaphoric gap** of an L-dislocated referent — the **referential distance** (RD) to its antecedent in the preceding discourse — is relatively large. A typical example of such usage may be seen in the following excerpt from a informal conversation:[15]

(15)　H:　...Well my dad was born in Sherman, that's close to where [...] is. He was born in Sherman in 1881, and he died in '75. Yeah. And ah, so, ah of course, **my great grandfather, they came in there**, I think, y'know, part of them from Tennessee and part of them from Illinois. And I don't really know much about that far back, Tom. **But my grand-dad, he was a hard-shelled Baptist preacher**, and he just, y'know, farmed and ranched.
　　　T:　In Texas?
　　　H:　Yeah, yeah.
　　　T:　So he was already in Texas?
　　　H:　They must've come there when he was small, y'know, 'cause he spent...
　　　T:　Your great grandfather moved and your grandfather was really raised in Texas.
　　　H:　Yeah, yeah. In other words, about three generations of us... were in Texas...
　　　T:　In Texas...
　　　H:　And of course we eh, **my dad, all he ever did was farm and ranch**...

To illustrate the relatively large anaphoric gap characteristic of L-dislocated referents, compare the referential distance (RD) values of subject NPs coded by five topic-coding devices. The averages were calculated from a continuous segment of a spoken narrative, the same one from which example (15) was taken.

(16)   **Average Referential Distance values for definite referents in spoken English**[16]

topic-coding device	# of tokens in the text	mean RD	median RD
zero anaphora	117 (16%)	1.0	1.0
anaphoric pronoun	423 (57%)	1.6	1.0
R-dislocation	4 (0.5%)	1.0	1.0
neutral DEF-noun	113 (15%)	10.0	8.5
L-dislocation	44 (6%)	**15.3**	**19.5**
other definites	24 (3.2%)		
total:	742 (100%)		

L-dislocation apparently is also used as a cue in the **turn-taking** system in conversation. In this connection, Duranti and Ochs (1979) have noted that L-dislocation in conversation is often used at **turn-initial** points, where a new speaker often wrestles the floor away from the previous speaker. This is to some extent predictable from the use of L-dislocation in referent tracking. When a new speaker grabs the floor, they often change the topic.[17] The referent they re-introduce thus reappears after a gap of absence, during which the previous speaker controlled the topic.

The reaching backward to a preceding turn — thus a preceding **thematic paragraph** — has a close analogue in a single-speaker narrative. As noted earlier,[18] contrastive topic-coding devices tend to find their anaphoric antecedent within the same thematic paragraph. They thus exhibit relatively short RD values. In contrast, L-dislocation tends to bring a topic back, across a gap of absence, from a preceding thematic paragraph. That is, the anaphoric antecedent of such L-dislocated topics is typically found across a thematic boundary. To illustrate this briefly, compare:

(17) **CONTEXT**:

> ...So **the king** went on a crusade, leaving **the queen** in the dilapidated old castle to fend for herself, taking care of the country, the children, and the hungry citizenry, which she undertook to do in a splendid fashion. She worked her butt off, in fact, nothing was too small or too insignificant to merit her attention

CONTINUATION:

a. **Following a period (new thematic unit)**:

   . **Now the king**, **he** found himself...

b. **Following a comma (same thematic unit)**:

   *, **now the king**, **he** found himself...

The context in (17) switches topicality from the king to the queen, which then dominates the thematic chain. If the chain is then closed with a period (17a), the use of L-dislocation to re-introduce the king seems felicitous. If the chain is not closed (17b), the use of L-dislocation is odd.

In written English, the function of L-dislocation is carried out by equivalent constructions. So that (17a) may be rendered by:

(18) a. **Now**, the king found himself...

   b. **In the meantime**, the king found himself...

   c. The king, **in the meantime**, found himself...

   d. **After a few months**, the king found himself...

   e. **As for the king**, he found himself...

Example (18e) is structurally as close to L-dislocation as the written register ever gets.

11.3.3.2. Syntactic characteristics

L-dislocation in the spoken register typically exhibits the following three syntactic characteristics:

(a) a **separate intonation contour** for the dislocated NP, signified in writing by a comma;

(b) **neutral case-marking** of the dislocated NP;

(c) an **anaphoric pronoun** referring to the dislocated NP inside the clause.

The pause feature (a) seems to also be associated with equivalent devices used in the written register. In some of those, the pause appears after the clause-initial adverb (18a,b,d,e), while in others it follows both the fronted topic and the adverbial (18c). The neutral case-marking morphology on the dislocated NP (b) may be illustrated in the following examples:

(19) a. **Subject**:
John, **he** wasn't there.
b. **Direct object**:
John, I didn't see **him** there.
c. **Indirect object (dative)**:
John, I talked **to him** later.
d. **Indirect object (associative)**:
John, I argued **with him** about it.

Within the clause, the coreferent anaphoric pronouns are appropriately case-marked. But the L-dislocated NP itself remains unmarked.[19] Finally, the anaphoric pronoun (c) is absent in most of the written-register equivalents of L-dislocation (18a,b,c,d).

11.3.4. Right dislocation

11.3.4.1. Syntactic characteristics

Syntactically, **right dislocation** (henceforth R-dislocation) is characterized by the same three features that characterize L-dislocation:
(a) intonation break between the clause and the dislocated NP;
(b) non-distinct case-marking of the dislocated NP; and
(c) an anaphoric pronoun inside the clause referring to the dislocated NP.
However, the dislocated NP here follows the clause in which its co-referent pronoun is found.

Much like L-dislocation, R-dislocation is confined primarily to the informal spoken register. But unlike L-dislocation, it is not clear what the functional equivalents of R-dislocation are in the written register. Typical examples of the use of this construction in the spoken register are:[20]

(20) a. **Subject**:
CONTEXT: ...We called **him** 'Cotton'. He was always a white-headed little kid, and [is] still pretty much white-headed and all curly-headed, y'know.
R-D: **He** lives in California, **Ol' Cotton-Ground**. But I...

b. **Direct object**:

CONTEXT: ...and [my Dad] looked down there and one of the ol' mares come in a-leadin' about, oh I imagine about **fifteen, twenty head of horses**, y'know,

R-D: she brought **them** back, yeah, **some of those ol' mares**. And so...

11.3.4.2. Functional characteristics

R-dislocation shares with L-dislocation the restrictions on reference and topicality. An R-dislocated NP is typically either definite or generic, but not referring-indefinite. Thus:

(21) a. **Definite**:

I saw **him** there yesterday, John

b. **Generic**:

I despise **them**, politicians

c. **REF-indefinite**:

?I saw **him** there yesterday, a politician

This suggests that, as in the case of L-dislocation, the R-dislocated NP has an anaphoric antecedent in the preceding discourse. And the study of R-dislocated NPs in spoken text shows that their anaphoric antecedent is typically found in the directly-preceding clause.[21] This can be seen in both examples (20a) and (20b) above. Whatever else prompts the use of R-dislocation, it seems to involve referents that are highly topical ('accessible', 'active') in the directly preceding discourse.

Early studies of the discourse-pragmatic function of R-dislocation assumed that it was an **afterthought** or a **repair** device.[22] Roughly, it was suggested that speakers use L-dislocation when they:

(a) assume that the referent is fully accessible, given its minimal referential distance, and therefore can be coded as an anaphoric pronoun;

(b) but then, after brief reflection (represented by a pause), decide that maybe the referent is not so fully accessible after all, and so it should better be re-coded as full NP.

The anaphoric context of anaphoric pronouns and R-dislocation indeed suggests a similarity. In both cases, the anaphoric antecedent is typically found in the **directly preceding clause**, i.e. with a typical referential distance of 1.0 (see table (16) above). But R-dislocation seems to be used as a **chain-final** topic-marking device. This is evident in both examples (20a) and (20b), where the R-dislocated NPs both precede a period. Anaphoric pronouns, on the other hand, are typically **chain medial**. And L-dislocated NPs are typically **chain initial**.

The contrast between R-dislocation and L-dislocation may be further illustrated in:

(22) **Context**:
    a. So **Mary** left **John** and went on to become an accomplished theoretical physicist. She built herself a hot career in low-temperature physics, and proceeded to dazzle the world with her discoveries.

    Possible continuation:
    b. **She** was quite a gal, **Mary** was.   (R-dislocation)
    c. *Now **Mary**, **she** was quite a gal.   (*L-dislocation)
    d. **Now John**, **he** didn't do so well.   (L-dislocation)
    e. ***He** didn't do so well, **John**.   (*R-dislocation)

The text frequency of R-dislocation, L-dislocation and anaphoric pronouns is radically different. Thus, in the text summarized in table (16), zero anaphora and anaphoric pronouns comprise fully 63% of all referents, as against 6% for L-dislocation and 0.5% for R-dislocation. These stark differences in text frequency suggest, albeit indirectly, that the discourse contexts in which the three devices are used are rather different. Given the strong indication of chain-final use of R-dislocation, it may be possible to view it as a **cataphoric** (rather than anaphoric) device,[23] signaling the end of a thematic chain. It may thus alert the hearer to the likelihood of **topic switching** in the next clause.

11.3.5. Dative-shifting

11.3.5.1. Preamble

    ABBOTT: Call me a cab.
    COSTELLO: You're a cab.
    ABBOTT: No, you idiot, call me a taxi!
    COSTELLO: OK, you're a taxi.
                [*Abbott and Costello*
                in Hollywood]

Dative shifting (or in more general terms, **promotion to direct object**) has been discussed initially in chapter 3, and again in chapters 8 and 9. It was noted there that in bi-transitive ("two object") clauses, the direct object tends to be more topical than the indirect object. In the following space we will focus more on the functional aspects of this grammatical device.

11.3.5.2. Semantic aspects

The promotion of indirect to direct objects in English is limited to primarily **dative** and **benefactive** objects. As noted in chapter 3, the most common bi-transitive verbs with an inherent dative-benefactive indirect object are 'give', 'tell', 'ask', 'show', 'teach', 'send', 'sell', 'promise' and 'bring'. As illustration of dative shifting as a syntactic process,[24] consider:

(23) a. She gave the book **to him** ⇒
                She gave **him** the book
      b. He told the story **to his son** ⇒
                He told **his son** a story
      c. She showed the house **to him** ⇒
                She showed **him** the house
      d. She taught French **to her children** ⇒
                She taught **her children** French
      e. They send their love **to you** ⇒
                They send **you** their love
      f. He sold the house **to her** ⇒
                He sold **her** the house
      g. He promised the car **to her** ⇒
                He promised **her** a car
      h. She brought the book **to him** ⇒
                She brought **him** a book

Dative shifting is also very common when an optional benefactive object is present, as in:

(24) a. She did a favor **for him** ⇒
                She did **him** a favor
      b. He washed a shirt **for her** ⇒
                He washed **her** a shirt
      c. They built a house **for him** ⇒
                They built **him** a house

    d. He caught two fish **for her** ⇒

          He caught **her** two fish

    e. She got the ticket **for him** ⇒

          She got **him** a ticket

The constraints on the promotion of optional benefactive objects to direct-object in English are primarily semantic, and have to do with case-role confusion. When the verb typically has a human patient, promoting another human to direct object may create semantic case-role confusion as to who is the patient and who the benefactive. As illustrations of this possibility, consider:

(25) a. He hit the/a guy **for her**

      b. *He hit **her** the/a guy

      c. Kiss your sister **for me**!

      d. *Kiss **me** your sister!

      e. She killed the general **for them**.

      f. *She killed **them** the general.

      g. Save my brother **for me**!

      h. *Save **me** my brother!

When the patient is not human, promotion seems less problematic. Thus compare (25g,h) with (26a,b); and (25e,f) with (26c,d):

(26) a. Save a seat **for me**!

      b. Save **me** a seat!

      c. Go kill a goat **for me**, OK?

      d. Go kill **me** a goat, ok?

It may well be, however, that some of the restrictions in (25) are at least in part pragmatic. This is evident from the fact that promoting a benefactive to direct-object seems much more natural when the patient/direct-object is indefinite, i.e. less topical. Thus compare:

(27) a. Kill me **a goat**!

      b. ?Kill me **the goat**!

      c. She wrote him **a letter**.

      d. ?She wrote him **the letter**.

      e. He built them **a house**.

      f. ?He built them **the house**.

As noted in chapter 3, something akin to dative-shifting can also take place with verbs that have an instrumental-locative alternation. That is:

(28) a. She sprayed the paint **on the wall**
     b. She sprayed the wall **with paint**

However, most event-frames that display this alternation require different lexical verbs in the two variants. That is:

(29) a. She stuck the knife **into him**
     b. She stabbed him **with a knife**
     c. He poured the wine **into the glass**
     d. He filled the glass **with wine**
     e. They gave the guns **to the guerrillas**
     f. They supplied the guerrillas **with guns**
     g. She spread the blanket **over the bed**
     h. She covered the bed **with a blanket**

Finally, instrumental, associative and locative objects in English typically cannot be promoted to direct-object along the same pattern as dative-benefactives. That is:

(30) a. She put the book **on the table**
     b. *She put **the table** a book
     c. She cut the meat **with a knife**
     d. *She cut **the knife** meat
     e. He cleared the field **with his brother**
     f. *He cleared **his brother** a field

The only possible interpretation of (30f) as a grammatical sentence is with 'his brother' as the benefactive.

11.3.5.3. Discourse-pragmatic aspects

In general, the direct object tends to be more topical than the indirect object. This is underscored by the functional distribution of topic-coding devices that mark direct and indirect objects in text. In one study of written English, it was found that the typically human dative-benefactive, which may appear as either indirect or direct object, appears 84% of the time as direct object (DO), and only 16% as indirect object. In contrast, the typically non-human locative object appears 100% of the time as indirect object. Further, the bulk of the dative-benefactives in text appeared as anaphoric pronouns. In contrast, the bulk of the locatives appeared as full NPs. These facts are summarized in (31) below.[25]

(31) **Distribution of dative shifting in written English**
(from Givón, 1984b)

grammatical coding device	dative-benefactive			locative		
	DO	IO	TOTAL	DO	IO	TOTAL
pronoun	34	0		0	0	
name	4	0		0	0	
full NP	0	7		0	50	
N:	38	7	45	0	50	50
%:	84%	16%	100%	/	100%	100%

Whenever there is a choice between coding a participant as either direct or indirect object, coding it as direct object tends to go hand in hand with the participant being more topical in discourse.

11.3.6. Raising

11.3.6.1. General characteristics

Raising is one of the most curious phenomena in English syntax. As a first approximation, it may be described as follows:

(a) A verb of mental activity — knowledge, perception, intention, belief, utterance etc. — has two senses, one involving a **nominal argument**, the other a **clausal argument**.

(b) Within the clausal argument, one NP is the important **topic**, thus typically the **subject**.

(c) That important topic is highlighted through raising, and is converted from an argument of a **subordinate clause** to an argument — either object or subject — of the **main clause**.

(d) In English, such "raising" also entails moving the nominal argument to an **earlier position** in the clause.

From another perspective, one may describe raising as a process of **analogical extension** of one syntactic pattern into another. Through this process, the syntactic pattern of the verb-sense that takes a nominal object is extended to the verb-sense that takes a clausal complement. Many verbs in the various sub-groups that allow raising indeed demonstrate the requisite dual sense distribution. For example:

(32) a. **Nominal object**:
            John wanted **an apple**
      b. **Clausal complement**:
            John wanted **to eat an apple**

(33) a. **Nominal object**:
            John knew **Mary**
      b. **Clausal complement**:
            John knew **that Mary had left**

(34) a. **Nominal object**:
            Mary saw **John**
      b. **Clausal complement**:
            Mary saw **that John left**

(35) a. **Nominal subject**:
            John is terrible
      b. **Clausal subject**:
            That John did it is terrible

Viewed as a grammatical process, raising is a heterogeneous mix of related phenomena. It is found in some complement-taking verbs but not in others. Wherever it is found, raising falls under two related sub-divisions:
      (a) Raising to object
      (b) Raising to subject
Both are limited to clausal complements of specific verbs or adjectives.[26] We will survey first some of the more common patterns.

11.3.6.2. Syntactic aspects

11.3.6.2.1. Raising to object

Raising to object most commonly involves verbs of intention, perception or cognition whose subject is semantically a **dative-experiencer**. Typical verbs in this group are 'see', 'know', 'believe', 'say', 'want' or 'consider'. The raised version may be viewed as a **syntactic blend** of the structure of the verb's two main senses — the one with a nominal object and the one with a clausal complement. Typical examples are:

(36) a. **Nominal object**:   She saw **Joe**
    b. **Verbal complement**: She saw **that Joe left**
    c. **Raised blend**:   She saw **Joe leave**

(37) a. **Nominal object**:   I believed **her**
    b. **Verbal complement**: I believe **that she was a crook**
    c. **Raised blend**:   I believed **her to be a crook**

(38) a. **Nominal object**:   She wanted **him**
    b. **Verbal complement**: She wished **that he would leave**
    c. **Raised blend**:   She wanted **him to leave**

(39) a. **Nominal object**:   We considered **him** (for the job)
    b. **Verbal complement**: We considered **that he was honest**
    c. **Raised blend**:   We considered **him honest**

(40) a. **Nominal object**:   She expected **a miracle**
    b. **Verbal complement**: She expected **that he would leave**
    c. **Raised blend**:   She expected **him to leave**

It has been traditionally assumed that the raised structure ((c) examples above) is a mere 'stylistic variant' of the verbal complement structure ((b) examples). That is, that the relationship between the unraised structure and the raised variant was a systematic **derivational relation**, rather than one of **semantic similarity**. A derivational relation would mean that the un-raised variants (36b-40b) represented the **deep structure** of the raised variants (36c-40c). This interpretation of the relationship between the variants may be illustrated by the following tree-diagrams, representing (40b) and (40c) above. Respectively:

(41) **Unraised (deep semantic structure):**

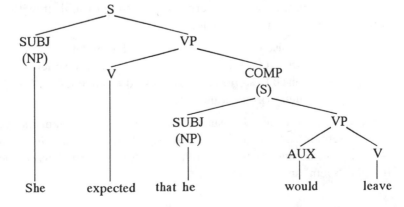

(42) **Raised (surface syntactic structure):**

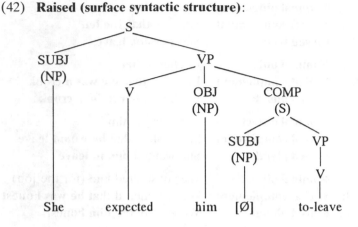

11.3.6.2.2. Raising to subject

Raising to subject sometimes involves the passive variant of verbs that allow raising to object. As illustrations, consider:

(43) a. **Unraised:**   We consider **that he is honest**
      b. **Raised to object:**   We consider **him honest**
      c. **Raised to subject:**   **He** is considered **honest**
      d. **Theme proposition:** He is honest

The existence of an active-passive relation between the raised-to-object variant (43b) and the raised-to-subject variant (43c) once again suggests a derivational relation between the two structures. That is, that in some sense raising to object must precede raising to subject, and is thus a prerequisite for it. This derivational interpretation encounters some difficulties when one notes that some verbs allow raising to subject, with a passive verb-form, but not raising to object:

(44) a. **Unraised:**   She said **that he left**
      b. ***Raised to object:** *She said **him to have left**
      c. **Raised to subject:** **He** is said **to have left**
      d. **Theme proposition:** He left

For other verbs, a raised-to-subject passive-marked variant indeed exists, but the semantically-related raised-to-object structure involves a different — though sometimes historically related — lexical verb. This can be seen in the pair 'seem' and 'see':[27]

(45) a. **Unraised**:   We saw **that John was leaving**
     b. **Raised to object**:   We saw **John leaving**
     c. **Raised to subject**:   **John** seemed (to us) **to be leaving**
                            John was seen **leaving**
     d. **Theme proposition**:   John was leaving

Raising to subject may also occur with some evaluative adjectives, whose intransitive nature precludes any corresponding raising-to-object structure. Here one can divide the adjectives involved into two main subgroups. In the first group, with adjectives such as 'easy' and 'hard', the adjective characterizes semantically the attributes of someone other than the raised NP. That other person is the subject of the underlying theme proposition, and the raised NP is its object. As an illustration of such a case, consider:

(46) a. **Unraised**:   **To please John** is difficult (for X)
     b. **Post-posed**:   **It** is difficult (for X) **to please John**
     c. **Raised to subject**:   **John** is difficult (for X) **to please**
     d. **Theme proposition**:   X pleases John

The most common use of the raised pattern in (46c) involves an **impersonal subject** in the theme proposition. That is, the subject of the theme proposition is non-referring and non-topical.[28] The syntactic structure of constructions (46a,b,c) above is represented in tree diagrams (47), (48) and (49) below; respectively:

(47) **Clausal subject (unraised)**:

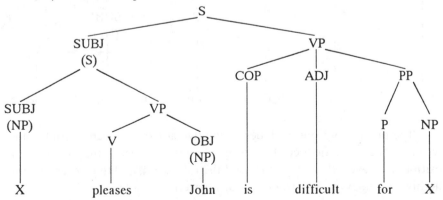

(48) **Post-posed clausal subject (unraised)**:

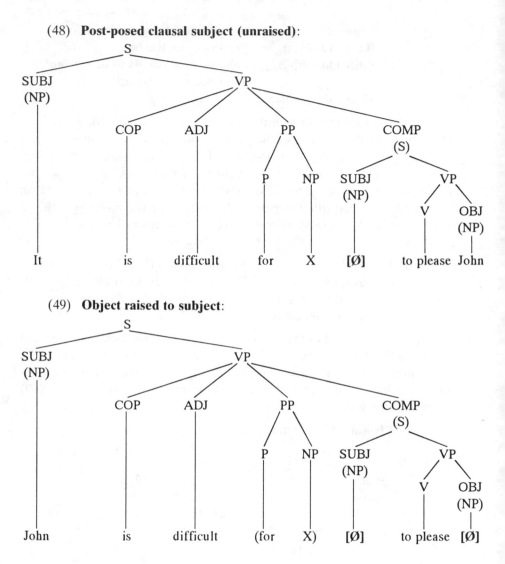

(49) **Object raised to subject**:

The other sub-group includes evaluative adjectives such as 'right' and 'wrong'. The semantic focus here is again on the subject of the theme proposition. However, that subject is itself the raised NP, and thus referring and highly topical. As an illustration of this pattern, consider:

(50) a. **Unraised**:   **For John to leave Mary** was wrong
      b. **Post-posed**:   **It** was wrong for **John to leave Mary**
      c. **Raised to subject**:   **John** was wrong **to leave Mary**
      d. **Theme proposition**:   John left Mary

The syntactic structure of constructions such as (50a,b,c) above is represented in tree diagrams (51), (52) and (53) below, respectively:

(51) **Clausal subject (unraised)**:

(52) **Post-posed clausal subject (unraised)**:

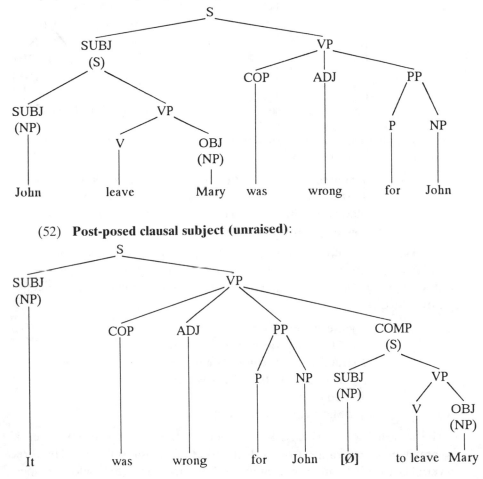

(53) **Object raised to subject**:

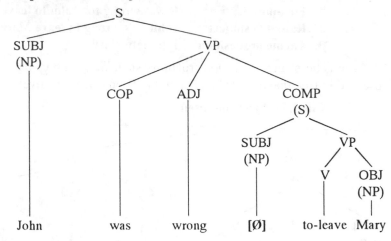

Other evaluative adjectives such as 'nice', 'kind', 'gracious', 'sneaky' etc. may take the same pattern, as in:

(54) a. **Unraised**:   **For you to have helped her** was nice
      b. **Post-posed**:   **It** was nice **of you to help her**
      c. **Raised to subject**: **You** were nice **to help her**
      d. **Theme proposition**: You helped her

There is, finally, another sub-type of raising that involves no inter-mediate derivational step of raising to object. This is because the clause out of which the topical subject is 'raised' begins semantically as the subject of a transitive verb:

(55) a. **Unattested deep structure**:
              ***That she was clever** struck me
      b. **Extraposed as V-complement**:
              It struck me **that she was clever**
      c. **Raised to subject**:
              She struck me as clever

The topical NP is thus raised-to-subject not from a deep-structure verbal complement, but rather from a deep-structure clausal subject.[29] The three variants (55a,b,c) are represented in (56), (57) and (58) below, respec-tively:

(56)

(57)

(58)

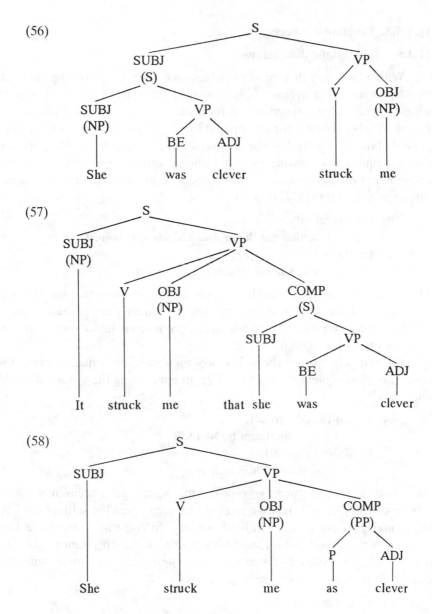

11.3.6.3. Functional aspects

11.3.6.3.1. Semantic dimensions

Within the generative tradition which coined the term, raising has been treated largely as a syntactic phenomenon, an optional stylistic variant whose semantic deep structure was represented by the unraised variant. In Postal's (1974) volume, for example, 13 pages out of 447 were allotted to possible functional correlates of raising, all of them semantic. They involve the consequences of having vs. not having a direct object that is directly encountered or experienced by the subject of the main clause. Consider, for example (Postal, 1974, p. 357):

(59) a. **Un-raised**:
          It struck me **that Julius Caesar was honest**
      b. **Raised**:
          Julius Caesar struck me as honest

The raised variant (59b) could have been uttered only by someone who had encountered Julius Caesar in person. The person who utters the un-raised (59a), on the other hand, need not have encountered Julius Caesar in person, nor even have been his contemporary.

Semantic effects not altogether dissimilar have been noted in our discussion of complementation (chapter 7), in contrasting the syntax of 'wish' and 'want':

(60) a. **Un-raised ('wish')**:
          She wished **that he had left**
      b. **Raised ('want')**:
          She wanted **him** to leave

We noted that a structure like (60b), with 'want' and a seemingly raised subject-of-complement, is more likely to be used when the subject has had **direct manipulative contact** with the object. In contrast, a structure like (60a), with 'wish' and an un-raised subject-of-complement, is more likely to be used when no such direct contact has taken place. A similar semantic effect may be seen with the verb 'see', as in:

(61) a. **Un-raised**:
          She saw **that he (had) left**
      b. **Raised**:
          She saw **him** leave

In the un-raised variant (61a), 'see' is used as a verb of inference, and its subject most likely did not see the subject of the complement. In the raised variant (61b), on the other hand, the two participants are more likely to have been on the scene together, and the subject of 'see' certainly saw the raised object.

11.3.6.3.2. Pragmatic dimensions

There are strong reasons for suspecting that raising a referent from a dependent clause to the role of grammatical object or subject in the main clause has the similar pragmatic effect as the one noted for other so-called **promotion rules** — respectively dative-shifting and passivization.[30] That is, in both cases:

> (a) The raised or "promoted" referents are more topical than their un-raised or "unpromoted" counterparts. And
>
> (b) Referents raised or "promoted" to subject are more topical than those raised or "promoted" only to object.

In the space below we will survey the arguments that support these assumptions.

a. **Definiteness and referentiality**

Much like Y-movement, L-dislocation and clefting, raising (at least with most verbs) seems to select definite or generic referents, and to reject REF-indefinites. Thus consider:

> (62) **Raising to object**:
> a. **Generic**:
>   We consider **in-laws** family
> b. **Definite**:
>   We considered **our in-laws** family
> c. **REF-indefinite**:
>   *We considered **an in-law** family

There is nothing wrong with (62c) *per se*, but 'an in-law' can only be interpreted there as non-referring. Similarly:

> (63) **Raising to subject**:
> a. **Generic**:
>   **Men** are hard to please
> b. **Definite**:
>   **This man** was hard to please
> c. **REF-indefinite**:
>   ***A man** was hard to please

Again, (63c) is perfectly acceptable if 'a man' is interpreted as non-referring. Similarly:

(64) **Raising to subject from an extraposed clause**:
   a. **Generic**:
      Romans strike me as honest
   b. **Definite**:
      Julius Caesar struck me as honest
   c. **REF-indefinite**:
      *__A Roman__ struck me as honest

Raised referents thus display the same restrictions seen earlier for topicalized NPs in cleft-focus, Y-movement or L-dislocation.

b. **Subjecthood and accessibility**

Under most circumstances, it is impossible to raise an NP to object unless it is the subject of the underlying theme clause. That is:

(65) a. **Unraised active complement**:
        They report that **John** rejected Mary
     b. **Raising to object**:
        They report **John** to have rejected Mary
     c. **Raising to subject**:
        John is reported to have rejected Mary
     d. *__Raising object to object__*:
        *They reported **Mary** John to have rejected (her)
     e. *__Raising object to subject__*:
        *__Mary__ is reported John to have rejected (her)

(66) a. **Unraised passive complement**:
        They report that **Mary** was rejected by John
     b. **Raising the subject-of-passive to object**:
        They report **Mary** to have been rejected by John
     c. **Raising the subject-of-passive to subject**:
        Mary is reported to have been rejected by John

The unacceptability of (65c,d), where the patient NP was an object of the active, is thus contrasted with the acceptability of (66b,c), where the patient of the very same verb is the subject of the corresponding passive. Similarly:

(67) a. **Un-raised active complement**:
          It seems that **Mary** dislikes John
      b. **Raising the subject-of-active to subject**:
          Mary seems to dislike John
      c. ***Raising the object-of-active to subject**:
          ***John** seems Mary to dislike (him)
      d. **Raising the subject-of-passive to subject**:
          John seems to be disliked (by many)

And similarly with raising adjectives:

(68) a. **Un-raised active complement**:
          It was wrong **for John** to leave Mary
      b. **Raising the subject-of-active to subject**:
          John was wrong to leave Mary
      c. ***Raising the object-of-active to subject**:
          ***Mary** was wrong for John to leave (her)

The subject-only restriction on raising is commonly interpreted as a purely syntactic restriction. While this interpretation describes the facts, it docs not go far in explaining them. A likely explanation of these syntactic facts is this: If raising is indeed a pragmatic operation that applies to **highly topical NPs**, then the restriction simply re-iterates the fact that the subject is the most topical grammatical role in the clause, and that it competes successfully with the less-topical direct object for further topicalization. We have, in fact, noted a similar case in the grammar of passivization (chapter 8) and its interaction with dative-shifting: The less-topical indirect object must be first promoted to DO before it can be further promoted to subject-of-passive.

(c) **The use of raising in text**

Not surprising, the best support for the idea that raising is a topicalizing device comes from observing the distribution of raising constructions in text. Raising constructions are not common in spoken English, nor are they that frequent in fiction. Where one finds them in relative abundance is in the news section of newspapers. Raising to subject appears to be the predominant type found. Typically, a raised NP is either:

(a) **Globally topical**: It is mentioned in the headline as the main topic of the report; or
(b) **Locally topical**: It is mentioned as an important topic in the clauses preceding the raised construction; or both.

Consider for example:[31]

(69) **MAN'S BEARD GETS HIM MISTAKEN FOR
BEAR AND SHOT IN LEGS, CHEST**
"...Nixon said he didn't know what **the man** was doing
in the Libby area but that **he** may have been picking
huckleberries. **He is thought to be** from Moyie Springs,
Idaho, the Sheriff said..."

Similarly:[32]

(70) **ISRAEL PLANS BIG DEFICIT**
"...In addition, **the Government suddenly reduced,
from 250,000 to 200,000**, the figure it is using for **the
number of soviet jews** that **is expected to arrive** here
next year. **The shift appears to be** largely a budgetary
maneuver..."

Similarly:[33]

(71) **CONOCO JET CARRYING 12 AMERICANS
REPORTED MISSING OVER MALAYSIA**
"...Kuala Lumpur, Malaysia, Sept. 4 (AP) **A Du Pont
Company jet** carrying 12 Americans **was reported
missing** over Malaysia today, officials said..."

Similarly:[34]

(72) **WIDOW OF COUP CONSPIRATOR ALSO
TAKES LIFE, SOVIETS SAY**
"...According to this account, **Mrs. Pugo** picked up her
husband's pistol but botched **her** suicide attempt. **She
was found alive**, covered with blood and slumped near
his body, the paper said..."

Similarly:[35]

(73) **HARDLINERS' LAST CHANCE MAY BE
SOVIET CONGRESS**
"...**They** are keeping quiet now, but **are very likely to
get together** against Gorbachov and against Democ-
racy..."

Similarly:[36]

(74) **SOVIET LEADER SAYS HIS WIFE IS RECOVERING**
"...During the live CNN interview, the Russian word
for "bout" was translated as "heart attack". But **Raisa
Gorbachov does not appear to have suffered** a heart
attack..."

Similarly:[37]

(75) **A FLYING TIGER FLIES HIGH**
"...The post-war US military never officially recog-
nized them as part of the war effort. Historians say
that's because the brass never stopped resenting **Gen.
Claire Chenault**, the outspoken army renegade who
led **the Tigers** in China...Meanwhile, controversial
Chenault, a career Army officer and pilot, had re-
signed his Army Air Corps commission in 1937...
Chenault, who **would be proven correct** in World War
II, had his own ideas about fighting tactics..."

Finally, in some cases the raising appears in the headline itself, as in:[38]

(76) **EX SALOMON TRADER SAID TO SEEK LEGAL AID**
..."**The trader** at the center of the Salomon Brothers
scandal has approached the government about the possibility of negotiating a deal, Wall Street lawyers said
yesterday..."

Of the 28 instances found in 2 issues of the local paper and one issue of
a national newspaper, only two involved raising to object, both within 5
lines of each other in the same article:[39]

(77) **BUSH STEPS UP CAMPAIGN AS
BUCHANAN LAYS OUT AN AGENDA**
"...Public opinion surveys taken over the last few days
show the president with a commanding lead over Mr.
Buchanan... similar polls conducted by The Globe last
month **found Mr. Bush leading his rival** by 58 percent
to 28 percent..."

Somewhat predictably, raising to subject involved, in all 26 instances, an **unspecified underlying agent**. This is consistent with the overwhelming passive or stative nature of 'raising' predicates, as well as with the nature of the passive as an agent-suppressing device. In contrast, neither of the raising-to-object instances in (77) are agent-suppressing. The distribution of the various 'raising' predicates in the three newspapers studies is given in (78) below:[40]

(78) **'Raising' predicates in newspaper English**

raising predicate	N	%
raising to subject		
stative predicates		
'seem'	6	
'appear'	4	
'be likely'	4	
passive verbs:		
'be expected'	3	
'be believed'	1	
'be supposed'	1	
'be proven'	1	
'be enabled'	1	
'be reported'	1	
'be found'	1	
'be thought'	1	
'be known'	1	
'be said'	1	
sub-total:	26	92.5
raising to object		
'show'	1	
'find'	1	
sub-total:	2	7.5
TOTAL:	28	100.0

The conclusions that one may draw from this discussion harken back to the major theme of our communicative approach to grammar: One syntactic structure is unlikely to be a "mere" stylistic variant of another. However subtle, variant grammar entails a variant communicative effect, and thus presumably a variant communicative goal. Subtle options of style are nothing but subtle options in the communicative use of grammar.

NOTES

1) Grammatical subject and object (chapter 3), reference, definiteness and anaphora (chapter 5), de-transitive voice (chapter 8), relative clauses (chapter 9), contrastive focus (chapter 10).

2) The other main focus is the grammar of tense-aspect-modality (and negation), morphologically clustered around the verb or verb phrase.

3) In the grammar of contrastive focus construction, the structural common denominator was stress.

4) See chapters 6, 7.

5) Several schools of linguistics have incorporated the notion 'topic' into their clause-level grammar (e.g. Dik, 1978; Foley & van Valin, 1984; Bresnan and Mchombo, 1987; *inter alia*). While this may be viewed as a formal device, the inference tends to persist that 'topic' is a clause-level functional notion.

6) As noted in chapter 5, the most accessible — continuous — referents are marked by zero or anaphoric pronouns.

7) These examples are taken from the spontaneous speech of 8-12 year old native speakers of American English. For further detail see Wright and Givón (1987).

8) See chapter 5, section 5.10.

9) *Ibid*.

10) The other main protagonist, the speaker herself ('I'), is obviously just as topical.

11) The examples are from various non-fiction articles in **The New Yorker** magazine (see R. Fox, 1985).

12) We already noted in chapter 9 that restrictive REL-clauses, which typically fall under the same intonation contour with the main clause, are used to establish either anaphoric grounding (for definite head nouns) or cataphoric grounding (for indefinite head nouns).

13) For the original discussion see Gary (1976).

14) See chapter 10.

15) From the conversation of a retired New Mexico rancher, recorded ca. 1978 (see Givón, 1983b)

16) See Givón (1983b).

17) This is characteristic of conversations with more than two participants (Duranti and Ochs, 1979). Two-participant conversations are often more collaborative, displaying greater referential and thematic continuity across turns.

18) See chapter 10.

19) One may wish to argue that this unmarked status corresponds to the norm for a nominative NP in English.

20) See note 15, above.

21) See Givón (1983b), as well as (16) above.

22) See Hyman (1975).

23) Hyman's (1975) notion of 'afterthought' is, in contrast, anaphorically based. That is, it involves the degree of accessibility of the referent in its anaphoric context.

24) The dative-shifted variant may be viewed as an independent though similar construction, rather than a variant that is 'syntactically derived' from the corresponding non-shifted construction.

25) Givón (1984b). In another language that has a much more extensive system of promotion to direct object (Nez Perce, a Sahaptian language of the Oregon-Washington-Idaho border), the higher topicality of direct object over indirect object was demonstrated by both anaphoric and cataphoric topicality measures (Rude, 1985).

26) For verbal complements and the verbs or adjectives that take them, see chapter 7.

27) The verb 'seem' is historically a Germanic middle-voice form of 'see', thus 'sort of a passive'.

28) For impersonal-subject constructions see chapter 8.

29) One could of course argue that the topical NP is raised only after its clause has been extraposed, in which case it is indeed raised from a clausal V-complement. It is not clear whether the argument here hinges on anything but formalism.

30) The term 'promotion' again carries the implicit sense of transformational derivation, whereby the un-promoted variant is the 'basic' or 'neutral' form ('deep structure'), while the promoted variant is 'derived' from it ('surface structure').

31) **The Eugene Register Guard**, Eugene (OR), 9-10-91, section A (news).

32) **The New York Times**, 9-5-91, section A (news).

33) *Ibid.*

34) *Ibid.*

35) **The Eugene Register Guard**, Eugene (OR), 9-2-91, section A (news).

36) *Ibid.*

37) *Ibid.*

38) **The New York Times**, 9-17-91, section A (news).

39) *Ibid.*

40) Two issues of **The Eugene Register Guard**, Eugene (OR), 9-2-91 and 9-10-91, section A (news); and one issues of **The New York Times**, 9-17-91, section A (news).

| NON-DECLARATIVE SPEECH ACTS

12.1. PRELIMINARIES

12.1.1. Speech acts

Until now, we have dealt almost exclusively with **declarative** clauses, in which the speaker's communicative goal — the intended **speech-act** — was most commonly **informative**. This focus on the declarative speech-act reflects a long tradition in linguistics and philosphy. While in some respects this tradition is natural and understandable, it has led to considerable distortions in the Western view of human language, and in particular to an excessive preoccupation with the role of language in the **mental representation** of knowledge, at the expense of its role in interaction and **communication**.

Linguists have always found it convenient, indeed almost inevitable, to begin their grammatical description with the grammar of declarative clauses.[1] This strong preference arises from two distributional facts, one about grammar per se, the other about the use of grammar in text:

(a) **The diversity of grammatical types**
The widest variety of grammatical phenomena, apart from those used specifically to code the speech-act value of the clause,[2] is found in declarative clauses. Non-declarative clauses tend to display a smaller sub-set of those phenomena.

(b) **The distribution of grammar in text**
At least in the two most prevalent discourse types — everyday conversation and narrative — declarative clauses predominate in terms of text frequency.

The differences in text-frequency between declarative and non-declarative speech-acts is illustrated in table (1) below, which summarizes the distribution of speech-act types in a written narrative that includes dialogue (i.e. conversation embedded in the narrative).

(1)   **Frequency of declarative vs. non-declarative clauses
      in written narrative and embedded dialogue**[3]

narrative						dialogue					
non-dec.		declar.		total		non-dec.		declar.		total	
N	%	N	%	N	%	N	%	N	%	N	%
/	/	81	**100%**	81	100%	22	**16%**	115	84%	137	100%

While the percent of non-declarative speech-acts is significantly higher in the dialogue portions of the text, declarative speech-acts predominate in both text types. The two distributional facts — diversity and text-frequency — may or may not be causally linked. Taken together, they explain — though perhaps not altogether vindicate — the considerable tilt in traditional grammatical descriptions toward declarative clauses. The preoccupation of philosophers with declarative speech-acts is another matter altogether. While understandable in its historical context, this self-imposed myopia has been an Achilles heel of the philosophers' view of language, mind and meaning since the dawn of **post-Socratic philosophy**.[4] It has allowed philosophers, and linguists in their wake, to ignore language as an instrument of communication and social interaction, and to focus almost exclusively on its capacity to express and interpret true or false propositions about the external world. Pre-Socratic Greek philosophers, such as the *sophists*, were keenly interested in non-declarative speech-acts. In this connection, Haberland (1985) characterizes the difference between the sophist Protagoras and Plato as follows:

> "...Protagoras distinguishes four parts of discourse..., namely "wish, question, answer and command"...Protagoras seems to have been interested in *speech acts*, not sentences in modern parlance. But... it is *statements* Plato is interested in..." (1985, p. 381; emphases added.)

Plato's role in narrowing the focus of the philosopher's interest in language to declarative propositions ('statements') is well documented. It stems from the Greeks' growing preoccupation — from Socrates onward — with the **truth value** of the propositions of science and, to a somewhat lesser degree, of ethics. Haberland (1985) characterizes Plato's position as follows:

"...For Plato...true knowledge — which, as he argues in this connection, does not coincide with perception — cannot aim at context-dependent truths; the truth of a sentence should not depend on who says it, in which situation, and to whom, and it should not, more specifically, depend on what the sentence is an answer to... But this interest of Plato's in statements...is again only understandable from a series of premises that are no longer self-evident. The first of these is that *truth is the main concern of the philosopher*. The second is that *analysis of language is ancillary to philosophical pursuits*. As a corollary from these two premises, we get that *linguistic analysis is mainly concerned with truth* as well. The third premise is that *truth is timeless and independent of context...*" (1985, pp. 381-382; emphases added).

Four major speech-act types turn out to be most distinctly and most consistently coded in the grammar of human languages. These recurrent **speech-act prototypes** are:

    (a) **declarative**
    (b) **imperative**
    (c) **interrogative**:
       (i) **yes/no question**
      (ii) **WH-question**

These prototypes are but the most salient stand-outs in a much larger array of sub-types and subtle variants. Nevertheless, the fact that they are so well coded and widely attested in human language makes them a convenient point of departure in describing the grammar of speech-acts. It also suggests that they may occupy major coordinates in the mental map of human language as an instrument of communication.

12.1.2. Assertion, presupposition and speech-act prototypes

Philosophical approaches to the distinction between declarative and non-declarative speech-acts have revolved around the notion of **truth**: Declarative speech-acts have **truth value**; questions and commands do not. In this section we will cover briefly some traditional arguments that re-surfaced in linguistics and philosophy due to the Ordinary Language Philosophers of the post-war period, most conspicuously Austin (1962).[5] We will consider first the balance of **assertion** and **presupposition** associated with the three major speech-act prototypes.

Consider the declarative clause (2a) below and the two possible responses to it, (2b) and (2c):

(2)   a. **Declarative**: Joe ate the salami.
      b. **Denial**: That's not true.
      c. **Affirmation**: That's true.

The truth value of a declarative speech-act such as (2a) can be either denied (2b) or affirmed (2c). The verbal exchange between the person uttering (2a) and another person responding with either (2b) or (2c) is reasonably coherent. Both (2b) and (2c) are, in principle, felicitous propositions in the context of the declarative proposition (2a).[6] Consider now the interrogatives clause in (3a) below:

(3)   a. **Interrogative**: Did John eat the salami?
      b. **Denial**: That's not true.
      c. **Affirmation**: That's true.

Neither the denial (3b) nor the affirmation (3c) is a coherent response to (3a). Similarly, neither the denial (4b) nor the affirmation (4c) are felicitous, coherent responses to the interrogative clause (4a):

(4)   a. **Interrogative**: Who ate the salami?
      b. **Denial**: That's not true.
      c. **Affirmation**: That's true.

And similarly, neither the denial (5b) nor the affirmation (5c) is a coherent response to the imperative clause (5a):

(5)   a. **Imperative**: Eat the salami!
      b. **Denial**: That's not true.
      c. **Affirmation**: That's true.

The inappropriateness, incoherence or infelicity of truth denials or truth affirmations of non-declarative clauses stems from the fact that truth is not an issue in non-declarative speech acts. This is so because the **communicative goal** of such speech-acts is not to assert that some information is either true or false. The goal is something else. A more appropriate challenge to non-declarative speech-acts focuses on their implicit **presuppositions**. In (6b,c,d,e) below, for example, various presuppositions associated with the WH-question (4a) ('Who ate the salami?') are challenged:

(6)   **Challenging the presuppositions of a WH-question**:
    a. Who says **anybody** did?
    b. How should **I** know?
    c. You were there watching, so **why ask**?
    d. Why should I tell **you**? What's in it for **me**?

The implicit presuppositions held by the speaker uttering the WH-question
(4a) that were challenged by (6a,b,c,d) were, respectively:

(7)   a. The event "Someone ate the salami" occurred.
    b. The hearer knows the answer.
    c. The speaker doesn't know the answer.
    d. The hearer is obliged to respond.

Similarly (8a,b,c,d) below challenge, in order, the presuppositions implicit
in the imperative speech-act (5a) ('Eat the salami!'):

(8)   **Challenging the presuppositions of an imperative clause**:
    a. I see **no salami** here.
    b. I've **already eaten** it.
    c. Who are **you** to tell **me**?
    d. I **can't** eat it, my hands are tied to the bed.

The presuppositions implicit in the imperative (5a) and challenged by
(8a,b,c,d) are, respectively:

(9)   a. A salami is there to be eaten.
    b. The hearer has not yet performed the act.
    c. The speaker has authority to command the hearer.
    d. The hearer is free to perform the act.

The presuppositions associated with non-declarative speech acts reveal
that truth or falsity — i.e. **epistemics** — is but a small portion of the functional domain of speech-acts. This may be further driven home by showing
that the same is also true for the declarative speech-act itself. In (10a,b,c,d)
below, the implicit presuppositions associated with our original declarative
clause (2a) ('Joe ate the salami') are challenged:

(10)   **Challenging the presuppositions of a declarative clause**:
    a. **Who** is John?
    b. **What** salami?
    c. Why should **I** care?
    d. Why are **you** telling me?

The challenges in (10a,b,c,d) pertain to the following presuppositions associated with the declarative speech-act (2a), respectively:

(11)   a. The hearer can identify the named subject.
     b. The hearer can identify the definite object.
     c. The hearer is interested in the information.
     d. The speaker has a legitimate reason for telling
        the information to the hearer.

Presuppositions (11a,b) seem to still be a matter of **epistemics**, i.e. concerning knowledge, truth or falsity of various propositions entailed by the speech-act. Presuppositions (11c,d), although stated as declarative propositions, are not about epistemics. Rather, they are about the **motivation** of the two participants. In the case of declarative speech-acts, the post-Socratic philosophical tradition tended to ignore such non-epistemic presuppositions, assuming — perhaps to some extent correctly — that they were less central to the speech-act.[7] In the case of the interrogative speech-act, one may wish to argue that questions of epistemics — truth or falsity of queried propositions — are still central to the speaker's goals. But even so, the interrogative speech-act purports to manipulate the actions of one's interlocutor. Consequently, socio-personal considerations of **status**, **power**, **obligation**, **entitlement**, **propriety** and **motivation** come to the fore. And this is even more true in the case of imperatives, where epistemic factors are even less central.

The communicative use of language is governed by conventions that may be subsumed together under **the communicative contract**. The communicative contract is a set of implicit, culturally-shared norms that govern human communication. Being culturally shared, they are understood by both speaker and hearer, and serve as implicit guidelines for the communicative interaction. As noted above, declarative speech-acts are just as strongly governed by the non-epistemic — interactional, **deontic**[8] — subclauses of the communicative contract as are non-declarative speech-acts. Still, the non-epistemic aspects of verbal communication manifest themselves more clearly in non-declarative speech-acts.

12.2. YES-NO QUESTIONS

12.2.1. Functional aspects

12.2.1.1. Truth and epistemic bias

Traditionally, logicians have rendered a yes-no question roughly as follows:[9]

(12)   "Given proposition P, tell me whether it is true or false".

Within this logical tradition, both questions (13a) and (13b) below assume, equally, that either the affirmative-declarative possible response (13c) or its corresponding negative-declarative (13d) is true. The hearer is simply asked to select which one:

(13)   a. **Affirmative question**:
              Did John eat the salami?
        b. **Negative question**:
              Didn't John eat the salami?
        c. **Affirmative response**:
              John ate the salami.
        d. **Negative response**:
              John did not eat the salami.

As Dwight Bolinger (1978) has pointed out, however, yes-no questions are not open alternative questions. Rather, an affirmative yes-no question such as (13a) exhibits a systematic bias toward the negative response (13d). And a negative yes-no question such as (13b) exhibits a systematic bias toward the affirmative response (13c). Indeed, in asking a yes-no question the speaker's **epistemic bias** toward either the affirmative or negative declarative is probably even more finely graded, yielding something like the following scale:

(14)   **strongest bias toward the negative**
        a. John **didn't** eat the salami, did he?
        b. Did John eat the salami?
        c. Didn't John eat the salami?
        d. John **did** eat the salami, didn't he?
        strongest bias toward the affirmative

The so-called **tag questions** (14a) and (14d) enrich the scale in both directions, allowing for at least four grammar-coded points between the two extreme biases. And there are grounds for suspecting that the scale is richer yet, with variant question forms in both directions of the bias scale, such as:

(15) a. Did John **really** eat the salami?
      b. Did John **really not** eat the salami?
      c. John **did** eat the salami, right?
      d. John **didn't** eat the salami, right?
      e. **Do you think** John ate the salami?
      f. **Don't you think** John ate the salami?

The multiplicity of subtle variants along the epistemic-bias continuum underscores Bolinger's suggestion that the normal pattern of yes/no questions is not a neutral, unbiased pattern. Rather, speakers use yes/no questions — including the more finely calibrated variants in (14a,d) and (15) — in situations where they have varying epistemic biases about the truth of the declarative proposition under query.

12.2.1.2. Alternative questions

A variant of yes-no questions that is much closer to the logician's traditional definition is the **alternative question**. In using this pattern, both the affirmative and negative — or even a longer list of alternatives — are overtly displayed, as in:

(16) a. Is it **raining**, or is it **not** (raining)?
      b. Is it **raining**, or is it **snowing**?
      c. Is it **raining**, or **did someone leave the sprinklers on**?
      d. Is it **raining**, **snowing**, or **hailing**?
      e. Did **Bill** do it, or did **Harry** or **Joe**?

Overtly given alternatives may not necessarily be exclusive of each other. Under some circumstances, they may be hierarchically organized as a progressive search procedure. With the conjunction 'or (just)', the search seems to progress from the specific to the generic. This may be seen in (17) below, where the opposite order — from the generic to the specific — would seem odd:

(17) a. Have you ever been to **Europe**, or just to the **East Coast**?
      b. *Have you ever been to the **East Coast**, or just to **Europe**?
      c. Do you ever go out for **Italian food**, or go out for
          another type of ethnic stuff, or just **go out** at all?

    d. *Do you ever **go out** at all, or go for **ethnic food**,
       or just for **Italian food**?
    e. Have you ever been a **boy scout**, or a member of a **youth
       group**, or any **social organization**?
    f. *Have you ever been a member of any **social organization**,
       or just a **youth group**, or just the **boy scouts**?

Other conjunctions, such as 'or (maybe) like', seem to code the opposite search procedure, from the generic to the specific, as in:

(18) a. Have you ever been a member of any **social organization**,
       like maybe a **youth group**, or like the **Boy Scouts**?
    b. *Have you ever been a member of the **Boy Scouts**,
       like maybe a **youth group**, or maybe like a **social
       organization**?

A general principle that is evident in the contrast between simple yes/no questions and alternative questions is this:

(19) **Explicit coding vs. inherent bias**:
    "The less there is an inherent implicit bias toward
    either one alternative or the other, the more likely
    it is that the alternatives will be spelled out
    explicitly".

Principle (19) is but a variant of a general coding principle that assigns less explicit coding to messages that are more transparent, more obvious, thus more redundant. Conversely, more explicit coding is reserved to messages that are less transparent, less obvious, thus less redundant.

12.2.1.3. Focused yes-no questions

So far we have considered only a version of yes-no questions that are, roughly speaking, somewhat neutral vis-a-vis the exact source of the speaker's uncertainty. We may assume that such questions are used when all the specific components of the state/event in question are known, but the event's **epistemic status** — 'true', 'probable', 'less certain', 'false' — is in doubt. Such neutral questions, as in (20a) below, are presumably abbreviated versions of their more expanded version, as in (20b):

(20) a. Did Joe kill the goat?
    b. Did the event "Joe killed the goat" take place?
       (>I do have my bias, but I want to be sure)

Quite often, however,[10] yes-no questions are used when the speaker's epistemic doubt concerning the proposition is much more specific. That is, when a proposition is assumed to hold true in the main, but one of its specific components — subject, object, verb, adverb — may be still in doubt. The uncertain element is then queried in a **focused yes-no question**. Consider for example questions (21) below, where contrastive stress is used to mark the focused elements:[11]

(21) a. Did **Joe** kill the goat?
            (> or did **someone else** do it?)
       b. Did Joe **kill** the goat?
            (> or did he only **kick** it?)
       c. Did Joe kill **the goat**?
            (> or did he kill **some other animal**?)

As noted earlier (chapter 10), when an optional adverbial is present in a declarative clause, the focus of assertion tends to be attracted to it. Such **focus attraction** also occurs in yes-no questions. Thus, the yes-no questions in (22) are obligatorily focused:

(22) a. Did Joe kill the goat **deliberately**?
            (> or accidentally?)
            (*> or did he not kill it?)
       b. Did Joe kill the goat **on Sunday**?
            (> or on Monday?)
            (*> or did he not kill it?)
       c. Did Joe kill the goat **in anger**?
            (> or in cold blood?)
            (*> or did he not kill it?)
       d. Did Joe kill the goat **in the barn**?
            (> or on the lawn?)
            (*> or did he not kill it?)
       e. Did Joe kill the goat **for Mary**?
            (> or for Sue?)
            (*> or did he not kill it?)

That the interrogative focus is attracted to optional constituents is further supported by the fact that when an optional adverbial is present, stressing another constituent in the clause is odd. In contrast, stressing the optional adverbial is natural:

(23) a. Did Joe kill the goat **on purpose**?
(> or did he do it **accidentally**)?
b. *Did **Joe** kill the goat on purpose?
(*> or did **someone else** do it on purpose?)
c. *Did Joe **kill** the goat on purpose?
(*> or did he **kick** it on purpose?)
d. *Did Joe kill **the goat** on purpose?
(*> or did he kill **another animal** on purpose?)

Two main themes emerge from our discussion of yes/no questions. First, speakers may have **varying degrees of certainty** or doubt about the epistemic status of a proposition. A whole range of variant grammatical patterns may be used to indicate these shades and gradations in the speaker's epistemic attitude. And second, speakers may have **varying reasons** for epistemic uncertainty about a proposition. Some syntactic variants of the basic yes-no question prototype may be used to indicate the more specific source of the speaker's epistemic uncertainty.

12.2.2. The syntax of yes-no questions

12.2.2.1. Intonation and subject-AUX inversion

Yes-no questions in English are coded syntactically by a combination of all three grammatical coding devices — intonation, morphology and word-order. Intonation is ever-present in whatever yes-no question pattern is used. Most conspicuously, yes-no questions display a raised, non-terminal melody. But word-order inversion is also part of the syntactic arsenal of English yes-no questions, always involving some **auxiliary** verb (or the verb 'be'). In illustrating the main pattern of English yes-no questions, it is perhaps useful to view the difference between a declarative clause and its corresponding yes-no question as a derivation, or **transformation** from declarative to interrogative. That is:

(24) **Subject-AUX inversion**:
a. John **is** eating dinner ⇒
Is John eating dinner?
b. Mary **has** come back ⇒
Has Mary come back?
c. He **will** forget ⇒
Will he forget?
d. She **is** ready? ⇒
Is she ready?
e. He **is** a crook ⇒
Is he a crook?

A declarative clause may also come without an auxiliary or 'be', in either the simple *past* or the *habitual*. As in the case of negation (chapter 4), English employs the auxiliary 'do' in yes-no questions. This auxiliary is then placed in the same clause-initial position as other fronted auxiliaries. For example:

(25) **The fronted auxiliary 'do'**:
    a. **Past**:
        John ate dinner ⇒
          Did John eat dinner?
    b. **Habitual (SG)**:
        She works for a living ⇒
          Does she work for a living?
    c. **Habitual (PL)**:
        They swim every day ⇒
          Do they swim every day?

12.2.2.2. Clefted yes-no questions

As noted in section 12.2.1.3. above, focused yes-no questions may be coded by intonation alone, i.e. by placing a prominent stress on the focused constituent. In addition, English also allows the use of the **cleft-focus** pattern in focused yes-no questions. As illustration of this pattern, consider:[12]

(26) a. **Declarative**:
        Joe killed the goat
    b. **Yes/no-Q, subject cleft**:
        Was it **Joe** who killed the goat?
    c. **Yes/no-Q, object cleft**:
        Was it **the goat** that Joe killed?
    d. **Yes/no-Q, verb cleft**:[13]
        ?Was it **killing** that Joe did to the goat?

In more formal terms, cleft-focused yes-no questions such as (26b,c,d) may be viewed as the product of a yes-no question 'transformation' applied to the corresponding declarative cleft-focus construction. That is, respectively:

(27) a. **Subject cleft-focus**:

It **was** JOE who killed the goat ⇒

Was it JOE who killed the goat?

b. **Object cleft-focus**:

It **was** the GOAT that Joe killed ⇒

Was it the GOAT that Joe killed?

Verb cleft-focus:

c. ?It **was** KILLING that Joe did to the goat ⇒

?**Was** it KILLING that Joe did to the goat?

12.2.2.3. Alternative choice questions

The conjunction 'or' is used in English to mark alternative choice questions. When a binary choice between the affirmative and negative is involved, the negation marker joins 'or'. Parts of the corresponding **negative yes-no question** may also appear following 'or not', as in:

(28) a. Is he coming **or not**?

b. Is he coming **or is he not**?

c. Is he coming **or is he not coming**?

(29) a. Did she leave home **or not**?

b. Did she leave home **or did she not**?

c. Did she leave home **or did she not leave home**?

(30) a. Are they home **or not**?

b. Are they home **or are they not**?

c. Are they home **or are they not home**?

The combined use of both the affirmative and negative yes-no question patterns, as in the more explicit (28c), (29c) and (30c), supports our earlier suggestion that the normal pattern — where either the affirmative or negative is used by itself — is indeed a biased question pattern. The totally open-ended alternative choice question requires more explicit coding. Given the general coding principle (19), one may conclude that the more general, neutral, unmarked pattern of yes-no questions in English is the biased pattern. Alternative-choice questions, on the other hand, with their added explicit coding, represent a more marked pattern.

12.3. WH QUESTIONS

12.3.1. Functional aspects

12.3.1.1. Focus and presupposition

WH-questions, also called **constituent questions**, are used typically when the speaker assumes that they and the hearer share the knowledge of a proposition concerning an event/state. That proposition is thus part of the presupposed background, the **pragmatic context** within which the WH-question is transacted. However, the speaker is still missing one element — information chunk — in the proposition. That missing element is then made the **interrogative focus** of the WH-question, typically pointing to the subject, object, verb, predicate, adverb, indirect object, time, place, manner, reason, etc. In principle, any constituent of the clause — a noun phrase, a prepositional phrase, a verb phrase or an adverb — may be placed under interrogative focus. To illustrate the more common pattern, consider the range of WH-questions that can be formed from the declarative proposition (31a) below:

(31) a. **Corresponding declarative clause**:
        Yesterday Mary sneakily gave a kiss to John
        in her father's barn.
   b. **Subject WH-question**:
        Who gave John a kiss? (= Mary)
   c. **Object WH-question**:
        What did Mary give to John? (= a kiss)
   d. **Indirect-object WH-question**:
        To whom did Mary give a kiss? (= to John)
   e. **Manner WH-question**:
        How did Mary give John a kiss? (= sneakily)
   f. **Time WH-question**:
        When did Mary give John a kiss? (= Yesterday)
   g. **Place WH-question**:
        Where did Mary give John a kiss? (= in the barn)
   h. **Possessor WH-question**:
        Whose barn was it? (= Mary's father's)

In addition to nominal participants of the clause, the whole clause, its verb phrase, its verb, a verbal complement or an adverbial clause may be made the focus of a WH-question:

(32) a. **Whole event WH-question**:
      What happened?
      (presupposed: 'Something happened')
   b. **Verb phrase WH-question**:
      What did John do?
      (presupposed: 'John did something')
   c. **Verb WH-question**:
      What did John do to Mary?
      (presupposed: 'John did something to Mary')
   d. **Verbal complement WH-question**:
      What did John decide to do?
      (presupposed: 'John decided to do something')
   e. **Reason/purpose ADV WH-question**:
      Why did John give Mary a kiss?
      (presupposed: 'John gave Mary a kiss for a reason')

In terms of information structure, the bulk of the WH-question clause is not under interrogative focus, but rather is presupposed. Under the communicative contract, the speaker assumes that the hearer will go along with the presupposed information and will not challenge it.[14] Only the focus element is under interrogative scope. Consider, for example, the following exchanges between the interrogating speaker and a respondent (hearer). The discrepancy between the speaker's and hearer's knowledge concerns the information under WH-focus. Since that information is not presupposed by the speaker, no serious disagreement ensues:

(33) SPEAKER: **Who** kissed John?
      HEARER: Sue.
      SPEAKER: You mean, it wasn't Mary?
      HEARER: No, she wasn't even there.

In both (34) and (35), on the other hand, the legitimacy of the background presupposition — "Someone kissed Mary" is under contention. Unless that presupposition is settled, the WH-question is infelicitous:[15]

(34) SPEAKER: **Who** kissed John?
      HEARER: Oh, did anybody kiss him?
      SPEAKER: What do you mean, you didn't see it happen?
      HEARER: I was right there and I didn't see any kissing.

(35) SPEAKER: **Why** did Mary kiss John?
      HEARER: What do you mean 'why'? She never kissed him.
      SPEAKER: She did too!
      HEARER: She sure as heck didn't!

12.3.1.2. The semantics of interrogative pronouns

The WH-pronoun ('question word') is also called the **interrogative pronoun**. The function of this pronoun is to mark the type of missing element that is under the interrogative focus. In English, several semantic distinctions are coded in interrogative pronoun.

(a) **Human vs. non-human**

For nominal participants in the clause — subjects, direct objects and indirect objects — the distinction here is between the human WH-pronoun 'who(m)' and the non-human one 'what':

(36) a. **Human subject**:
        Who fell into the river?
    b. **Non-human subject**:
        What fell into the river?
    c. **Human object**:
        Who(m) did you see?
    d. **Non-human object**:
        What did you see
    e. **Human indirect object**:
        Who(m) did you build the house **with**?
    f. **Non-human indirect object**:
        What did you build the house **with**?

(b) **Subject vs. object**

For human participants only, a distinction can be made between the subject WH-pronoun 'who' and the object WH-pronoun 'whom', as in:

(37) a. **Subject WH-pronoun**:
        Who saw her?
    b. **Object WH-pronoun**:
        Whom did she see?
    c. **Indirect object WH-pronoun**:
        Whom did she go **with**?

This distinction, at least in American English, is nearly obsolete. The form 'who' may be used in both contexts, and 'whom' is falling into disuse. The best evidence for this process comes from instances of **hyper-correction**. These are cases where speakers use the object WH-pronoun 'whom' for the subject role, presumably conscious of their tendency to under-use it in the object role. An example of this may be seen in (38) below, where the object WH-pronoun 'whom' is used to mark the predicate-nominal role. If one goes by the more conservative grammar, predicate nouns take the subject

> (38)   "Holland's belief in a strong deanship extends to his
>   advice to his successor, **whomever** that person may
>   be..."[16]

(c) **Prepositional (indirect object) case-roles**

For prepositional objects, human or non-human alike, the appropriate preposition marking the semantic case-role of the participant must be added, most naturally as a post-verbal 'dangling' preposition:

> (39) a. **Dative-recipient:**
>   **Who** did he give the book **to**?
>   b. **Benefactive:**
>   **Who** is she doing this **for**?
>   c. **Instrument:**
>   **What** did she cut herself **with**?
>   d. **Associative:**
>   **Who** did she run away **with**?
>   e. **Locative:**
>   **Where** is she coming **from**?

(d) **Adverbial roles**

Several adverbial roles in English have their special WH-pronouns. These roles may be either verb-phrase participants, such as locative or manner, or ADV-clause roles (see chapter 13). For example:

> (40) a. **Locative:**
>   **Where** did he go to school?
>   b. **Time:**
>   **When** is she coming?

  c. **Manner**:
     How did they do it?
  d. **Reason/purpose**:
     Why did she leave?

For each of these adverbial roles, more specific WH-questions can be
made, using the appropriate preposition, as in:

(41) a. **Locative**:
         Where did he go **to**?
      b. **Time**:
         What date is she arriving (**on**)?
      c. **Manner**:
         In what way did they do it?
      d. **Reason/purpose**:
         What did they fire him **for**?
         What did she send him there **for**?

Some of these examples are stilted, and more natural variants do exist. The
pattern of syntactic variants of WH-questions to some extent parallels the
variation seen in REL-clauses (chapter 9).

(e) **Definiteness and reference**
    English marks reference and definiteness distinctions in WH-questions
in a fairly systematic way, by augmenting the interrogative pronouns with
appropriate quantifiers or nouns. As an illustration, consider the restrictions
on possible answers to the WH-questions. In (42) below the normal WH-
pronoun is used. This pattern does not restrict the definiteness or referentiality of possible answers:

(42) **Unrestricted WH-pattern**:
      Who murdered Smith?
          (a) **Definite**:   Joe.
          (b) **REF-indefinite**: Some woman I used to know.
          (c) **NON-REF**:   A pervert.

All of the responses (42a,b,c) are equally appropriate. On the other hand,
the WH-question in (43) below is aimed specifically at eliciting a **definite**
response. The REF-indefinite response (43b) or the non-referring response
(43c) are incompatible with such a question:

(43) **Definite WH-pattern**:
      Which one did it?
    (a) **Definite**:   Joe.
    (b) ***REF-indefinite**: *Some woman I used to know.
    (c) ***NON-REF**:   *A pervert.

In (44) below, the WH-question is aimed specifically at eliciting a **non-referring** response. Now the definite response (44a) and the REF-indefinite response (44b) are incompatible with the question:[17]

(44) **NON-referring ('type') WH-pattern**:
      What kind of a person did it?
    (a) **Definite**:   *Joe.
    (b) **REF-indefinite**: *Some woman I used to know.
    (c) **NON-REF**:   A pervert.

(f) **Number and class/gender**

To both the definite pattern (43) and the non-referring pattern (44), number and class/gender distinctions may be added. The question can be thus focused more and more finely, either toward the specific **referential identity** of the focused constituent, or its specific **class membership**. To elicit a more specific definite response, the pronoun 'which' is combined with a specific noun, as in:

(45) **More specific definite WH-pattern**:
    a. **DEF, SG, human**:
       Which man did it?
    b. **DEF, PL, non-human**:
       Which houses did you see?

(46) **More specific non-referring WH-pattern**:
    a. **NON-REF, SG, non-human**:
       What kind of a town is this?
    d. **NON-REF, PL, human**:
       What kind of people are they?

12.3.1.3. Quantifier WH-questions

The WH-questions we have seen thus far focus on major constituents, such as noun phrases, prepositional phrases, verb phrases, verbal complements, verbs or adverbs. But WH-questions can also focus on some sub-constituents of those. Two such elements are:

(a) The **quantity** of head nouns within the NP; that is, what is marked in the declarative clause by **quantifiers**.

(b) The **extent** of verbs or adjectives; that is, what is coded in the declarative clause by **extent adverbs** that modify verbs or adjectives.

(47) **Quantifier on a count noun**:
    a. **Declarative**:   She saw **three** mules.
    b. **WH-question**: **How many mules** did she see?

(48) **Quantifier on a mass noun**:
    a. **Declarative**:   He drank **lots of** water.
    b. **WH-question**: **How much water** did he drink?

(49) **Extent of predicate adjective**:
    a. **Declarative**:   She is (**very**) big.
    b. **WH-question**: **How big** is she?

(50) **Extent of modifying adjective**:
    a. **Declarative**:   He has a (**very**) big house.
    b. **WH-question**: **How big a house** does he have?

(51) **Extent of manner adverb**:
    a. **Declarative**:   She worked (**very**) hard.
    b. **WH-question**: **How hard** did she work?

When the quantification in the declarative clause involves more exact measure units, those may appear in the corresponding WH-question. Thus compare:

(52) a. **Declarative**:   This car can do **65 miles per hour**.
    b. **WH-question**: **How many miles per hour** can it do?

(53) a. **Declarative**:   He weighed **185 pounds**.
    b. **WH-question**: **How many pounds** did he weigh?

But the complex quantification in declaratives such as (52a) and (53a) can just as easily be elicited by more general quantifier questions:

(54) a. **How fast** can it go?
    b. **How much** did he weigh?

12.3.1.4. Multiple interrogative focus

The general search strategy in using WH-questions as a tool for eliciting information is parsimonious: One presupposes the entire clause except for one element, and then focuses on that missing element. Under certain conditions, however, one can form a **multiple WH-question**, whereby more than one WH-pronoun appears in the same interrogative clause. Examples of this special pattern are:

(55) a. **Who** gave **what** to **whom**?
      b. **Who** said **what**?

Multiple WH-questions are used under specific discourse conditions: The speaker has failed to hear the information supplied in the preceding turn. That preceding turn may have identified a group — two or more — of **parallel events**, listing the parallel roles (subject, direct object, indirect object) too fast for the hearer to absorb. For example, a description of the two parallel events in (56) below may have precipitated the multiple WH-question (55a):

(56) Mary gave a book to John, and Sally gave a rose to Bill.

Alternatively, the speaker may have misheard — or disbelieved — an item in a WH-question, other than the focused one. The multiple-WH pattern is then used as a way of querying that extra item. For example, the simple WH-question (57) below could have precipitated the multiple WH question (55b) above:

(57) **Who** said that Joe was dead?

While multiple WH-questions are a possible pattern in English, they are clearly not a very common one.

12.3.2. The syntax of WH-questions

12.3.2.1. Word-order

Two main features characterize the syntactic order of English WH-questions:

(a) Pre-posing of the WH-pronoun
(b) Subject-AUX inversion

The pre-posed — or **clause initial** — position of WH-pronouns can be seen in all the examples above. However, subject-AUX inversion does not apply to subject-WH-questions. The use of auxiliaries in WH-question clauses follows, in the main, their use in negation (chapter 4) and yes-no questions (section 12.2.). If the clause has an auxiliary — *be*, *have* or *modal*, that auxiliary is placed directly after the WH-pronoun. This, together with subject-AUX inversion, is illustrated in (58) below:

(58) **Subject-AUX inversion in WH-questions**:
    a. **Declarative**:   She **will** do it ⇒
       Interrogative: What **will** she do?
    b. **Declarative**:   He **has** seen the house ⇒
       Interrogative: What **has** he seen?
    c. **Declarative**:   They **are** leaving tomorrow ⇒
       Interrogative: When **are** they leaving?

In forming WH-questions, the main verb 'be' is treated as an auxiliary, and thus undergoes subject to subject-AUX inversion:

(59) a. **Declarative**:   John **is** at home ⇒
       Interrogative: Where **is** John?
    b. **Declarative**:   Mary **is** tall ⇒
       Interrogative: How tall **is** Mary?
    c. **Declarative**:   They **are** politicians ⇒
       Interrogative: What **are** they?

Finally, in the simple past and habitual tense-aspects, where no auxiliary exists in the declarative clause, the auxiliary 'do' is used in the WH-question, and is placed after the WH-pronoun. The subject then follows 'do', and the main verb then takes the bare stem form:

(60) a. **Declarative**:   Mary read the book ⇒
       Interrogative: What **did** Mary read?
    b. **Declarative**:   They work hard ⇒
       Interrogative: How hard **do** they work?
    c. **Declarative**:   George hates broccoli ⇒
       Interrogative: Why **does** George hate broccoli?

12.3.2.2. Un-inverted WH-questions

In colloquial English, one also finds a WH-question pattern that dispenses with the word-order strategy described above. In such a pattern, the WH-pronoun merely replaces the focused constituent *in situ*, and the WH-question then looks superficially like a declarative clause. However, a strong stress and raised intonation then mark the WH-pronoun. Indeed, this is an **emphatic interrogative** pattern. For example:

(61) a. **Declarative**:   She will do **it** ⇒
    Interrogative: She will do **what**?
   b. **Declarative**:   John has met **Bill** ⇒
    Interrogative: John has met **who**?
   c. **Declarative**:   John is leaving **tomorrow** ⇒
    Interrogative: John is leaving **when**?
   d. **Declarative**:   Mary went **home** ⇒
    Interrogative: Mary went **where**?

The un-inverted WH-question pattern is used in contexts of disbelief or faulty hearing, somewhat akin to double-focus questions (12.3.1.4.). In the case of the double-focus question, a constituent in a preceding question was misperceived or disbelieved. In the case of un-inverted question, a constituent in a preceding declarative clause is misperceived or disbelieved.

12.3.2.3. Clefted WH-questions

WH-questions share many of the syntactic characteristics of cleft clauses. In both constructions, the bulk of the clause is presupposed and only a single — fronted — constituent is in focus. Clefted WH-questions seem to be another emphatic pattern, presumably in the context of a misperceived or disbelieved clefted declarative:

(62) **Subject focus**:
   a. **Cleft declarative**:
      It's **John** who saw Mary.
   b. **Cleft WH-question**:
      It's **who** that saw Mary?

(63) **Object focus**:
   a. **Cleft declarative**:
      It's **Mary** that John saw
   b. **Cleft WH-question**:
      It's **who** that John saw?

12.3.2.4. Embedded WH-clauses

A certain group of perception-cognition-utterance verbs allow, in addition to declarative complements, also WH-like complements:

(64) a. **Subject**:   I know **who came first**
      b. **Direct object**:   She suggested to me **whom I should see**
      c. **Indirect object**: She wondered **who I gave it to**
      d. **Benefactive**:   Nobody knew **who she did it for**
      e. **Location**:   He discovered **where the key was**
      f. **Time**:   They told her **when they were coming**
      g. **Manner**:   I forgot **how it was done**
      h. **Purpose**:   He finally remembered **what he came to do**
      i. **Reason**:   She guessed **why it happened**

Not all perception-cognition-utterance verbs can take such WH-complements. Thus compare:[18]

(65) a. *I thought **who came first**
      b. *She regretted **why it happened**
      c. *He hoped **where the key was**
      d. *He said **whom I should see**
      e. *I wish **how it was done**
      f. *She doubted **who did it**
      g. *He was afraid **why they fired her**

All the verbs that allow WH complements are epistemic verbs, i.e. verbs that involve either knowledge or certainty. In contrast, most of the verbs that reject such complements are verbs of preference. However, non-preference verbs such as 'think' or 'say' also reject WH-complements, so that the distinction of epistemic vs. preference does not tell the entire story.

Verbs that allow WH-complements also tend to allow **nominal complements** modified by a REL-clause. Further, the meanings of the two constructions are deceptively close — though by no means identical. Thus, compare (66) below to (64) above:

(66) a. **Subject**:   I know **the person who came first**
      b. **Direct object**:   She suggested to me **the woman that I should see**
      c. **Indirect object**: She wondered **who it was that I gave it to**

    d. **Benefactive**: Nobody knew **who it was that he did it for**
    e. **Location**: He discovered **the place where the key was**
    f. **Time**: They told her **the date when they were coming**
    g. **Manner**: I forgot **the way it was done**
    h. **Purpose**: He finally remembered **the thing he came to do**
    i. **Reason**: She guessed **the reason why it happened**

The close semantic similarity between the constructions in (66) and (64) suggests that WH-complements in (66) are not WH-questions, but rather **headless REL-clauses**. Some support for this hypothesis comes from the fact that an important syntactic feature of WH-questions — the obligatory subject-AUX inversion — is absent in such WH-complements:

(67) a. **Subject**: I know **who came first**
     b. **Direct object**: *She suggested to me **whom should I see**
     c. **Indirect object**: *She wondered **who did I give it to**
     d. **Benefactive**: *Nobody suspected **who did he do it for**
     e. **Location**: *He discovered **where was the key**
     f. **Time**: *They told her **when were they coming**
     g. **Manner**: *I forgot **how was it done**
     h. **Purpose**: *He finally remembered
         what did he come to do
     i. **Reason**: *She guessed **why did it happen**

Note, finally, that the very same WH-like clauses that appear in verbal complements in (66) can also occupy the subject position, in main clauses whose predicates take sentential subjects:

(68) a. **Who did it** remains a mystery
     b. **Why it happened** is not clear
        (*Why did it happen** is not clear)
     c. **Where the key was** perplexed her
        (*Where was the key** perplexed her)
     d. **Who I should see** is still a question
        (*Who should I see** is still a question)
     e. **How it was done** was never discovered
        (*How was it done** was never discovered)
     f. **What he did** is none of your business
        (*What did she do** is none of your business)

Here again, the subject-AUX inversion characteristic of WH-questions is unacceptable. This supports the idea that these embedded structures are not WH-questions, but either headless REL-clauses or perhaps, a syntactic hybrid.[19]

12.4. MANIPULATIVE SPEECH-ACTS

12.4.1. Preamble

The traditional generic label **imperative** covers a wide range of functionally-related speech-acts and grammatical constructions. We have already noted that interrogative speech-acts are in fact manipulative, since they are used to manipulate the hearer toward supplying information via a verbal response. The goal of interrogative speech-acts thus remains epistemic. In contrast, manipulative speech-acts are used primarily to elicit the hearer's non-verbal response, i.e. **action**.

12.4.2. Functional aspects

12.4.2.1. The communicative contract

Manipulative speech-acts are verbal acts through which the speaker attempts to get the hearer to act. Under the **communicative contract** that governs the interaction between speakers and hearers, the following conventions tend to apply to manipulative speech acts:[20]

(69) **Conventions governing manipulative speech-acts**:
    (a) **State of the world**:
        "The *desired* state of affairs that is the *goal* of the manipulation is different from the *current* state of affairs".
    (b) **Power to act**:
        "The manipulee — hearer — is free to act in the desired direction".
    (c) **Authority**:
        "The manipulator — speaker — has legitimate authority over the manipulee".

To illustrate how these clauses govern manipulative speech-acts, consider the use of the canonical imperative in:

(70) Get up!

Clause (69a) of the communicative contract renders (70) inappropriate if the manipulee is already standing. Clause (69b) renders (70) inappropriate if the manipulee is tied securely to his/her seat. Clause (69c) renders (70) inappropriate for a small child addressing a venerable elder.

12.4.2.2. Manipulation, power and status

Clearly, clause (69c) of the communicative contract involves the social-personal relations between the speaker and hearer. The balance of **status**, **power**, **obligation** or **entitlement** between the two participants determines the exact manipulative construction to be used. Questions of **politeness**, **propriety**, **respect**, and **fear** — or **potential social consequences** of improper usage — are all germane to the choice of a manipulative construction. These factors are not independent of each other, but enter into predictable interactions. Those interactions may be summarized as the following conditional associations:

(71) a. Higher speaker's power/status ⇒
        (i) greater hearer's obligation to comply
       (ii) lesser speaker's need to be deferent
    b. Higher hearer's power/status ⇒
        (i) lesser hearer's obligation to comply
       (ii) greater speaker's need to be deferent

While the associations (71a,b) are fairly general, a vast array of intimate, culture-specific conventions determine the proper use of manipulative constructions in any particular language. In this domain, the grammar of verbal manipulation shades gradually into the grammar of **deference** on the one hand, and of **epistemic certainty** on the other.

Consider the following gradation from the canonical **imperative** to a deferent **request**, where constructions are ranked according to manipulative strength:

(72) **highest manipulative strength**
    a. Get up!
    b. Get up, will you.
    c. Would you please get up?
    d. Would you mind getting up?
    e. Do you think you could get up?
    f. Would you mind if I asked you to get up?
    lowest manipulative strength

The gradation in (72) reveals a number of coding principles that are used to express manipulative strength. Manipulations seem to be systematically weakened by the following devices:

(73) **Devices that weaken manipulative strength**:
    a. increased length
    b. the use of question forms
    c. explicit mention of the manipulee pronoun ('you')
    d. use of irrealis modality on the verb
    e. use of negative form
    f. embedding the manipulative clause under
       the scope of a modality or cognition verb

One may also view the devices in (73) as **politeness conventions**. By using them, alone or in various combinations, the manipulation becomes more polite, indirect, deferential, circumspect. We will return to discuss this further in section 12.5., below.

12.4.3. The syntax of manipulative speech-acts

12.4.3.1. The canonical imperative clause

The imperative verb-form in English is the simple bare-stem form of the verb, the same one that appears after modals or the auxiliary 'do'. Further, the imperative clause is most typically subjectless, a feature that is predictable from the fact that the subject is always the addressee, i.e. *you*.[21] As a bare-stem form, the imperative also shows a very restricted range of tense-aspect-modality marking. This is again predictable from the fact that a manipulative speech-act is by definition in the irrealis, future projecting mode. In terms of verbal modalities, the canonical imperative verb-form is thus less-finite.[22] There is neither past imperative nor present imperative in English, and the use of either the progressive or perfect aspects is severely restricted:

(74) a. **Simple**:   Do the dishes!
     b. **Progressive**: *Be doing the dishes!
     c. **Perfect**:   *Have done the dishes!

The restriction on the progressive (74b) is probably due to the fact that the progressive is a state, and imperatives in general are aimed at eliciting action, i.e. an event. Similar restrictions tend to crop up in the complements of manipulative verbs:[23]

(75) a. **Simple complement**:
   She told him to **shut** the door.
   b. **Progressive complement**:
   *She told him to **be shutting** the door.

12.4.3.2. Prohibitive or NEG-imperatives

NEG-imperatives, or **prohibitive** clauses, require the negative auxiliary 'don't', as in:

(76) a. Wash the dishes! ⇒
   Don't wash the dishes!
   b. Leave! ⇒
   Don't leave!

One may consider the NEG-imperative as roughly an equivalent, in terms of directness or manipulative strength, of the 'canonical' imperative. Less direct, weaker prohibitive expressions come with their own negative form.

12.4.3.3. Weaker manipulative constructions

As seen in (72) above, English has a wide array of manipulative constructions, most of them less direct, more deferential, or weaker — in terms of the speaker's authority over the hearer — than the canonical imperative. In this section we will briefly survey some of the more common variants.

12.4.3.3.1. The hortative imperative

The plural **hortative imperative** in English involves the inclusion of the speaker — together with the hearer — as dual or plural subject of the manipulative clause. Typically, such an exhortation is marked with the contraction 'let's' ('let us'), followed by the verb in its non-finite bare-stem form. A **negative-exhortative** would then include 'not':

(77) a. **Let's** get out of here!
   b. **Let's not** worry about it!

12.4.3.3.2. The jussive clause

The verb-derived marker 'let' may also be used to signal a peculiar speech-act, the **jussive**, which purports to elicit the action of a third person, rather than of the hearer:

(78) a. Let **her** do it then!
   b. Let **George** do the dishes instead!

The origin of this construction is transparently as an imperative form of the manipulative verb 'let' (see chapter 7). But it does not necessarily involve directing the hearer to either take action, make a third person take action, or allow the third person to take action. This is clear from the fact that there may be no hearer present, or that the hearer may have no control over the third-person subject of the exhortative clause. Thus consider:

(79) a. **Let** Congress rot in Washington till Christmas then!
      b. **Let** the storm rage, who cares!
      c. **Let** time take its inevitable course.

The jussive construction seems to be an expression of **preference**, **oath**, or **resignation** toward states or events. This explains the compatibility of stative clauses, non-agentive subjects or even agentless passives with the jussive construction. Such non-agentive constructions would be incompatible with more direct, stronger manipulations. Thus compare:

(80) a. **Let** there be light!
          (*Be there light!)
          (*I told there to be light)
      b. **Let** her be!.
          (*Be)
          (*I told her to be)
      c. **Let** the trees rot!
          (*rot!)
          (*I told the trees to rot)
      d. **Let** there be no mistake about it!
          (*Be there no mistake about it!)
          (*I told there to be no mistake about it)
      e. **Let** her be sent home!
          (*be sent home)
          (*I told her to be sent home)

12.4.3.3.3. Weaker yet verbal manipulation

As noted in (72) and (73) above, modals, conditionals, questions, irrealis markers and other devices can be used systematically to weaken manipulative speech-acts. Such devices make the manipulation less direct, less forceful, less authoritarian, more polite. With the use of such devices, the imperative may gradually shade into **request**, **plea**, **begging**, **suggestion**, or a weak expression of **preference**. Many weakening devices allow the speaker-manipulator to appear overtly as co-subject of the clause. In others, the speaker is the only subject, excluding the hearer. For example:

(81) a. **Shall** we go now?
      b. **Please, would you** leave me alone?
      c. **Should** we **perhaps** do something about it?
      d. **Could** we leave now?
      e. **Would it be OK if** we left?
      f. **Would you mind** moving over one seat?
      g. **Would you mind** Joe coming over now?
      h. **May** I join you?
      i. **Would you mind very much if** we skipped the party?
      j. **Would you object to** Jill joining us?
      k. **Would you be kind enough to** move over?

Syntactically, these weak manipulative devices shade gradually into other speech-act areas, such as questions.

12.5. INDIRECT SPEECH-ACTS: THE CONTINUUM

12.5.1. Preamble

In the preceding discussion, except in the very last section, we dealt primarily with the three prototypical non-declarative speech-acts: yes-no question, WH-question, and the canonical imperative. In noting the weaker manipulative speech-acts in (81), however, one can already observe the use of non-manipulative grammatical forms, such as yes-no questions, to express various shades of manipulation. In this section we will discuss somewhat more systematically various aspects of this phenomenon, which has traditionally gone under the label of **indirect speech-acts**. In a somewhat simplified way, one may define an indirect speech-act as:[24]

(82) **Indirect speech-act**:
      "An indirect speech-act is a construction used to perform
      one speech-act even though its grammatical form is more
      commonly associated with another speech-act".

Within the framework pursued here, this use of particular forms to convey specific speech-acts is not an accident, but rather involves a systematic extension-by-similarity of well-established form-function correlations. In other words, the syntax of indirect speech acts is functionally well motivated.[25]

12.5.2. From imperative to interrogative

Consider first the continuum in (83) below, between prototypical imperative and interrogative speech acts:

(83) **most prototypical imperative**
a. Pass the salt.
b. Please pass the salt.
c. Pass the salt, would you please?
d. Would you please pass the salt?
e. Could you please pass the salt?
f. Can you pass the salt?
g. Do you see the salt?
h. Is there any salt around?
i. Was there any salt there?
most prototypical interrogative

The extreme points of scale, (83a) and (83i), correspond to the imperative and interrogative prototypes, respectively. The mid-points on the scale — (83c,d,e) — exhibit intermediate features both functionally and syntactically. Finally, intermediate (83b) is more like the imperative prototype (83a), while intermediates (83f,g,h) are closer to the interrogative prototype (83i).

One may consider the intermediate points in (83) as a continuum of **extension-by-similarity** [26] between the distinct prototypes of imperative and interrogative. The following parameters are probably involved in the meaning dimensions that underlie the continuum:

(84) a. The **power gradient** between speaker and hearer
b. The degree of the **speaker's ignorance** concerning a state of affairs about which he wishes to learn
c. The degree of the **speaker's sense of urgency** or **determination**.

The individual parameters suggested in (84) are scalar. Taken together, they seem to define a multi-dimensional mental space. As we shall see below, some of these parameters also pertain to the continuum among other speech-act prototypes.

12.5.3. From imperative to declarative

Consider next the continuum in (85) below, spanning the space between the prototypes of imperative and declarative:

(85) **most prototypical imperative**
  a. Wash the dishes!
  b. You better wash the dishes!
  c. You might as well wash the dishes.
  d. I suggest you wash the dishes.
  e. It would be nice if you could wash the dishes.
  f. It would be nice if someone could wash the dishes.
  g. The dishes need to be washed.
  h. The dishes are dirty.
  i. The dishes were dirty.
  most prototypical declarative

Expression (85a) is syntactically a prototype imperative. Intermediates (85b,c,d,e) explicitly code the subject/agent 'you'. The manipulative force of the speech-act gradually decreases, as the syntactic form is slowly changed toward the declarative prototype. In (85f) 'you' is replaced by 'someone', an impersonalization that further decreases the manipulative power. The impersonalization is further underscored with the passive form (85g). Finally, both (85h,i) are syntactically fairly prototypical declaratives. And the shift to past tense in (85i) makes a situation-bound imperative interpretation untenable.

Of the underlying socio-pragmatic dimensions in (84) above, the two that pertain to imperatives — (84a,c) — are presumably also involved in continuum (85). In addition, the following features are also likely to be involved:

(86) a. The speaker's **subjective certainty** about the information
  b. The speaker's assessment of the **hearer's ignorance** of the information
  c. The speaker's assessment of the strength of the **hearer's motivation** to learn that information

The degree of syntactic similarity of the constructions along scale (85) probably represents, isomorphically, the degree of their functional similarity.

12.5.4. From declarative to interrogative

A graded continuum also exists between the prototypes of declarative and interrogative. Consider first the scale involving yes-no questions:

(87) **most prototypical declarative**
   a. Joe is at home.
   b. Joe is at home, I think.
   c. Joe is at home, right?
   d. Joe is at home, isn't he?
   e. Is Joe at home?
   most prototypical interrogative

This continuum involves, among other things, a clear decrease in the speaker's subjective certainty concerning the information in their possession. It thus involves the *irrealis* — uncertainty — epistemic modality as an intermediate point (87b) on the scale between *realis*-assertion and yes-no question.

Consider finally the continuum between the declarative and WH-question prototypes:

(88) **most prototypical declarative**
   a. Joe called, and...
   b. What's-his-name called, and...
   c. Whoever it was that called, tell them...
   d. I don't know who called.
   e. Who knows who called...
   f. Who called?
   most prototypical interrogative

The gradation here is similar to that in (87), moving gradually from *realis*-assertion ('high certainty') through *irrealis*-assertion ('low certainty') to question.

12.6. MOOD: THE INTERACTION BETWEEN EPISTEMIC AND MANIPULATIVE MODALITY

12.6.1. Preamble

As noted earlier, the traditional discussion of propositional modalities, from Aristotle onward, has taken for granted a clear division of the epistemic (declarative) from the non-epistemic (interrogative, imperative) modes. Among the former, irrealis is the well recognized mode of possible truth.

A cursory look at the distribution of the irrealis modality in grammar[27] reveals a consistent association of irrealis with non-declarative clauses, both interrogative and manipulative. In this section we will consider a range of facts, all pointing out to systematic shading between **epistemic**, **intentional** and **manipulative** modality. One conclusion that one could draw from this shading is that there are no discrete boundaries between the epistemic ('declarative') and the manipulative ('deontic') modes, but rather a continuum. Within that continuum, weak epistemic certainty shades into weak preference; and strong preference shades into weak manipulation.

The grammatical phenomenon of **subjunctive mood** tends to cover the mid-portion of the continuum, from weak epistemic certainty, through preference, to weak manipulation. Perhaps the best example of this continuum is found in the complementation scale (see chapter 7):

(89) **The complementation scale**   **modality**

manipulative extreme

a. She **let go** of the knife
b. She **made** him **shave**
c. She **let** him **go** home   STRONG MANIPULATION
d. She **had** him **arrested**   (REALIS)
e. She **caused** him **to switch** jobs

f. She **told** him **to leave**
g. She **asked** him **to leave**   WEAK MANIPULATION
h. She **allowed** him **to leave**

i. She **wanted** him **to leave**   STRONG PREFERENCE
j. She **expected** him **to leave**

k. She **suggested** that he **leave**
l. She**'d like for him to leave**
m. She **wished** that he **would leave**   WEAK PREFERENCE
n. She **preferred** that he **leave**
o. She **hoped** that he **might leave**
p. She **was afraid** that he **might leave**

q. She **suspected** that he **had left**
r. She **thought** that he **had left**   WEAK CERTAINTY
s. She **was sure** that he **had left**

t. She **knew** that he **left**   STRONG CERTAINTY (REALIS)

epistemic extreme

We have already noted, in an earlier discussion of the communicative contract, that notions such as certainty and probability of challenge necessarily shade into the domain of intent, preference, power, and action. This shading is not logically necessary. Rather, it involves pragmatic inferences about likelihoods and norms.

12.6.2. The subjunctive mood: From weak certainty to weak manipulation

The main modal steps along the semantic modal continuum of complementation scale are summarized in (90) below:

(90) **Main semantic steps on the complementation scale:**
      manipulative extreme

sub-mode	modality
a. successful causation ("implicative")	REALIS
b. intended manipulation ("non-implicative") c. preference/aversion d. epistemic anxiety e. epistemic uncertainty ("non-factive")	LIKELY RANGE OF SUBJUNCTIVE MOOD
f. epistemic certainty ("factive")	REALIS

epistemic extreme

The subjunctive is a grammatical category that appears in many languages, but is normally ignored in English. In languages where it does occur,[28] the subjunctive tends to crop up within the modal space of irrealis, in the continuum space between weak epistemic certainty and weak manipulation. In contemporary English, the old grammatical category of subjunctive has almost disappeared. Older or more formal speakers — or usages — may still show two subjunctive forms. One subjunctive form is coded by the bare-stem form of the verb. It is found in the complements of manipulative verbs, but is also the form taken by main verbs following a modal auxiliary ('should', 'must', 'will' etc.), as well as the bare-stem imperative form. Another subjunctive is coded by the past tense form of the verb.

The connection between subjunctive and the English modals is not accidental. English modals — especially their historical past-tense forms[29] — in fact code the very same modal ranges that in other languages are coded by subjunctive forms. Typically, the use of both the residual subjunctive form and modals in manipulative-verb complements signals weaker, less-direct, less-coercive manipulation. As illustrations of the use of the **bare-stem subjunctive** form, consider:

(91) a. I insist that she $\left\{\begin{array}{l}\textbf{leave}\\ \textbf{*leaves}\end{array}\right\}$ at once.

b. She asks that her record $\left\{\begin{array}{l}\textbf{be}\\ \textbf{*is}\end{array}\right\}$ wiped clean.

c. They suggest that she $\left\{\begin{array}{l}\textbf{retake}\\ \textbf{*retakes}\end{array}\right\}$ the exam.

d. They prefer that she $\left\{\begin{array}{l}\textbf{do}\\ \textbf{*does}\end{array}\right\}$ it right away.

e. I'd rather she $\left\{\begin{array}{l}\textbf{not come.}\\ \textbf{*doesn't come.}\end{array}\right\}$

f. She better $\left\{\begin{array}{l}\textbf{behave}\\ \textbf{*behaves}\end{array}\right\}$ herself.

Many speakers, especially younger ones, do not recognize the bare-stem subjunctive form. As an illustration, consider the following passage of newspaper prose:[30]

(92) "...Elaine Franklin, Packwood's chief of staff, said she called Baucus' campaign manager after seeing the ad Friday "and said it would be our preference that Sen. Packwood **is** not in this race"..."

The second subjunctive form in English, the **past-form subjunctive**, is found in the modal range of strong preference and — at least implicitly — indirect manipulation. While the past verb-form is used here, the modal meaning is just as future projecting as other irrealis modes. Thus consider:

(93) a. I'd rather she **didn't come** at all.
      b. I'd appreciate it if he **didn't show up**.
      c. We'd prefer it if she **went** somewhere else.
      d. Would you mind if I **did** it tomorrow?

There is a subtle modal contrast between the bare-stem and past-form subjunctives. The choice seems to hinge on:

(a) the expected degree of **resistance** on the part of the
    implied manipulee;
(b) the speaker's **uncertainty** about the outcome, and
(c) perhaps the speaker's **anxiety** about the outcome.

Thus contrast:

(94) a. **Bare-stem ('present') subjunctive**:
         I'd rather she **go** somewhere else.
      b. **Past-form ('past') subjunctive**:
         I'd rather she **went** somewhere else.

In using the past-form subjunctive (94b), there is somehow a stronger inference that the subject of 'go' may resist, that her compliance is more in
doubt, and that the speaker is more anxious — perhaps more adamant —
about the desired outcome.

The past-form subjunctive is also used in the more epistemic range of
irrealis, in the context of **lower certainty**. As an illustration, consider:[31]

(95) a. I'd be really surprised if she **showed** up now.
      b. If she **left** tomorrow, it would be a relief.
      c. If you **did** that, her brother would kill you.

In these epistemic contexts, one can again contrast the past-form subjunctive form with the present-form conditional, as in:

(96) a. **Present conditional**:
         I'd be surprised if she **shows** up.
      b. **Past-form subjunctive**:
         I'd be surprised if she **showed** up.
      c. **Present-form conditional**:
         If she **leaves** tomorrow, it **will** be a relief.
      d. **Past-form subjunctive**:
         If she **left** tomorrow, it **would** be a relief.

In using the past-form subjunctive in (96b,d), the speaker conveys a strong
sense that the projected future event is less certain, as compared with the
present-conditional (96a,c).

12.6.3. The subjunctive range and modal auxiliaries

In more informal spoken English, the subjunctive forms noted above,
especially the present-form subjunctive, are less likely to appear. In that
register, the modal range of irrealis between weak manipulation and lower

epistemic certainty is more likely to be coded by modals. Consider, for example, the systematic use of the modals 'should' and 'must' in covering three irrealis sub-domains:

(97) **Epistemic uncertainty**:
   a. This **must** be his house.
      (> I am convinced this is his house)
   b. He **must** have done it then.
      (> I am convinced he did it)
   c. She **should** be here in five minutes.
      (> I am sure she will be here in five minutes)

(98) **Description of weak manipulation**:
   a. She told him that he **must** leave.
   b. He told her she **should** go.

(99) **Weak manipulation**:
   a. You **must** leave immediately!
   b. You **shouldn't** stand there!

The very same three sub-domains of irrealis that are covered by English modals above are coded by the subjunctive mood in languages that have this explicit verb-form.[32] The irrealis range covered by the English modals is considerably wider than the traditional range of the subjunctive mood. Nonetheless, the overlap between the semantic range of English modals and the subjunctive mood is indeed striking.

12.7. CERTAINTY, POWER AND DEFERENCE

12.7.1. Preamble

In the preceding section we divided the irrealis modality into two distinct sub-ranges: the manipulative or **preference** ('valuative', 'deontic') modes, and the **epistemic** ('certainty') modes. While this division is analytically sound,[33] it is not absolute. We have seen, for example, that several grammatical forms in English — subjunctive verb-forms and modal auxiliaries — span the irrealis range across the divide between valuative and epistemic sub-modes. Such overlapping of grammatical forms across neighboring meaning domains is a common phenomenon, most likely motivated by the diachronic process of **extension by similarity**.[34]

The systematic shading from epistemic to valuative ('deontic') modality — and thus from the declarative to the manipulative speech-act — is most likely motivated by the following set of one-way pragmatic inferences:[35]

(100) a. truth > knowledge
     b. knowledge > certainty
     c. certainty > status
     d. status > power

None of the inferences in (100) are logically necessary. Rather, they seem to represent conventional norms associated with the communicative contract. The communicative contract is itself embedded within a wider context, a well-regulated and highly culture-specific matrix of social **interaction**. In this section we will briefly survey some of the clauses of the communicative contract that govern the interaction between the epistemic and non-epistemic aspects of speech-acts.

12.7.2. Epistemic deference

The communicative contract seems to involve both epistemic dimensions (knowledge, certainty) and socio-personal dimensions (authority, status, power, obligation, entitlement). It has been noted (Syder and Pawley, 1974) that in facing an interlocutor of higher status, speakers tend to scale down their expressed certainty, by using hedges that place assertions in a lower — irrealis — epistemic range. This is not done, necessarily, because of a contrary attitude on the part of the higher-status interlocutor. Rather, toning down is a hedge against the possibility that the higher authority might hold a contrary belief. Such **epistemic deference** to higher powers is a pervasive feature of many, perhaps all, cultures. As an example of such status-induced epistemic deference, compare (101) and (102) below:

(101) **Reporting to a lower-status interlocutor**:
     a. The contract is in the bag.
     b. The report is ready.
     c. This is the wrong solution.

(102) **Reporting to a higher-status interlocutor**:
     a. **It seems that** the contract **might** be in the bag.
     b. The report **must be** ready, **I think**.
     c. This is **perhaps not** the **only possible** solution.

12.7.3. Negation, authority and politeness

Negative assertions are contrary, denying speech-acts. One would thus expect their use to be extremely sensitive to the perceived social status of the interlocutor. In contexts where one's interlocutor is of higher status, authority or power, speakers — probably universally and regardless of culture — tend to tone down their disagreement; they couch their contrary opinions in a variety of softening devices, many of which are sub-varieties of irrealis. Some common gambits for toning down a negative assertion in the face of a higher-status interlocutor are:

(103) a. Quite, quite.
     b. Yes, I see.
     c. I see what you mean.
     d. That's interesting.
     e. I suppose you got a point there.
     f. Perhaps not quite so.
     g. Perhaps you may wish to consider an alternative.
     h. Well, I'm not sure about that, maybe...
     i. Now if it was up to me, I would suggest...

In more traditional cultures, including our own rural small-town societies, it is not always easy to find overtly-marked negation in speech directed toward perceived superior, outsiders, or even *bona fide* members of the social network. Contrariness has its obvious social costs in a stable, closely-knit society of intimates. Outside the immediate family circle, the social norms of small-town society seem to counsel against overt confrontation, even when the issue seems to be merely epistemic.

Somewhat paradoxically, negation can itself be used as a softening device in the face of perceived higher authority. This toning down function of negation seems to apply to both epistemic and manipulative speech-acts. Thus consider:

(104) a. **Won't** you come in please?
        (> Do come in)
     b. I suppose he **isn't** done yet.
        (> I wonder if he's done)
     c. I **don't** suppose he's done yet?
        (> I wonder if he's done)
     d. **Wouldn't** it be better if...
        (> It'd be better if...)
     e. I suppose you **couldn't** spare a fiver...
        (> I wish you could)

This use of negation — often in conjunction with other irrealis operators such as modals, subjunctives, conditionals and yes-no questions — is widespread. Its deference value may derive from the overlap between negation and irrealis, along the psychological dimension of **low subjective certainty**.

12.7.4. Certainty, responsibility and blame

In most cultures, claiming direct personal responsibility for transacted information may be a serious social error, to be avoided in any but the most intimate, well protected, social contexts. Strong claims to direct authorship of transmitted information, with the attendant marking of high **subjective certainty** and strong **evidential support**, are often shunned. In carrying out communication under these cultural constraints, a variety of well-regulated conventional strategies are used, including indirection, disclaimer, oblique attribution, impersonalization, masking assertions as questions, negation and — universally — various forms of irrealis. The guiding principles behind these usages are probably:

(105) **The hazardous information principles**:
   a. Knowledge is power, but power is responsibility.
   b. Information may be coveted, it may also be hazard-
      ous and socially destabilizing.
   c. Transmitting new information may yield a clear
      social advantage, but it also incurs some risks.
   c. Therefore, being identified explicitly as the author
      — or even conduit — of information may be
      unwise, and must be avoided.

The application of principles (105) is again more conspicuous in small, rural, scattered communities, where residents of isolated homesteads are adept at coaxing fresh gossip, preferably malicious, out of the occasional visitor. In spite of their geographic scatter, such communities are intimate social units, where one's business is everybody's business, and where the most mundane news disseminates with lightning speed. The transmission of fresh gossip may indeed be the real purpose of a visit. Yet the transmitter must tread lightly, lest he be later identified as the author of the information.

NOTES

1) We noted earlier (chapter 1) that in the theme-and-variations format of grammatical description, the main, declarative, affirmative, active clause-type is used as 'theme'. Relative to that theme, subordinate, non-declarative, negative, passive clauses are 'variations'.

2) This exception is obvious: Grammatical devices used to code non-declarative speech-act values are, by definition, absent from the declarative clause.

3) The written text, narrative interlaced with dialogue, was pp. 68-71 of L. McMurtry's **Leaving Cheyenne** (1963). 'Embedded dialogue' are the direct-quote portions, i.e. conversation attributed by the author to the novel's various characters.

4) Post-Socratic philosophy harkens back to Plato and Aristotle.

5) The later work of Ludwig Wittgenstein (1953) gave the initial impetus for this tradition; see also Searle (1970) or Grice (1968/1975).

6) Following the Ordinary Language Philosophy tradition, a proposition is said to be 'infelicitous', regardless of its truth value, if it is used inappropriately in its discourse context. Put another way, an infelicitous proposition is incompatible with the presuppositions associated with other propositions within the same coherent discourse.

7) The 'submerged' presuppositions of the declarative speech-act go much further, involving various norms and conventions that govern the propriety of the declarative transaction. Some of those are discussed under the heading of conversational postulates and sincerity conditions in Grice (1968/1975). Other components of the declarative transaction have to do with the conditions under which speakers are expected to back up their assertions with supporting evidence, or are prepared to entertain and deflect a challenge from the hearer. These are discussed, under the general heading of evidentiality, in Chafe and Nichols (eds, 1986).

8) The distinction between 'epistemic' and 'deontic' aspects of communication arose initially from the study of propositional modality (see chapter 4; see also Palmer, 1979, 1986; Coates, 1983; Bybee *et al*, in press).

9) A more flexible definition was suggested by Sadock and Zwicky (1985): "...the yes-no (nexus) question, one that seeks comments on the degree of truth of the questioned proposition..." (1985, p. 179).

10) Perhaps most commonly; the frequencies in natural communication are yet to be determined.

11) The focus element in a yes-no question can also be marked by word-order and morphology; see further.

12) The cleft-focus pattern was discussed in chapter 10.

13) As noted in chapter 10, cleft-focusing on the verb is a less-likely pattern in declarative clauses.

14) Under the strict logical definition of presupposition, the information under its scope is presupposed to be 'true'. But as we have seen repeatedly, the notion of 'presupposition' that is more relevant in language is not truth, but rather the hearer's presumed belief, familiarity, or even mere quiescence.

15) Within the logical tradition, such 'failure of presupposition' is supposed to make the proposition — or in this case the WH-question — meaningless. This is so presumably because if the presupposition does not hold, an asserted proposition has no truth value. While this approach (cf. Strawson, 1950), was historically important, it is not particularly well suited for characterizing the communicative use of language. The proposition 'Someone kissed John' is perfectly well-formed and has a truth value from the speaker's perspective, and there is no reason to assume that the hearer considers it aberrant. The hearer is simply contending that it is not part of the agreed upon background for the communicative transaction in (34). What is violated is not a rule of logic, but rather a clause in the communicative contract.

16) From a report in the **Oregon Daily Emerald**, a student-run campus newspaper, 8-19-91 (p. 7). There is a raging confusion in current American English about this very issue. In the declarative clause, the colloquial usage seems to be gravitating toward the *object* form of pronouns placed in the nominal-predicate slot, as in 'It's me', 'It's him', 'It's us'. Usages such as 'It is I' or 'This is she' are decidedly non-colloquial.

17) While the general WH-pronoun pattern, as in (41), may allow the question to elicit a REF-indefinite response, there seems to be no specific WH-question pattern in English that focuses only on such a response. This restriction may be grounded in general pragmatic considerations, but those remain to be elucidated.

18) The semantic motivation for the restrictions on WH-like complements is discussed in chapter 7, section 7.5.3.

19) New syntactic hybrids are created by analogy with two (or more) existing structures, in this case verb complements, WH-questions and headless REL-clauses. English is rather promiscuous in giving rise to many such constructions (see e.g. our discussion of raising in chapter 11), but the general phenomenon is widespread.

20) This formulation of the convention goes back to (at least) Austin (1962) and Grice (1968/1975).

21) John Haiman (in personal communication) notes cases such as "Nobody move!" or "Everybody get up!" where a subject — albeit a non-referring one — is present in an imperative clause. While possible, these are less typical and less common imperatives.

22) We noted at several points above (chapters 6, 7) that finiteness is not a binary distinction between finite vs. infinitive, but rather a matter of degree.

23) See chapter 7.

24) For some of the traditional discussion of indirect speech-acts, see Sadock (1970), Green (1975), Searle (1975), Davison (1975) or Gordon and Lakoff (1971).

25) The traditional discussion of indirect speech-acts (see note 24 above) tended to leave the impression that the couching of one speech-act in the guise of another was somewhat capricious. An exception to this may be seen in Brown and Levinson (1978).

26) Or metaphoric extension.

27) See chapter 4, section 4.4.

28) For a comprehensive cross-linguistic survey, see Bybee *et al* (in press, ch. 7).

29) See Bybee (1992) for the historical development of the past modals in English.

30) From the **Eugene Register-Guard, Eugene, OR, 11-4-90.**

31) Examples (95b,c) are of conditional ADV-clauses, discussed more extensively in chapter 13.

32) E.g. Spanish.

33) For some linguists, the soundness of this division is so profound that it overrides the semantic unity of irrealis (Bybee *et al*, in press).

34) See discussion in Heine (1992); Palmer (1979, 1986); Coates (1983).

35) Unlike logically-necessary deductive inference, pragmatic inference depends on likelihoods, norms and probabilistic judgement.

13 | INTER-CLAUSAL CONNECTIONS AND DISCOURSE COHERENCE

13.1. INTRODUCTION

13.1.1. Subordination and coordination

The subordinate clauses we have discussed thus far have been **embedded clauses**. That is, they were clauses placed in well-defined syntactic positions within other ('host') clauses, falling under the same intonation contour as their host clause. Thus, clausal subjects and objects occupy a **grammatical role** within a host clause (chapters 3,6). Relative clauses and noun complements occupy a **modifier** position in a noun phrase inside a host clause (chapters 6,9). And verb complements occupy an **object-like** position in the verb phrase inside a host clause (chapter 7).[1] An embedded clause is tightly bound to its host main clause. It tends to fall under the same **intonation contour** with it. It also tends to abide by more stringent syntactic constraints, such as those that apply to subjects, objects and noun modifiers.

Many of the constraints between embedded clauses and their host clauses are semantic in nature. Thus, for example, sentential subjects and objects are compatible only with a small group of semantically-specific verbs. Verbal complements exhibit strong semantic bonds with their main verbs. Noun complements are associated, predominantly, with complement-taking verbs, via nominalization. And relative clauses involve intricate remedial strategies for recovering the semantic role of their unexpressed ('deleted') argument.

The inter-clausal connections discussed in this chapter are much looser. Traditionally, they have been grouped into two main types:

(a) adverbial-subordinate clauses

(b) conjoined ('coordinated') clauses

Both clause-types tend to fall under their own independent intonation contour. But adverbial-subordinate clauses have been considered traditionally dependent — syntactically and semantically — on their adjacent main clause. Conjoined clauses, on the other hand, have been considered more independent of their immediate clausal environment. This distinction is not absolute but is a matter of degree. No clause is totally independent of its immediate clausal context in connected **coherent discourse**. Consequently, if a conjoined clause is part of a coherent discourse, some strands — semantic or pragmatic — must connect it to its immediate clausal environment. And such strands of connectivity ('coherence') tend to come with concomitant **grammatical dependencies**. The close parallel between semantic-pragmatic ('functional') and grammatical ('formal') **inter-clausal dependencies** reflects the same iconic tendencies we noted in the grammar of verbal complements:

(1)   **Iconicity of event-integration and clause-integration**:
        "The more semantically or pragmatically connected two
        events/states are in the discourse, the more grammati-
        cally integrated will the two clauses be".

13.1.2   Thematic coherence and grounding

The functional relation between a clause and its immediate clausal environment in coherent discourse has been traditionally described along semantic or logical dimensions. On the semantic end, one finds traditional rhetorical notions such as temporality, conditionality, causality, concession, purpose, reason and so on. On the logical end, one finds notions such as conjunction, disjunction and conditionality, as well as paraphrase, tautology and contradiction. The utility of these traditional categories goes only a certain distance, most commonly when the discourse is confined to two successive propositions. When one considers longer strings of coherent discourse, a more complex notion of discourse connectivity emerges, that of **thematic coherence**.

Thematic coherence is a more global meta-phenomenon, made out of many sub-components or **coherence strands**. The most easily observable coherence strands, and the ones most likely to be coded by grammar, are:

(2)   **Strands of thematic coherence**:
        a. Referential continuity
        b. Temporal continuity
        c. Spatial continuity
        d. Action continuity

These strands are clearly the most concrete, salient, observable links between clauses in coherent discourse. But the phenomenon of discourse coherence is richer yet. First, coherence strands may connect — or **ground** — the clause either to the current text, to the current speech situation, or to generic-lexical knowledge.[2] Second, coherence strands may extend either locally, between adjacent clauses, or globally, across larger text-structures. Third coherence strands may be either semantic or pragmatic in nature. Finally, the strands may ground the clause in either an anaphoric or a cataphoric direction.[3] The formal coding apparatus — syntax, grammar — is involved in all of these facets of thematic coherence.

13.2. LOCAL COHERENCE LINKS OF ADVERBIAL CLAUSES

13.2.1. Preamble

Thus far, we have defined the contrast between the semantic and pragmatic components of communicative function by two criteria:

(a) **Scope**: Semantic aspects of meaning are more localized, and do not depend on a wider context. Thus, the proper domain of lexical semantics are individual words, and that of propositional semantics the individual clause.

(b) **Lexical dependence**: Semantic aspects of meaning are more heavily dependent on the semantics of lexical words. Thus, semantic transitivity and the case-frames of clauses are defined by the semantic properties of both the nouns and the verbs inside them (chapter 3). And the bond between main verbs and their verbal complements is heavily dependent on the semantic properties of main verbs (chapter 7).

By these criteria, the coherence strands of both adverbial clauses and conjoined clauses to their immediate clausal environment are primarily pragmatic. The relevant local connection of an adverbial clause (hence-forth ADV-clause) is then defined as its meaning relation with its main clause, to which it is "subordinate".[4] All ADV-clauses are then divided into various types according to their specific meaning relations.

13.2.2. Temporal ADV-clauses

The temporal connection between an adverbial clause and its adjacent main clause can be divided into several sub-types, many of which are marked by explicit **adverbial subordinators**. Some of the more common explicitly marked temporal adverbials are:

(3) **Temporal links of adverbial clauses**:
   a. **Precedence**:
      Before she came, he left.
   b. **Subsequence**:
      After she came, he left.
   c. **Simultaneity**:
      While she was working, he left.
   d. **Point coincidence**:
      As she was coming, he saw her.
   e. **Terminal boundary**:
      Till she left, he worked steadily.
   f. **Initial boundary**:
      (Ever) since she came, he's been ignoring her.
   g. **Intermediacy**:
      Between her starting the project and
      her quitting in a huff, nobody slept.

While semantically specific subordinators as in (3) are readily available in English, quite often a generic time-ADV subordinator such as 'when' is used even when more specific temporal relations are in fact intended. Such a less-marked coding strategy is adequate when the semantic specificity of the temporal relation can be inferred from other information present in the two clauses. Such information is most commonly available either from the tense-aspect-modality of the two clauses, or from the lexical-semantic specificity of the two verbs. As illustrations of inferences guided by tense-aspect-modal information, consider:

(4) a. **Precedence**:
      When she **came**, he **had** already left.
         (inferred from the perfect aspect of the main
         clause)
   b. **Subsequence**:
      When he **got** up, she **did** too.
         (inferred from the past/perfective aspect in
         both clauses)

c. **Simultaneity**:

> When she **lived** there, everybody **was** real friendly.
>> (inferred from the stative verb of the ADV-clause and the stative aspect of the main clause)

d. **Point coincidence**:

> When he was just **beginning** to open the door, she **shot** him.
>> (inferred from the inceptive 'begin' in the ADV-clause and the past/perfective aspect in the main clause)

e. **Terminal boundary**:

> When you're **done**, let me know.
>> (inferred from the perfect aspect of the ADV-clause)

f. **Initial boundary**:

> When you **start**, just **keep** going.
>> (inferred from the inceptive 'start' in the ADV-clause and durative aspect of the main clause)

g. **Intermediacy**:

> When he's **done** and she's **not yet** started, that's when you should enter.
>> (inferred from the perfect and NEG-perfect aspects of the conjoined ADV-clause)

The lexical meaning of the verbs in the two adjacent clauses can also guide inferences about local temporal (and other) links between them. Such inferences depend on culture-shared knowledge about **conventional action sequences** and their likely temporal relations.[5] This may already be part of the strategy in (4), but it could also be the entire strategy in discourse contexts where tense-aspect-modality is not specific enough. For example:

(5)   a. **Precedence**:

> When I got tired, I slept.
> When she got hungry, she ate.
> When she knocked, he let her in.

   b. **Simultaneity**:
      When she slept, she dreamed of home.
   c. **Point coincidence**:
      When she fell, he caught her.
   d. **Terminal boundary**:
      When they ate, they went to sleep.

Such a lexically-guided strategy of temporal inference is of course most prominent in clausal coordination, where the grammar supplies fewer temporal clues than in subordination.

When temporal inference relies more heavily on lexical-cultural knowledge rather than on grammatical clues, stronger restrictions on sequencing tend to occur, as in:

(6) a. **When** she got tired, she slept.
    b. ?**When** she slept, she got tired.
    c. She slept **when** she got tired.
    d. ?She got tired **when** she slept.

In contrast, when the temporal relation is marked more explicitly by grammar, one can code event sequences that are less culturally stereotyped, less conventional. Thus compare:

(7) a. **After** she got tired, she slept.
    b. **After** she slept, she got tired (again).
    c. She slept **after** she got tired.
    d. She got tired (again) **after** she slept.

13.2.3. Conditional clauses

Conditional ADV-clauses are divided into three main types:
(a) simple irrealis conditionals
(b) subjunctive irrealis conditionals
(c) counter-fact conditionals.
We will discuss them in order.

13.2.3.1. Simple irrealis conditionals

Irrealis conditional clauses fall under the scope of the irrealis modality. Like other irrealis clauses, they are said to have **no truth value**. Being in this case dependent ADV-clauses, their truth value depends on the truth value of their associated main clause. Those main clauses are most commonly also in the irrealis mode, and thus have no truth value either.

Irrealis conditional clauses have an **implied futurity**, with the main clause itself marked by either future, or modal or some other irrealis operator:

(8)   a. **Modal**:
          If you finish on time, you **can** have this.
      b. **Future**:
          If she comes, they'**ll** see her.
      c. **Imperative**:
          If you see him, **please** tell him I'm alright.
      d. **Yes-no question**:
          If this is true, then aren't we being a bit hasty?
      e. **Indirect request**:
          If she comes, I **would like** to know.
      f. **Verb-coded low certainty**:
          If she agrees to do it, then **I think** we're in good shape.

The unresolved truth value of IRR-conditional clauses also persists when they are cast in the *habitual* mode, again with a sense of prediction (or some other irrealis sub-mode) associated with the main clause. As examples of this, consider:

(9)   a. If he **works** that hard, he (**surely**) has no time for this.
      b. If she **lives** here, she (**must**) be in serious trouble.
      c. If this **goes** on here regularly, then we **better** quit right now.
      d. If you **work** here, **how come** I never see you?
      e. If they **earn** that much, they **should** pay more taxes.

The unresolved truth value of the irrealis conditional clause can also pertain to past events, as in:

(10) a. If she **did** it, it (**surely**) will make a difference.
             (> I'm not sure, but if it turns out she did...)
      b. If they **arrived** late, they **must be** tired.
             (> I'm not sure, but if they were indeed late...)
      c. If she **was** here, then she surely knows that...
             (> I'm not yet sure, but if it turns out she was...)
      d. If she **was** there, she **must have** seen it.
             (> I'm not yet sure, but if she indeed was there...)

An irrealis conditional clause can be marked with the temporal subordinator 'when', as long as the modality of both clauses remains irrealis. The slight semantic difference between a temporal and a conditional interpretation of a 'when'-marked irrealis clause is inferred from the context. Thus compare:

(11) **When** you bring it to me, I'll pay you.
　　　a. **Conditional interpretation**:
　　　　...And if you don't bring it, I won't pay you.
　　　　So it's up to you to decide which it'll be.
　　　b. **Temporal interpretation**:
　　　　...So just go ahead and bring it to me,
　　　　so that I can pay you.

Under the conditional interpretation (11a), the speaker assigns lower certainty to the proposition. Under the temporal interpretation (11b), they assign it higher certainty. What the two interpretations share is the general logical structure of irrealis conditionals, one that stands at some variance from the deceptively similar logical connector. That is, both seem to be linked by a **bi-conditional** implication:[6]

(12) a. **Temporal**:
　　　　When you bring it, I'**ll** pay you
　　　　　(> but **until** you bring it, I **won't**)
　　　b. **Conditional**:
　　　　If you bring it, I'**ll** pay you
　　　　　(> but **if** you **don't** bring it, I **won't**)

Both the irrealis 'if' and 'when' seem to allow the inference:

(13) (A > B) > (not-A > not-B)

Finally, English also possesses special **negative-conditional** subordinators that in some sense combine the meaning of "if not". As an illustration, consider the rough meaning equivalence of (14a,b) below:

(14) a. **Unless** you pay up, we'**ll** have you arrested.
　　　b. **If** you **don't** pay up, we'**ll** have you arrested.

13.2.3.2. Subjunctive conditionals

"...Honey, I have uh...an unusual request...uh...y'see, I've been on this uh...island...for a long time uh...without uh...the companionship of a uh...female...so I been uh..uh...wonderin'...uh...if I **gave** you two coconuts..."

Ed Sanders as Robinson Crusoe
The Fugs' **It Crawled into my Hand Honest**
Reprise Records RS-6305 (ca. 1967)

An oft-ignored sub-type of conditional clause in English is the **subjunctive conditional**. It corresponds, in form, meaning and use, to subjunctive-marked conditional clauses in other languages.[7] For example, in the following passage, an English translation of dialogue in Pedro Almodóvar's movie "Dark Habits", the Spanish original corresponding to the past-marked verb in the English sub-titles used the Spanish *past subjunctive*:

(15) (**Context**: Two nuns in the convent are debating whether to ask a guest, a singer, to sing at a party for the Mother Superior's Saint's Day. They strongly suspect the singer would refuse.)
"...Yolanda...we want to invite you to sing for the Mother Superior's Saint's Day... We usually do it ourselves, but she **would** be so happy if you **did** it..."[8]

The contrast between the subjunctive conditional and the simple irrealis conditional in English may be illustrated as follows:

(16) a. **Simple irrealis conditional**:
          If she **agrees** to come, we **will** go on and...
      b. **Subjunctive conditional**:
          If she **agreed** to come, we **would** give her the sky!

(17) a. **Simple irrealis conditional**:
          If you **do** that, you'**ll** be rewarded.
      b. **Subjunctive conditional**:
          If you **did** that, you **would** be insane!

(18) a. **Simple irrealis conditional**:
          If she **is** fired, she **can** get another job.
      b. **Subjunctive conditional**:
          If she **was** fired, she **could** sue the heck out of you!

(19) a. **Simple irrealis conditional**:
If he **does** that, they **may** go along.
b. **Subjunctive conditional**:
If he **did** that, they **might** do anything!

The lower certainty value of both the subjunctive conditional clause and its adjacent main clause is coded on both clauses. In the conditional clause, the verb is marked by the *past* form, contrasting with the *habitual* in the main clause following the simple irrealis conditional. In parallel, one finds the historical *past* form of the modal in the main clause associated with the subjunctive conditional, contrasting with the *simple* form in the main clause following the simple irrealis conditional.

The event or state coded in the subjunctive conditional clause is deemed by the speaker to be less likely but not altogether impossible. The subjunctive conditional clause is often used to render counter normative states or events, ones that often carry dire, undesirable consequences:

(20) a. **If** we **released** him, he **would surely** skip bail.
(> Since we don't want him to skip bail,
it'd be silly to release him)
b. **If** we **were** to release him, he **would** have to
stay put.
(> But since he's not likely to stay put,
we better not release him)
c. **Were** I to agree, you **would have** to pay through the nose.
(> But you're surely not likely to want to do that,
so what's the point of agreeing?)
d. **Should** she want to do that, she**'d better** shape up.
(> But I doubt it that she wants to, so her
shaping up is probably a moot point)

When the subordinator 'if' is not used, as in (20c,d), the modal auxiliary — 'were', 'should' — undergoes subject-AUX inversion.[9]

Finally, the past-marked subjunctive form can be also found in other irrealis ADV-clauses, as in the following bit of dialogue from a bestselling novel. The discussion, between a detective and a woman trapped by a sadistic killer, is whether and when the guy would kill her, surely a dire prospect:[10]

(21)   "...You know he'd do it to you, just like he'd do it
         to anybody else".
         "I don't think he'd ever bushwack me — it's rude,
         and he wouldn't get to ask any questions that way.
         Sure he'**d** do it as soon as I **bored** him..."

13.2.3.3. Counter-fact conditionals

Unlike irrealis conditionals, whose truth value is unresolved, the truth value of **counter-fact conditionals** (or 'hypothetical conditionals') is firm — but negative. The adjacent main clause codes a proposition that could, would or might have been true — if only another proposition, the one coded in the counter-fact clause, were true. But since that conditional-clause proposition is in fact false, the main-clause proposition is also false.

Counter-fact conditionals can be marked with the combination of the subordinator 'if' and either the **perfect-past** or just the **past** tense-aspect. The corresponding main clause is then marked with a **modal-perfect**. For example:

(22)   a. **If** she **had** known, she **would have** done it.
           (> but since she didn't know, she didn't do it)
       b. **If** I only **knew**, I **would have** left early.
           (> but since I didn't know, I didn't leave early)
       c. **If** you **had** only told me, I **could have** come.
           (> but you didn't tell me, so I didn't come)
       d. **If** I only **knew**, I **might have** agreed.
           (> but I didn't know, so I didn't agree)

The counter-fact clause may also be if-less; but then **perfect** marking, including the auxiliary 'have', must be retained (not just the past); and sub-ject-AUX inversion must be applied, as in:

(23)   a. **Had** I known, I would have done it.
       b. *****Knew** I, I would have done it.
       c. *****I **had** known, I would have done it.

The counter-fact mode in main clauses need not be associated with a counterfact conditional clause. It is also found in main clauses in other dis-course contexts. For example:

(24) a. You **should have** told me he was here
          (> but you didn't)
      b. I **would have** loved to see him
          (> but I didn't)
      c. It **might have** worked
          (> but it didn't)
      d. He **could have** done it
          (> but he didn't)

There may be a weak hypothetical-conditional inference attached to many of these seemingly-independent clauses, such as "if things had turned out to be different, then...". And a near counter-act flavor is associated with *perfect modals* in WH-questions, as in:

(25) a. Who **would have** imagined that it **could** happen to her?
      b. How **could have** anybody contemplated that?
      c. Why **would have** anyone wanted to do that?
      d. Who **could've** she possibly given it to?

Both 'might have' and 'could have' can also signal a simple irrealis reading, i.e. with the truth-value of a possible past event yet unresolved. In this sense, they share some of the meaning of 'may have', as in:

(26) Yeah, you're right, he $\left\{ \begin{array}{l} \textbf{could have} \\ \textbf{might have} \\ \textbf{may have} \end{array} \right\}$ done it.

      So let's find out.

Finally, the counter-fact modality may also be found in verb-complement clauses, as in:

(27) a. She knew that it **could have** been her
          (> but it wasn't)
      b. I wish you **were** here
          (> but you aren't)
      c. I told her she **should have** come
          (> but she didn't)

The conditional adverbial clause is thus only one environment where the counter-fact modality appears.

13.2.3.4. Concessive conditionals

Concessive conditional clauses involve the optional addition of 'even' to the subordinator 'if'. Alternatively, when 'even' is not added to the ADV-clause, the adverb 'still' is used in the main clause. Concessive conditional clauses are used when the information in the main clause should, under normal expectations follow from the conditional clause. But in fact it doesn't follow. Rather, the information is **contrary to expectations**. For example:

(28) a. **Even if** she left him, he'd (**still**) go on living there.
> (> One would expect him to vacate if she left him,
>   but in fact he'll stay on)

   b. **If** he gives it to me for free, I **still** don't want it
> (> You expect me to take it when given for free,
>   but I still won't)

13.2.4. Concessive clauses

Concessive ADV-clauses involve a presupposed **contrast** or **counter-expectancy**, with the ADV-clause supplying the grounds for the expectation, and the main clause supplying the unexpected or less-likely event or state. A wide range of subordinators may mark concessive ADV-clauses. Some of the more common ones are:

(29) a. **Although** he liked her, he stayed away.
>   (Normally, if you like a person you stay close)

   b. **In spite of** liking him, she spoke harshly.
>   (Normally, if you like a person you speak kindly)

   c. **In spite of the fact that** she liked him, she sent him away.
>   (Normally, if you like a person you keep them near)

   d. **Even though** she disapproved, she went along.
>   (Normally, if you disapprove, you decline to
>   participate)

   e. **Though** I had met him, I didn't really know him.
>   (Normally, meeting a person is a step toward
>   knowing them)

   f. **No matter** how hard he worked, he wasn't promoted.
>   (Normally, a hard-working person gets promoted)

   g. **Except for** her meddling in his affairs, he loved her.
>   (Normally you don't love someone who meddles in
>   your affairs)

The ADV-clauses in (29b) and (29g) display a reduced **participial** clausal structure (see further below).

13.2.5. Substitutive clauses

Closely linked semantically to concessive clauses are substitutive ADV-clauses. Here the ADV-clause codes an event or state that is expected to be the case, but in fact is not. Rather, something else is the case, and that something else is then spelled out in the main clause. The expectation coded in the ADV-clause may arise from diverse sources, including rather subtle pragmatic presuppositions. And the substitutive ADV-clause is often **participial** or **less-finite**, with its subject left unexpressed. This is possible when the subject of the ADV-clause is co-referential with that of the main clause.[11] For example:

(30) a. **Rather than** do the dishes, he watched TV.
      b. **Instead of** doing her homework, she loafed.

The main difference between substitutive and concessive ADV-clauses has to do with **logical incompatibility**. In the case of concession, the main-clause proposition is not logically incompatible with the ADV-clause proposition, but only surprising, given the normative expectation associated with the latter. In the case of substitution, the main and adverbial clauses are logically incompatible. Thus compare:

(31) a. **Concession**:
         In spite of being tall, Joe was quite agile.
            (> Though tall people are expected to be clumsy,
                Joe was both tall and agile)
      b. **Instead of** being tall, John was short.
            (> Though expected to be tall, Joe was in fact short)

13.2.6. Additive clauses

An additive ADV-clause is used when the main clause adds information that amplifies on the information in the ADV-clause. There is an associated inference here, to the effect that normally the first piece of information should be enough. The ADV-clause is again typically participial, or non-finite as in:

(32) a. **In addition to** having your hand stamped,
         you must (**also**) show your ticket stub.
            (> Normally one would expect that stamping
                the hand would be enough)

b. **Besides** missing my bus, I (**also**) got my feet all wet.
(> Missing one's bus is bad enough)

c. **On top of** being born rich, she (**also**) inherited
a fortune from her aunt.
(> Being rich is good enough)

An additive ADV-clause may also have an overtly-expressed subject that need not be co-referential with the subject of the main clause, as in:

(33)   **Not only** did I miss the bus, but the driver who finally
picked me up turned out to be a jerk.

13.2.7. Cause and reason clauses

The subordinator 'because' is used in English to mark ADV-clauses that are said to be either the **cause** or the **reason** for the main clause. Semantically, one can argue that the two notions are distinct, but have a predictable one-way conditional association:

(33)   cause > reason
(but not necessarily vice versa)
or:
"A cause is necessarily a reason, but some reasons
may be due to things other than a cause".

The difference between 'cause' and 'reason' involves the speaker's perspective. Typically, a cause tends to involve an **external relation** between an event and a resulting event or state. The speaker's perspective is that they are merely reporting that causal relation. A reason, on the other hand, may also involve the speaker's **evaluative perspective** concerning their — or someone else's — grounds for belief or motivation for expressing the belief. That is:

(34)   a. **Cause**:   Some external state or event either
(i) causes an **agent** to **act**, or
(ii) causes a **state** to **be**.

b. **Reason**: The speaker — or another observer — considers
some state/event as the **reason** for either
(i) some other state/event taking place; or
(ii) for **saying** or **thinking** some proposition
about that state/event.

To illustrate this general division, as well as some of its subtleties, consider first some obvious contrasts:

(35) a. **Eventive external cause**:
          Because he bumped me, I dropped the glass.
      b. **Stative external cause**:
          Because it was freezing, the water-pipes broke.
      c. **Eventive external reason**:
          Because she showed up there, I left.
      d. **Stative external reason**:
          Because it was cold, I put my coat on.
      e. **Eventive internal reason**:
          Because my leg began to hurt, I stopped running.
      f. **Stative internal reason**:
          Because the lecture was boring, I left.

When a 'cause' perspective is adopted, as in (35a,b), the connection between cause and effect is considered necessary. Even if the effect involved a human subject, that subject has no choice and no control. When a 'reason' perspective is adopted, the affected subject is considered being in control, they have a choice, they decide to act — for the stated reason.

Since 'cause' and 'reason' is often a matter of point of view, the very same event may be invoked as either cause or reason for another event or state. Thus, for example, (35a) is normally interpreted from a 'cause' perspective. But if the speaker got disgusted and deliberately dropped the glass, then (35a) would become a 'reason'.

The invocation of 'reason' is often subtle or even opaque. Consider, for example, the multiplicity of 'because' answers that may be given to a 'why?' question:

(36) A: -"This is a bad idea".
      B: -"Why?"
      A: a. -"Because you made a mistake in your assessment".
         b. -"Because it's not this kind of a problem".
         c. -"Because I plainly don't see how it could work".
         d. -"Because suppose you were right, where can we go
             next?"
         e. -"Because the boss won't like it".

     f. -"Because I can detect a fallacy right here".

     g. -"Because I don't like it".

     h. -"Because I say so".

     i. -"Because Joe told me all about it".

The inferential complexity of all these reasons is totally unconstrained. Anything that strikes the speaker as relevant may be cited as reason.

13.2.8. Purpose clauses

Purpose ADV-clauses most typically have a subject that is co-referential with the subject of the main clause. This is only to be expected, since they typically signal the agent's purpose for performing the action coded in the main clause. The main clause is thus typically eventive, active, agentive. And the purpose ADV-clause is typically non-finite, with its verb marked by either 'to' or 'in order to'. For example:

(37) a. He went out **to** look for his boy.

       b. **To** go there, you must take the train.

       c. **In order to** finish on time, she had to cut corners.

The semantic restriction on the main clause does not hinge so much on being active *per se*, but rather on the subject-agent having choice or control. Thus, the main clause associated with a purpose ADV-clause may be stative, as long as control by the subject is plausible:

(38) a. **To** do this, you must **be brave**.

          (> You can **act** brave even if you are a coward)

       b. **To** play basketball, one had better **be tall**.

          (> You must **decide** whether you're tall enough
            to play basketball)

Like other ADV-clauses in English, purpose clauses may either precede or follow their main clause. There is a considerable functional difference, both semantic and pragmatic, between a pre-posed and a post-posed purpose clause. We will discuss this difference in section 13.4. below.

13.3. PARTICIPIAL ADVERBIAL CLAUSES

13.3.1. Local coherence and non-finiteness

Participial ADV-clauses can be viewed as being more closely integrated with their adjacent main clauses. Functionally, this closer integration involves two major components of thematic coherence:

(39) **Components of discourse coherence relevant to participial ADV-clauses**:

    a. **Referential coherence**:
        Participial ADV-clauses have the **same subject** as their main clause.

    b. **Temporal coherence**:
        Participial ADV-clauses tend to exhibit a rigid **temporal aspectual relation** vis-a-vis their main clause, most commonly either:
        (i) **Simultaneity** (progressive participial)
      (ii) **Anteriority** (perfect participial)

Structurally, participial ADV-clauses display clear features of **low finiteness**, chiefly in terms of two major clusters in the grammar of finiteness:[12]

(40) **Grammatical features of finiteness relevant to participial ADV-clauses**:

    a. **nominal inflections**
        (i) unexpressed (zero-marked) subject
       (ii) genitive case-marking of the subject (if present)

    b. **verbal inflections**
      (iii) reduced tense-aspect-modality
      (iv) no subject agreement

The grammatical features of nominal inflections (40a) pertain to coding the **referential coherence** (39a) of the participial clause. The grammatical features of verbal inflections (40b) pertain to the coding of the **temporal coherence** (39b) of the participial clause.

13.3.2. Progressive participial clauses

The verb in the **progressive participial clause** is marked with the suffix *-ing*. As noted earlier, this suffix is ambiguous, serving to mark either one type of *infinitive* or the *progressive aspect*. The progressive meaning of this suffix accounts for the simultaneous temporal coherence of at least some participial ADV-clauses. This temporal-simultaneous interpretation is found most typically in post-posed participial ADV-clauses, as in:

(41) a. He stayed home all day **working** on his taxes.
      b. She swam across the pool **thinking** of her mother.

The simultaneous-temporal interpretation of the participial clause is only possible if both events are non-punctual, i.e. have temporal duration. When one of the two clauses is punctual, a simultaneous interpretation is sometimes odd. Thus compare:

(42) a. ?He stayed home all day **deciding** not to worry.
      b. ?He **closed the door** working on his taxes.
      c. ?She swam across the pool **remembering** she hadn't had lunch.

But sometimes a simultaneous temporal interpretation is possible in spite of the main-clause being punctual, as in (cf. 41b):

(43) She **plunged into** the pool thinking of her mother

There is a tendency, probably not absolute, to interpret a pre-posed participial ADV-clause as *anterior* — thus *temporally sequential* — rather than progressive-simultaneous. This is clearly seen when the order of the odd (42a,c), in which the punctual ADV-clause cannot receive a simultaneous interpretation, is reversed:

(44) a. **Deciding** not to worry, he stayed home all day.
      b. **Remembering** she hadn't had lunch, she swam across the pool in a hurry and got out.

In both (44a,b), the punctual event in the ADV-clause temporally precedes the more stretched event in the main clause.

The tendency to interpret a pre-posed participial clause as sequential-anterior is further demonstrated when one pre-poses a participial clause whose semantic interpretation can be either punctual or non-punctual, as in:

(45) a. **Finishing** his tax returns, he stayed home.
      b. He stayed home **finishing** his tax returns.
      c. **Thinking** of her mother, she hurried home.
      d. She hurried home **thinking** of her mother.

In the pre-posed order (45a), 'finishing' is interpreted as punctual and anterior to 'stayed home'. In the post-posed order (45b), 'finishing' is interpreted as non-punctual and simultaneous with 'stayed home'. Likewise, in the pre-posed (45c) 'thinking' is interpreted as punctual and anterior to 'hurried home'. In the post-posed order (45d), 'thinking' is interpreted as non-punctual and simultaneous with 'hurried home'.

13.3.3. Perfect participial clauses

The **perfect participial clause** incorporates the *perfect-anterior* aspect, marked by the auxiliary 'have'. It shares with the progressive participial clause the main grammatical features of non-finiteness:
(a) unexpressed (zero) subject
(b) no subject agreement
(c) reduced tense-aspect-modality
(d) *-ing* marking on 'have'

In signalling local temporal coherence, the perfect-participial clause can only be interpreted as sequential-anterior relative to the main clause, regardless of syntactic order.[13] Thus compare:

(46) a. **Having worked** on his taxes all day, he went home.
  b. He went home, **having worked** on his taxes all day.
  c. **Having thought** of her mother, she kept swimming.
  d. She kept swimming, **having thought** of her mother.

13.3.4. Chained participial clauses

Either progressive or perfect participial clauses may appear in chains of more than one clause. Consider for example the following chain of three *-ing*-marked participial clauses followed by one — chain-final — finite clause:

(47) a. **Coming** out of the house,
  b. **stopping** to check the mail
  c. and **adjusting** his hat,
  d. **he turned** to look for the paper.

The chained clauses in (47) render events in temporal sequence. And the sequential interpretation is maintained even when the chained participial clause follows the finite main clause:

(48) a. He **came** out of the house,
  b. **stopping** to check the mail,
  c. **adjusting** his hat
  d. and **turning** to look for the paper.

But chained -*ing*-marked clauses need not always be temporally sequential. This is most clear when they are semantically stative, as in:

(49)   a. **Suffering** from the gout,
     b. **being** old and decrepit,
     c. and **not having** much to live for,
     d. **he woke up** one day and said: "The heck with it!"

The stative chained participial clauses (49a,b,c) code states that are roughly simultaneous. In some sense, however, they are nonetheless temporally anterior to the event in the finite chain-final clause (49d). This anteriority may be due to the fact that the depicted states (49a,b,c) at least started prior to the event in (49d). But the main clause itself could also be stative, in which case no anteriority is imparted:

(50)   a. **Suffering** from the gout,
     b. **being** old and decrepit,
     c. and **not having** much to live for,
     d. **he was** indeed a mess.

Long chains of participial clauses are relatively rare in contemporary English, where multiple clause-chaining of this type is not the main paragraph-level strategy.[14] In 19th century written prose this chaining strategy seemed more common. But even there long participial-clause chains preceding a finite main clause are not common. The following two examples, with two or three chained participial clauses, are more typical:[15]

(51)   "...**Proceeding** leisurely,
     first **taking** off one thing,
     then another,
     and **with the help** of scissors,
     I quickly **rid** her of every covering..."
                                  (Anon, 1828, p. 119)

(52)   "...**Feeling** assured I should not be troubled by the day
     for some time,
     and **finding** myself much overcome from what I had
     undergone,
     I **rang** for the light..."
                                    (Anon, 1828, p. 57)

Perfect participial clauses may also appear in chained sequences, as in:

(53) a. **Having first tended** toward the offer,
      b. and **having then vacillated** for two weeks,
      c. and **having written** a withdrawal letter,
      d. **he** finally **accepted**.

The events in (53) are chained in a temporal sequence. But the perfect-marked clauses in a chain may also signal the off-sequence value of the *pluperfect*, as in:

(54) a. **Having tended** toward the offer,
      b. having **earlier** vacillated for two weeks,
      c. and having **earlier yet** even written a withdrawal letter,
      d. **he** finally **accepted** the job.

Event (54b) is anterior to (54a), and (54c) is anterior to (54b), while all three chained perfect-marked events (54a,b,c) are anterior to the finite-clause event (54d).

13.3.5. Preposition-headed -*ing*-participial clauses

The -*ing*-marked participial ADV-clause may be further marked with a temporal preposition, thereby assuming an explicit temporal ADV-clause function. Examples illustrating this construction are:

(55) a. **In** assessing his chances, John took into account...
      b. **While** waiting in the hall, Mary kept thinking about...
      c. **On** finding out the results, John immediately...
      d. **Upon** receiving permission, Mary went over to...
      e. **After** arriving at the terminal, they stopped by...
      f. **Before** accepting the ride, she checked with...

The co-reference constraints on these ADV-clauses are the same as seen in other -*ing*-marked participial clauses above.

13.3.6. Participial ADV-clauses without co-reference constraints

One of the main non-finiteness features exhibited by participial ADV-clauses thus far was the missing subject, coupled with a strong constraint on **subject co-reference** between the main and adverbial clause. But in some participial ADV-clauses the subject is not missing, and strict subject co-reference is not required. The first example of such clauses involves subjects that are possessed — sometimes as part or kin — by the subject of the main clause:

(56) a. **His** heart pounding, **Joe** opened the box.
     b. **His** wife sick and **his** children gone, **Bill** ran away.
     c. **Her** mother following behind, **Sarah** barged in.
     d. **Her** career in shambles, **Wendy** went home to Cleveland.
     e. **The book** arrived, **its** cover promising adventure.
     f. **His** wife having left, **Joe** moved in with Myrna.
     g. **His** quest having been concluded, **the knight** rested.

The possessive relation between the subject of the participial ADV-clause and the subject of the main clause need not be grammatically marked, but may also be implicit. It may in fact be even more vague, to the point where one may wish to characterize it not as 'possession' but rather as relevance. Consider for example:

(57) a. **The house** being old, **Joe** sold it for a pittance.
         (> The house **belonged** to Joe)
     b. **The war** having been won, **they** were all discharged.
         (> They **fought in** the war)
     c. **Food** being scarce, **they** foraged in the bush.
         (> They intended **to eat** the food)
     d. **English** being too easy, **she** switched to Math.
         (> She was **studying** English)
     e. With **the state of the world** being what it is,
       Joe converted his condo to gold bullion.
         (> Joe **lived in** this world)

What these examples suggest is that, in essence, referential continuity is but a sub-type of the **thematic coherence** that must bind a participial ADV-clause to its adjacent main clause. When such coherence involves subject — i.e. main topic — continuity, the participial-clause subject is zero-marked. But even when the two clauses do not share their subject, other coherence strands may still bind them.

13.4. OTHER NON-FINITE ADVERBIAL CLAUSES

In addition to participial clauses, other types of non-finite clauses can also be used as subordinate ADV-clauses.[16] In this section we survey several types of those.

13.4.1. For-to adverbial clauses

For-to ADV-clauses may be viewed as a sub-type of purpose clauses (see 13.2.8.). As in the case of purpose clauses, the event coded in the ADV-clause constitutes the reason or purpose for the action by the subject of the main clause. However, the subject of for-to ADV-clauses is not co-referential with the subject of the main clause. Consider for example:

(58) a. **(In order) for** John **to** get the job,
          she had to cashier three union employees.
      b. **For** them **to** agree,
          she had to offer some inducement.
      c. **For** that **to** take place,
          someone had to change the rules.

The combination of a for-to ADV-clause with its main clause thus describes two causally-linked events, involving the action of two distinct agents. One event, coded in the ADV-clause, is the projected desired end. The other event is initiated earlier by the subject/agent of the main clause in order to make possible or facilitate the desired end.

13.4.2. Truncated copular-participial clauses

Copular clauses in English may lose their semantically-empty main verb 'be' in several complex-clause contexts. We have already noted that REL-clauses based on copular sentences, including copular auxiliaries, often appear verb-less.[17] A similar situation may be found in copula-based participial ADV-clauses:

(59) a. **Prepositional predicate**:
          (With) his career in ruins, John...
              (> His career *was* in ruins)
      b. **Prepositional predicate**:
          (With) her head on the floor, Mary...
              (> Her head *was* on the floor)
      c. **Adjectival predicate**:
          His face livid with rage, he...
              (> His face *was* livid with rage)
      d. **Nominal predicate**:
          Her face a blank mask, she...
              (> Her face *was* a blank mask)

    e. **Perfect-participle predicate**:
       (With) her parents gone for the summer, Cindy...
       (> Her parents *were* gone for the summer)
    f. **Passive-adjective predicate**:
       (With) his shirts neatly folded on the shelf, he...
       (> His shirts *were* neatly folded)
    g. **Progressive verbal predicate**:
       (With) senility slowly creeping on him, Fred...
       (> Senility *was* slowly creeping on him)

The truncated copular ADV-clauses in (59) display no equi-subject constraint relative to their main clause. Rather, they abide by the more lax coherence constraints discussed earlier. The subject of the ADV-clause may be possessed by the subject of the main clause. But looser yet coherence links are also possible, as in:

(60) a. With the end of summer rapidly approaching, John...
       (> The end of summer *was* rapidly approaching)
    b. With the country in total chaos, Gorbachov...
       (> The country *was* in total chaos)

13.4.3. Nominalized ADV-clauses

Fully-nominalized clauses may also serve as ADV-clauses, most commonly temporal ADV-clauses headed by a temporal preposition. The subject of such ADV-clauses may be co-referential with that of the main clause, in which case it is expressed as a pronoun — the possessive determiner in the nominalized clause. Thus:

(61) a. **Following** *their* rapid drive to the coast, *the troops*...
       (> The troops drove to the coast)
    b. **During** *their* approach to the airport, *they*...
       (> They approached the airport)
    c. **After** *their* surrender, *the conspirators*...
       (> The conspirators surrendered)
    d. **With** *her* ascent to the throne, *Elizabeth* also...
       (> Elizabeth ascended to the throne)
    e. **Upon** *her* arrival at the palace, *she*...
       (> She arrived at the palace)

The co-referential subject may also be implicit, with the nominalized verb displaying another determiner, as in:

(62) a. **Following** *the* rapid drive to the coast, *she* tried...
          (> She drove to the coast)
      b. **After** *the* approach to the airport, *they* began...
          (> They approached the airport)
      c. **After** *a* rapid descent, *the plane* pulled level and...
          (The plane descended rapidly)

In principle, these ADV-clauses need not abide by an equi-subject condition, as long as coherence constraints are observed. Thus compare:

(63) a. **Following** *the union's* collapse, *Gorbachov* decided...
          (> The union collapsed)
      b. **After** *the new queen's* ascent to the throne,
          the army mutinied and...
          (> The new queen ascended to the throne)
      c. **Upon** the arrival *of winter*, *they* all packed up and...
          (> Winter arrived)

While subject co-reference is not an absolute grammatical requirement in these clauses, it does play a strong role in insuring cross-clausal coherence. One facet of nominalized clauses in English is that the possessor of the nominalized verb can be, at least in principle, either the agent or the patient of the event. Thus compare:

(64) a. **Agent possessor**:
          Forty years after **her** discovery (of radium),
          Mme Curie finally received the Nobel Prize.
      b. **Patient possessor**:
          Forty years after **its** discovery (by Mme Curie),
          radium remains as rare and mysterious as ever.

One way of characterizing the difference between (64a) and (64b) is by suggesting that 'discovery' is a nominalized active verb when the agent is expressed as the possessor (64a), but a nominalized passive verb when the patient is the possessor (64b). The constraints on co-reference thus appear uniform, since the possessor-patient in (64b) is still the subject of the underlying clause — albeit the subject of a passive clause.

While patient possessor (64b) is indeed a grammatical option in English, its less-than-judicious application can lead to incoherent usage. Consider, for example, the following lead to a news report:[18]

(65) "...Decades after **their** discovery, **renegade scholars**
publish part of the tightly guarded **Dead Sea Scrolls**..."

Only with a considerable delay of one's mental computations is it possible
to reject two successive misleading interpretations of (65):

(66)   a.   Decades after **the renegade scholars** had been
discovered, someone finally published...

 b.   Decades after **the renegade scholars** discovered
the Dead Sea Scrolls, they finally published...

The correct interpretation can of course be computed by access to the
rather convoluted history of the subject. And indeed, in the full news-story,
the record is set perfectly straight:[19]

(67) "NEW YORK. — More than 40 years after the Dead Sea
Scrolls were discovered by Bedouin shepherds in caves
near Jerusalem, computer-reconstructed tests from the
long-suppressed documents were published Wednesday by
a renegade band of aging and embittered scholars who had
been prevented from studying the originals..."

13.5.   THE DISCOURSE-PRAGMATICS OF ADVERBIAL CLAUSES

13.5.1. Scope and direction of grounding

In the preceding sections we have dealt primarily with the various **local
coherence** links of adverbial clauses, those obtaining between ADV-clauses
and their adjacent main clauses. In this section we deal with more **global
coherence** links of these clauses. These links are more diffuse and span
across larger chunks of discourse, providing ADV-clauses with **anaphoric
grounding**. More specifically, we also deal here with the communicative-
pragmatic difference between ADV-clauses that precede (are 'preposed'
to) the main clause and those that follow (are 'post-posed' to) it. The local
grounding connections of both types are often similar. It is their longer-dis-
tance anaphoric links that are quite different.

13.5.2. Pre-posed vs. post-posed ADV-clauses

13.5.2.1. Local vs. global coherence links

The functional difference between pre-posed and post-posed ADV-
clauses has been studied in some detail by Thompson (1985) in her work on

purpose clauses. Thompson first observed that the exact semantic scope of 'purpose' in the two possible orders of the purpose clause was rather different. Post-posed purpose clauses most typically describe the purpose of the main-clause subject in initiating the event. In contrast, pre-posed purpose clauses often deal with the purpose of someone else, often someone who is not explicitly mentioned in either clause. Consider for example:

(68) **Post-posed**:
    a. Then he came over **to fix the plumbing**.
    b. *__To fix the plumbing__ (,) (then) he came over.

(69) **Pre-posed**:
    a. **To illustrate this**, consider the following passage.
    b. *Consider the following passage **to illustrate this**.

In the felicitous (68a), the post-posed purpose clause furnishes the motivation for the action by the subject of the main clause. Further, the semantic contents of the two propositions strongly militates toward such a local-scoped interpretation of 'purpose'. This renders the pre-posed order in (68b) odd, since such an order begs for a more global-scoped interpretation. In (69), where 'purpose' is the speaker's (and the subject of the main clause is the hearer), the natural tendency would be to pre-pose the purpose clause (69a). Here again the semantic contents of the two clauses biases against a local interpretation of 'purpose'. For this reason the post-posed order in (69b) seems odd.

The equi-subject condition that is more typical of post-posed purpose clauses, i.e. a stronger constraint on referential continuity, is again a reflection of the fact that the two clauses in this order display tighter local coherence. Interjecting the speaker into the discourse, on the other hand (cf. (69)), the scope of the purpose-clause's coherence links widens. Not only reference, but also point of view now shifts between the main and subordinate clause.[20]

13.5.2.2. Anaphoric grounding

Consider next a case where the semantics of the two clauses makes either the pre-posed and post-posed order permissible, and where subject co-reference obtains in both:

(70) a. **Post-posed**:
      He came home early **(in order) to fix the plumbing**.
    b. **Pre-posed**:
      In order to fix the plumbing, he came home early.

The purpose clause in both (70a) and (70b) refers to the subject's motivation for coming home early, so that one might be tempted to consider their
coherence links equally local. But in the pre-posed (70b) there is a strong
inference that the topic of the faulty plumbing and fixing it had come up in
the preceding discourse. In the post-posed order (70a) such an inference is
not as natural. The pre-posed ADV-clause in (70b) indeed exhibits a strong
local-coherence link to its main clause. This link — the equi-subject constraint — is also found in the post-posed ADV-clause in (70a). In (70b) it
serves as the **cataphoric grounding** of the ADV-clause. But the pre-posed
ADV-clause also exhibits a more global coherence link, one that is totally
absent in the post-posed ADV-clause — its **anaphoric grounding**. By
exhibiting both directions of grounding, anaphoric and cataphoric, the pre-
posed purpose clause in (70b) functions as a **coherence bridge** to the preceding discourse.

13.5.2.3. Pre-posed ADV-clauses as coherence bridges

Post-posed ADV-clauses appear typically in **paragraph medial** contexts. Pre-posed ADV-clauses, on the other hand, tend to appear at **thematic breaks** in the discourse, typically at the opening of new thematic paragraphs. We will use an extended text example from a western novel to illustrate the use of pre-posed ADV-clauses as coherence bridges and the wide
scope of their anaphoric links. The first passage (71) opens the book, intro-
ducing the main character and furnishing the general background for the
narrative:[21]

(71) "For seven days in the spring of 1882 the man called
      Shalako heard no sound but the wind. No sound but the
      wind, the creak of his saddle, the hoofbeats of his horse.
      Seven days riding the ghost trails up out of Sonora, down
      from the Sierra Madre, through Apache country, keeping
      off the skylines, and watching the beckoning fingers of the
      talking smoke..." (p. 1)

In the next example (72), three successive paragraphs appear, each of the
last two opening with an ADV-clause:[22]

(72)   "...Circling, Shalako discovered where the ambushers had
       lain in wait. Four men... Four Apaches. He studied the
       droppings of the horses, kicking them apart with a boot
       toe. He recognized in those droppings seeds from a plant
       found in the foothills of the Sierra Madre, but not farther
       north. These were no reservation Indians from San Carlos
       then, they were some of Chato's outfit, just up from below
       the border. Their trail when they left Wells's body lay in
       the direction he himself was taking, and that meant the
       waterhole was off limits for Shalako unless he wished to
       fight them for it, and no man in his right mind started a
       fight with Apaches.

       When the time came for fighting, the man Shalako
       fought with a cold fury that had an utterly impersonal
       quality about it. He fought to win, fought with deadly effi-
       ciency, with no nonsense about him, yet he did not fight
       needlessly.

       Despite his weariness and that of his horse, he began
       backtracking the dead man. Peter Wells was not likely to
       be alone, so his presence indicated a camp nearby..." (pp.
       7-8)

The second paragraph in (72) involves a *habitual*, *irrealis* description of
Shalako's normal fighting style, initiating a thematic break from the *sequential*, *perfective*, *realis* mode of the preceding paragraph. The ADV-clause
reaches over anaphorically into the preceding paragraph, linking there with
'fight'. The third paragraph returns to the *sequential realis* mode of the first.
The opening ADV-clause reaches backward anaphorically in a way that is
impossible to circumscribe. The weariness of Shalako and his horse is a diffuse, cumulative inference from the entire early text.

   The coherence and grounding functions of pre-posed ADV-clauses
may be summarized in the following diagram:

(73) **Coherence and grounding function of pre-posed ADV-clauses**:

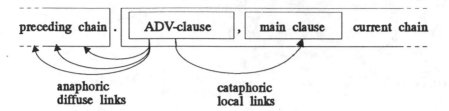

Pre-posed ADV-clauses — as well as other pre-posed adverbials — perform their coherence-bridging function by having coherence links in both directions, anaphoric and cataphoric. Their anaphoric links are more diffuse and global, reaching back to thematic information anywhere in the preceding thematic chain, paragraph or even episode. Their cataphoric links are strictly local, anchoring the ADV-clause to the main clause, which then launches the new thematic unit. Pre-posed ADV-clauses may thus be viewed as **thematic re-orientation** devices, used to re-establish coherence across a major thematic boundary. The consistent presence of a preceding period and a subsequent comma associated with pre-posed ADV-clauses in written text — both concomitants of pausing in natural speech — is a reflection of the **cognitive re-orientation** that must accompany thematic re-orientation, in both discourse production and discourse production and discourse comprehension.[23]

13.6. CONJOINED ('COORDINATE') CLAUSES

13.6.1. Preamble

The traditional definition of conjoined clauses assumes that — in contrast with subordinate clauses — they are **independent** of their immediate clausal environment. To substantiate such independence, logicians and linguists have traditionally constructed pairs of clauses such as:[24]

(74) John is in the house and Mary is at school

for which the following type of syntactic description was furnished:[25]

(75)

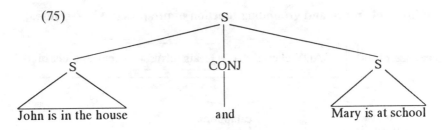

Within this tradition, conjunction was viewed as a local syntactic relation between two adjacent clauses, rather than a thematic relation between adjacent clauses in a continuous coherent text. The syntactic form of conjoined clauses was then described in terms of various **reductive transformations**, an economy-producing device, given the presence of recurrent elements in the two conjoined clauses. If no such recurrent elements occurred, as in (74)/(75), no **conjunction reduction** took place. At the other extreme, when only one non-recurrent element occurred — either the subject, object, indirect object or an adverb — **NP conjunction** applied (see chapter 6). Within such a purely syntactic approach, the referential continuity of topical subjects in connected discourse, syntactically expressed by zero anaphora or anaphoric pronouns, is viewed as a sub-type of conjunction reduction, in this case **VP conjunction**, as in e.g.:[26]

(76)   I can sing and dance

characterized by the following type of syntactic description:

(77)

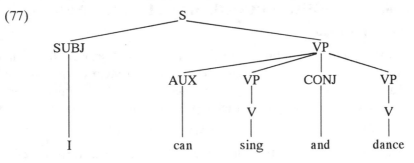

There is a vast array of types and degrees of reductive clausal structures associated with conjunction in English.[27] For example, maximally-integrated conjoined structures such as (76)/(77), falling under a unified single-clause intonation contour, can be shown to be members of a continuum of conjoined expressions. Along this continuum, the degree of both **thematic connectivity** and **syntactic integration** of the conjoined clause relative to the preceding clause, and thus also the degree of **syntactic reduction** of the conjoined clause, grows weaker and weaker:

(78)   a. She sang and played the guitar.
       b. She sang and also played the guitar.
       c. She sang, and she also played the guitar.
       d. She sang, and then she played the guitar.
       e. She sang. Then she played the guitar.
       f. She sang. Later on she played the guitar.

Of the wide range of conjunction types in English, we will focus here primarily on the most common clause-type found in connected discourse, the one that falls under a separate intonation contour in the spoken register, roughly corresponding to examples (78c-f) above. Such conjoined clauses predominate in chain-medial contexts, and most commonly involve subject continuity. One studies such clauses from two parallel perspectives. spectives.

(a) **Functional dependency: Degree of thematic connectivity**
     In connected natural discourse, the total independence of any clause, be it most loosely connected, from its environment is a mirage, an artifice created by the linguist. A clause that is thematically — pragmatically — independent of all other clauses in connected discourse is a sure locus of incoherence. Therefore, the thematic dependency — connectivity, coherence — of a clause relative to its immediate discourse context can be taken for granted. What remains to be determined is the type and degree of cross-clausal connectivity. And conjoined clauses in connected discourse indeed can code different degrees of **coherence transition**, some tighter, others increasingly looser. From this perspective, the difference between subordinate ADV-clauses and conjoined clauses may be summarized as follows:

(i) **Scope of coherence links**:
The coherence links of conjoined clauses tend to be more local. In this they resemble the more local links post-posed ADV-clauses, but sharply contrast with the more global links of pre-posed ADV-clauses.

(ii) **Direction of coherence links**:
The connectivity of conjoined clauses can be described more fruitfully in terms of anaphoric links. In this way, conjoined clauses resemble the local

anaphoric links of post-posed ADV-clauses, but contrast with the local cataphoric links of pre-posed ADV-clauses.

(b) **Grammatical dependency: Degree of clause integration**

The more thematically connected a conjoined clause is with an adjacent clause — the more strands of thematic coherence it shares with that adjacent clause — the more likely it is to appear reduced, less finite, syntactically integrated with that other clause. Here, the same principle observed earlier for verb complements (chapter 7) and ADV-clauses (above) governs the syntax of conjoined clauses:[28]

(79) **Isomorphism between functional and structural integration**:
"The more functionally integrated — more tightly coherent — two adjacent states/events are, the more syntactically integrated will the two clauses that code them be".

13.6.2. The components of thematic coherence

Thematic coherence is a complex meta-phenomenon, made out of a number of more concrete 'strands'. The main strands are:

(80) **Components of thematic coherence**:
More concrete, local strands:
a. referential continuity
b. temporal continuity
c. spatial continuity
d. action continuity
More abstract, global strands:
e. modal continuity
f. speech-act continuity
g. perspective continuity

The degree of cross-clausal thematic coherence, or its converse, thematic disruption, can be expressed in terms of the number of individual strands that either continue or change with the cross-clausal transition.

Of the two groups of coherence strands listed in (80), a more concrete, local strand (80a-d) can change in the middle of a chain without necessarily precipitating the termination of the chain. On the other hand, a change in one of the more abstract, global strands (80e-g) tends to be associated with

the end of the entire chain. The degree of cross-clausal continuity of conjoined clauses is finely coded by the combination of **punctuation** (or **intonation**), **conjunctions** and **clause-initial adverbs**. But the grammar of these
inter-clausal connectors interacts intimately with two other grammatical
sub-systems:

(a) the grammar of tense-aspect-modality that signals
temporal and modal coherence (chapter 4)

(b) the grammar referential coherence (chapter 5)

Some more common thematic coherence transitions coded by the combination of punctuation and conjunctions or adverbs may be seen in:

(81) a. **Comma/'and' conjunction**:
She came in, [Ø] stopped, [Ø] looked around
and [Ø] froze.
b. **Period conjunction**:
She came in, [Ø] stopped and [Ø] looked around.
She froze.
c. **Period-'then' conjunction**:
She came in and [Ø] looked around. **Then she froze**.
d. **Period-'later on' conjunction**:
...She froze and [Ø] blacked out.
Later on she woke up in a strange room...

The thematic continuity of the last clause in examples (81) is highest in
(81a), lower in (81b), lower yet in (81c) and lowest in (81d). This is true
even though referential continuity is never broken.

In the next example, various mid-chain disruptions in the more concrete individual coherence strands occur without terminating the chain:

(82) **Low-level mid-chain coherence breaks**:
a. **Break in referential continuity**:
She came in and **he** followed.
b. **Change in temporal continuity**:
She flew in **at midnight** and [Ø] left **the next day**.
c. **Break in both referential and temporal continuity**:
She ran in, but **he** had left **earlier**.
d. **Break in spatial continuity**:
She lived **in Chicago** and [Ø] worked **in Cleveland**.

e. **Break in action continuity**:
   (i) She went to the fridge, [Ø] opened the door,
        [Ø] took out the bacon and [Ø] unwrapped it,
   (ii) then [Ø] fetched a frying pan, [Ø] turned on
        the stove and [Ø] fried four strips.

In example (82e), two distinct tightly-bound and highly conventionalized **action clusters** occur,[29] the first (i) depicting the routine of removing an item from the fridge, the second (ii) depicting the routine of frying bacon. The use of the conjunction 'then' between the two clusters signals a slight discontinuity, relative to the maximal action continuity within each cluster.

In all the passages in (82), one could render the very same cross-clausal transitions thematically more disruptive by using the appropriate combination of punctuation (i.e. intonation) and conjunctions. Thus compare:

(83) **Chain-ending coherence breaks**:
   a. **Break in referential continuity**:
      She came in. **He** followed.
   b. **Change in temporal continuity**:
      She flew in **on Monday**. But she left **the next day**.
   c. **Break in both referential and temporal continuity**:
      She ran in. But **he** had left **earlier**.
   d. **Break in spatial continuity**:
      She lived **in Chicago**. But she worked **in Cleveland**.
   e. **Break in action continuity**:
      (i) She went to the fridge, [Ø] opened the door,
           [Ø] took out the bacon and [Ø] unwrapped it.
      (ii) Then she fetched a frying pan, [Ø] turned on
           the stove and [Ø] fried four strips.

The more abstract, global strands of coherence, those pertaining to the continuity of modality, speech-act and perspective, are all associated with the speaker's assignment of **point of view**. A break in any of those would typically involve a **major thematic boundary**, the beginning of a new chain or a new paragraph. Thus compare:

(84) **Discontinuity of modality**:
   a. She **came** in and **sat** on the bed.
      She **would** soon move out for good.
   b. *She **came** in and **sat** on the bed,
      [Ø] **would** soon get married and move out.

(85) **Discontinuity of speech act**:
   a. She came in and sat on the bed.
      Was she thinking about him?
   b. *She came in and sat on the bed,
      was she thinking about him?

(86) **Discontinuity of perspective**:
   a. She came in and sat on the bed.
      She was tired, she thought.
   b. *She came in and sat on the bed,
      she was tired, she thought.

In (84a), the first chain is given in the realis (past) mode, the second in an irrealis (future) mode. Juxtaposing the two without a chain-breaking period (84b) is infelicitous. In (85a), the first chain combines two declarative clauses, the second adds an interrogative. Juxtaposing them without a chain-breaking period (85b) seems infelicitous. Finally, in (86a) the first chain is given from the narrator's perspective, the second from a character's perspective. Juxtaposing them without a chain-breaking period would again yield an infelicitous sequence.[30]

13.6.3. Conjunctions, punctuation and thematic coherence

The strong association between conjunctions, punctuation and referential continuity has been studied by Hayashi (1989). The results of that study, first those pertaining to punctuation, are summarized in (87) below.

(87) **Cataphoric referential continuity associated with zero, comma, period and paragraph indentation, with 'and' and 'then' in written English**
(Hayashi, 1989)

conjunction type	% subject switch (DS) across the conjunction
and	15%
, and	70%
. And	81%
and then	16%
, and then	36%
. And then	100%
,then	50%
. Then	56%
. PARAG/Then	100%
comma (alone)	10%
period (alone)	72%

The ranking of the various punctuation devices in (87) yields the scale:

(88) **highest referential continuity**
zero
comma
period
paragraph indentation
lowest referential continuity

This ranking suggests an inverse correlation between the length of the inter-clausal pause — mimicked by the punctuation mark — and the degree of referential continuity across the inter-clausal boundary:

(89) "The more continuous — coherent — is reference across the clause boundary, the smaller the pause between the clauses".

13.6.4. Conjunctions and thematic contrast

Some conjunctions, such as 'but', are said to be contrastive. Others, such as 'and', are said to be non-contrastive. There appears to be a systematic connection between the use of contrastive conjunctions on the one hand, and low referential and thematic continuity on the other. Thus, clauses conjoined with 'and' signal a milder transition and tighter cross-clausal coherence; while clauses conjoined with 'but' signal more abrupt transition, and thus weaker coherence. For example:

(90) a. He gutted the fish, cleaned it **and** cut off the head.
      b. ?He gutted the fish, cleaned it **but** cut off the head.

One could of course dream up a presuppositional background that would render (90b) felicitous and (90a) odd. For example:

(91) We love eating fish-heads.

But such a background is clearly at variance with the cultural norms of action continuity that render (90a) more felicitous.

There is a strong statistical association between contrastive conjunctions and referential discontinuity, and likewise between non-contrastive conjunctions and referential continuity. The following figures are again cited after Hayashi (1989).

(92) **Cataphoric referential continuity and contrastive conjunctions in written English** (Hayashi, 1989)

conjunction	% subject switch (DS) across the conjunction
and (all punctuations)	29%
, while	77%
but (all punctuations)	85%
, though	100%
. Yet	100%

The contrastive — counter-expectancy — conjunctions 'while', 'but', 'though' and 'yet' are strongly associated with **subject switching**, while the non-contrastive 'and' is strongly associated with subject continuity.

The correlations reported above should not be taken to mean that conjunctions and punctuation are used primarily to signal varying degrees of referential continuity. Most likely, their primary function is to signal degrees of thematic coherence. But since one of the main concrete strands of thematic coherence is referential continuity, a strong statistical association exists between thematic and referential continuity.

As noted earlier (chapter 10), contrast may be due to any strand of discourse coherence, certainly including reference, as in:

(93) **Purely referential contrast**:
   a. Joe came, **but** Sally didn't.
   b. I found Sally, **but** couldn't locate Joe.

But contrast may be due to other strands of coherence, often in combination with reference:

(94) a. **Switch verb**:
        Mary sat down, **but** got up immediately.
     b. **Switch time**:
        She was here yesterday, **but** not today.
     c. **Switch place**:
        She was supposed to go to Cleveland, **but** wound up
        in Chicago.
     d. **Switch subject & verb**:
        Mary sat down, **but** Bruce stayed on his feet.
     e. **Switch object and verb**:
        Mary loved lettuce, **but** loathed spinach.
     f. **Switch subject, object & verb**:
        Mary played chess, **but** Bruce detested board-games.

Contrastive conjunctions such as 'but' are used when some expectations have been pre-established concerning either individual or types of states, activities, subjects or objects that are expected to behave in a certain way, but then turn out not to. The expectations may be based on cultural norms, as in (90) above, involving the normal way in which some event-types are expected to follow others. They may be also set up in the preceding discourse for specific occasions and participants. Contrasts based on overtly-constructed discourse-specific expectations, as in (93) and (94) above, merely represent more obvious cases. But ever-more-subtle contrasts are possible, provided the appropriate expectations are pre-established and then violated. Consider:

(95)   She was a famous physicist **but** loved potatoes.

On the surface, (95) seems odd, a non-sequitur. But if via some inference, or a chain of inferences however long and complex, one could derive an expectation such as either (96a) or (96b) below, (95) would then lose its oddity:

(96)   a.   When a woman is a famous physicist
            She does not love potatoes.
       b.   When one is a famous physicist
            One does not love potatoes.

The pragmatic motivation for contrastive conjunction is thus, in principle, unconstrained.

13.6.5. The syntax of conjoined clauses

13.6.5.1. Finiteness and inter-clausal connectivity

As noted earlier, the semantic and pragmatic links of conjoined clauses to their clausal environment in continuous coherent discourse are the loosest of all cross-clausal connections. It is hardly surprising then that the cross-clausal syntactic connectivity — or dependency — of such clauses is also the loosest. But conjoined clauses in connected discourse still display some syntactic adjustment to their context. In the case of loosely-conjoined chain-medial clauses, the relevant structural expressions of their connectivity clusters around three major grammatical foci:

(a) the grammar of tense-aspect-modality
(b) the grammar of referent-marking
(c) conjunction words and pauses/punctuation

All three foci have been described in considerable detail earlier above.[31]

The two syntactic adjustments most commonly found in loosely-conjoined clauses involve foci (a) and (b), and may be described in terms of **reduced finiteness**. In the marking of referents, reduced finiteness involves zero-anaphoric coding of the recurrent referent — most commonly the recurrent subject — in the chain-medial clause. In the marking of tense-aspect-modality, decreased finiteness involves reduced expression of the recurrent tense-aspect-modal auxiliaries.

13.6.5.2. Clause chaining and zero-marked subjects

Both aspects of reduced finiteness in chain-medial clauses have already been noted in chained participial clauses, as in:[32]

(97) a. "...[Ø] **Proceeding** leisurely,
      b. first [Ø] **taking** off one thing,
      c. then [Ø] another,
      d. and [Ø] with the help of scissors,
      e. **I** quickly **rid** her of every covering...."

In all but the chain-final clause in (97), the subject is left unexpressed, and the verb (if present) is stripped of tense-aspect-modality marking.[33]

The dominant clause-chaining strategy in English is not the one in (97). In the more common strategy, the **chain-initial clause** is the most finite clause. All non-initial clauses are, in one way or another, grammatically less finite. Non-initial clauses may be participial-like, as in the short examples below:[34]

(98) a. "...**He paused** again by a clump of ironwood,
         [Ø] **enjoying** the fragrance from the yellow blossoms..."
      b. "...He **started** his horse,
         [Ø] **walking** it to keep the dust down..."
      c. "...For a while a chaparral cock **raced** ahead of him,
         [Ø] **enjoying** the company..."
      d. "...He **circled** it as wearily as a wolf,
         [Ø] **studying** it from all angles..."

In such short sequences, the participial clause in fact tends to be durative-stative, with the state being often simultaneous with the main-clause event.[35]

Most commonly in English, the non-initial clauses in the chain includes what seems, at least on the face of it, a finite verb, as in:[36]

(99) "...He **swung** his leg over the saddle,
      then [Ø] **stood** in the saddle..."

In the next section we will review the evidence of reduced finiteness in the tense-aspect-modal marking of such chain-medial verbs.

13.6.5.3. Finiteness and verbal inflections

Several verbal inflections in English are marked by auxiliaries. Consider first the perfect, durative marking in the clause-chain:

(100) a. Mary **has been** com**ing** here every summer,
     b. gather**ing** plants,
     c. watch**ing** birds,
     d. collect**ing** rocks
     e. and just rest**ing** and hav**ing** a quiet time.

Semantically, both the perfect and durative aspects in (100) persist through the entire chain, as does the subject referent. But only the chain-initial clause (100a) has fully marked subject and tense-aspect. The non-initial clauses (100b,c,d,e) are less marked in terms of all three features.

When the tense-aspect-modal continuity of a clause-chain such as (100) is disrupted, the chain must be terminated. Whereby the initial clause of the new chain must revert to more finite marking, in terms of both tense-aspect-modality and explicitly-coded subject. For example:

(101) **Maximally-coherent initial sequence**:
     a. She **was** writ**ing** to her parents,
     b. [Ø] tell**ing** them about her new flat,
     c. [Ø] describ**ing** the furniture
     d. [Ø] and pok**ing** fun at the neighbors. [BREAK]
     e. She **was going** to tell them...
     Unacceptable alternative continuation:
     *e. , [Ø] **was going** to tell them...

In the same vein, breaking the continuity of sequential action — i.e. the perfective-past tense-aspect — also yields an ill-formed chain. For example:

(102) **Maximally-coherent initial sequence**:
     a. He **came** into the room,
     b. [Ø] **stopped**,
     c. [Ø] **saw** the woman on the couch,
     d. [Ø] **looked** at her briefly
     e. [Ø] and **wondered** why she was there. [BREAK]
     f. He **had thought** that someone...
     Unacceptable alternative continuation:
     *f. , [Ø] **thought** that someone...

The temporal-thematic discontinuity associated with the use of the perfect aspect is vividly demonstrated in the following passage, in which a series of marked — rather than implicit — perfects follow each other in succession:[37]

(103) a. "...The dead man **had ridden** a freshly shod horse
into the playa from the north,
b. and when *[Ø]* shot he **had tumbled** from the saddle
c. and the horse **had galloped** away.
d. Several riders **had then approached** the body
e. and one **had dismounted** to collect the weapons..."

While the perfect aspectuality persists across the chain, other aspects of thematic coherence keep being disrupted. In clause (103b), a pre-posed ADV-clause breaks the thematic continuity. And in clauses (103c), (103d) and (103e), the referential continuity is disrupted. These deviations from maximal continuity are enough to precipitate a more explicit finite marking of the clauses, in terms of both overtly-marked subject and overtly-marked perfect aspect. In the same vein, the continuity of modality also results in less explicit marking of the auxiliary in conjoined chain-medial clauses, as in:

(104) **Maximally coherent initial sequence**:
a. She **should go** there,
b. [Ø] **stop** by,
c. [Ø] **pick up** a pound of salami
d. and [Ø] **take** it home. [BREAK]
e. She **can** rest then...
Unacceptable alternative continuation:
*e. , [Ø] **can** rest then...

The break in modal continuity between (104d) and (104e) again requires terminating the chain with a period in (104d). Following the break, explicit coding of the new modality is required, as well as explicit re-coding of the subject, in spite of referential continuity.

13.6.6. Truncated chain-medial clauses

So far, the zero-coding of the recurrent elements — coherence strands — in conjoined chain-medial clauses has involved either the subject or tense-aspect-modal auxiliaries. But fluent coherent discourse, both spoken and written, allows more extensive **truncation** of conjoined chain-medial clauses. Thus, for example, the main verb 'be' is easily dropped in chain-medial stative clauses, as in (with the truncated parts restored):[38]

(105) a. "...The man called Shalako **was** a brooding man,
   b. [he was] a wary man,
   c. [he was] a man who trusted no fate,
   d. [he was a man who trusted] no predicted destiny,
   e. [he was a man who trusted] no luck..."

And similarly:[39]

(106) a. "...The margin of error **was** slight,
   b. [it was] a dry waterhole,
   c. [it was] a chance fall,
   d. [it was] a stray bullet...
   e. or [it was] an Apache he missed seeing first..."

And similarly:[40]

(107) a. "...Seven days **riding** the ghost trail up out of Sonora,
   b. [riding] down from the Sierra Madre,
   c. [riding] through Apache country..."

The general coding principle evident in such truncations remains the same: Once a chain-initial clause has been coded explicitly by more finite grammatical markers, predictable recurrent elements may be left unmarked in the following chain-medial clauses.

13.6.7. Equi-object anaphoric reference

The referential continuity we dealt with above, as part and parcel of thematic coherence, pertained exclusively to subject continuity. But at least in spoken English one finds on occasion some stranger conjoined clauses where the referential continuity involves object-to-subject transition. The following example of such a switch was taken from a newspaper article:[41]

(108) a. "...""I made the decision
   b. that we could no longer pay **him** a salary
   c. **and him not** perform a function"
   d. said Lt. Bob McManus,
   e. who is in charge of the sheriff's patrol division..."

While admittedly non-standard, the conjoined clause (99c) above nonetheless attempts to abide by the generalizations noted above. The object of (99b) switches to subject of (99c), enough of a discontinuity to warrant overt marking — but in the object case ('him'). And except for the negative marker, the verb in (99c) remains non-finite.

13.6.8. Incoherent clause-chaining

The dexterous manipulation of the grammar of thematic coherence — punctuation, conjunctions, adverbs, referent-coding and tense-aspect-modal coding — gives rise to more coherent paragraphs. Less expert control of these elements of grammar give rise to a well known type of text — seemingly grammatical but incoherent, and hard on the cognitive processor. The four examples below were culled from a James Kilpatrick's cautionary column:[42]

> (109) "...Oil Change Express, which opened about 10 days ago, caters to that customer with a van in which a mechanic will bring the oil and filter to the car, provide the needed service in about 20 minutes without someone having to wait around one of the service stations still offering full service or reworking an entire day's schedule to drop the car off and then return for it later..."

> (110) "...His father had planned to move the family to North Carolina this week to escape the urban mayhem that in recent months has claimed a 5-year-old hit in the head while sleeping by a stray bullet fired by his mother's former boyfriend, and a 10-year-old killed by stray bullets in a store when an argument between a customer and the owner erupted in gunfire..."

> (111) "...The operators of the house were serving alcohol to guests and/or providing 'setups' at an in-house bar, which requires a city liquor license, which the house does not have and could not get one, according to revenue director Carlton West, because it is in a residential area and within 100 yards of a school, Notre Dame Academy..."

(112) "...After twisting and screaming for 15 of his 22 points to break open a game distressingly tight after three quarters, Kemp could not nominate this as his ranking final period against Hart, whom he starred in a club record 50-point Sonic outburst last year at home..."

13.7. CLAUSAL DISJUNCTION

So far we have surveyed the most common, syntactically-loose clausal coordination or **conjunction**. Another, less common inter-clausal coordination type also exists, called **disjunction**. The main marker differentiating disjunction from conjunction is the conjunction 'or', sometimes augmented with 'either'. In this section we will briefly discuss the semantics and grammar of disjunction.

13.7.1. Disjunction and logic

Disjunction is a well-defined propositional connector in logic, whose value can be summarized in the following **bi-conditional** equivalencies:

(113) a. (**either**) A is true **or** B is true ⇔
        if A is **not** true, then B is true
     b. **if** A is **not** true, then B is true ⇔
        if B is **not** true, then A is true

The logical equivalency (113a) allows the substituting 'if not' for 'or', and vice versa. The logical equivalency (113b) establishes the two disjuncts, A and B, as truly exclusive of each other.

Disjunction in language follows logic only up to a point. The bi-conditional translation from 'or' to 'if not' indeed holds. That is:

(114) a. (**either**) do this **or** you'll be sorry ⇔
        If you **don't** do this, you'll be sorry.
     b. (**either**) come forward now **or** forever hold you peace ⇔
        If you **don't** come forward now, hold your peace forever.
     c. **Either** he comes up with it **or** we go belly up ⇔
        If he **doesn't** come up with it, we go belly up.

However, easy bi-conditional substitution between the two disjuncts is not always felicitous. That is:

(115) a. **If** you **don't** do this, you'll be sorry.

?⇔

If you **won't** be sorry, you'll do this.

b. **If** you **don't** come forward now, hold your peace forever.

?⇔

If you **don't** hold your peace forever, come forward now.

c. **If** he **doesn't** come up with it, we go belly up.

*⇔

If we **don't** go belly up, then he comes up with it.

Nor is there an easy bi-conditional substitution between the two disjuncts with 'or':

(116) a. (**Either**) do this **or** you'll be sorry

*⇔

(**Either**) you'll be sorry **or** do this

b. (**Either**) come forward now **or** forever hold your peace

*⇔

(**Either**) hold your peace forever **or** come forward now

c. (**Either**) he comes up with it **or** we go belly up

*⇔

(**Either**) we go belly up **or** he comes up with it

This is one more example of how sequential order in language is not the neutral arrangement it is in logic (or mathematics), but rather is likely to involve directional biases that are more characteristic of thematic coherence in natural text.

13.7.2. Disjunction and modality

The modal scope of both disjointed clauses is clearly **irrealis**. This is probably predictable from the fact that the disjointed clausal relation is translatable into a **conditional** relation, where both clauses are irrealis. It is thus not surprising to find disjunction of **non-declarative** clauses such as yes-no questions and imperatives. Both types of non-declarative speech-acts typically fall under irrealis modal scope. As illustrations, consider:

(117) a. Would you like tea, **or** [would you like] coffee?

⇔

If you **don't** like tea, would you **then** like coffee?

b. Answer **either** this question **or** [answer] that one.

⇔

If you **don't** answer this one, **then** answer that one.

The inherent irrealis modality of disjunctions explains why they tend to sound odd, perhaps with a strong flavor of logical tautology, in many **strong-assertion** contexts, as in:

(118) a. **Past**: ?John did his homework **or** (he) didn't (do it).

b. **Present**: ?John is doing it **or** (he) isn't (doing it).

c. **Habitual**: ?He's either a crook or he isn't (a crook).

d. **Negation**: ?He **didn't** either do it or not do it.

In contrast, in irrealis contexts of **weak assertion**, such disjunctions do not induce the same tautological flavor:

(119) a. **Modal**:

He **might** do it, **or** he might not, we'll see.

b. **Weak certainty**:

She **never knew if** he'd show up **or** not.

c. **Weak doubt**:

He **wondered whether** what he heard was true **or** not.

By suggesting that tautological expressions such as (118) are odd, one does not suggest that there is anything "ungrammatical" about tautology. As both Levinson (1983) and Wierzbicka (1987) have pointed out, many tautological expressions in language — some of them in fact disjunctions — can be assigned a meaningful interpretation, given various pragmatic or culture-specific conventions, as in:[43]

(120) a. War is war

(> What can you expect? War has always been this way.)

b. Either John will come or he won't.

(> There's nothing we can do about it, we'll just have
to wait and see.)

c. If he does it, he does it.

(> We have no control over the situation,
we'll have to accept whatever he does.)

d. Boys will be boys.
(Regardless of how we feel about it, boys will continue to behave in a frustrating, objectionable way.)

13.8. COHERENCE, SYNTACTIC PARALLELISM AND CLAUSE INTEGRATION

13.8.1. Preamble

So far, we have focused our discussion primarily on the loosest type of clausal conjunction, the one that is predominant in chain-medial clauses. In this type of conjunction, the grammar marks primarily two concrete features of thematic continuity:

(a) **subject continuity** (reduced subject marking)
(b) **tense-aspect-modality continuity** (reduced TAM marking)

In this section we will examine briefly conjunction types where cross-clausal coherence is much greater, involving many more components of the clause. Those components may include the verb, the direct object, indirect object or adverbs. With an increasing number of shared clausal elements (or shared coherence strands) across two adjacent clauses, an increase in the **syntactic integration** of the two clauses takes place. Thus, the types of clausal conjunction described below tip the scale gradually toward increased **syntactic parallelism** as precondition for eventual **conjunction reduction**.

13.8.2. Syntactic parallelism and mutual relevance

Consider first the loosest syntactic parallelism between two clauses, where they seem to share no major constituent, but only *tense-aspect-*modality. The type of coherence involved here is, most commonly, that the two events had a strong spatio-temporal link, and that the two subjects — topics — were relevant to each other. For example:

(121) a. Mary **read** the paper and Marvin **watched** TV.
     b. ?Mary **read** the paper and Marvin **will watch** TV.
     c. ?Mary **read** the paper and Marvin **watches** TV.
     d. ?Mary **read** the paper and Marvin **is watching** TV.

The oddity of (121b,c,d) arises from lack of spatio-temporal coherence between the two clauses. Given a query such as:

(122) What did Mary and Marvin do Sunday morning?

one can only answer it with (121a), but not with (121b,c,d). This reveals a more subtle element of the underlying coherence that motivates a conjunction such as (121a): The two subjects/topics must somehow "belong together", or have some **mutual relevance**.

A breach of mutual relevance may spring from a variety of sources. For example:

(123) a. ?Mary read the Sunday papers and Marvin **was a dodo**.
   b. ?Mary read the Sunday papers and Marvin **loved Bach**.
   c. ?Mary read the Sunday papers and Marvin **killed a rat**.
   d. ?Mary read the Sunday papers and **G. Bush** watched TV.
   e. ?Mary loved tomatoes and Marvin hated **Hitler**.
   f. ?Mary **saw** Sally and Marvin **killed** his aunt.

The oddity of (123a,b) arises from an attempt to conjoin an activity verb with a permanent state. The oddity of (123c) arises from conjoining an activity with a fast-moving event. The oddity of (123d) arises from conjoining clauses whose subjects have no obvious mutual relevance. The oddity of (123e) arises from conjoining clauses whose objects have no mutual relevance. Finally, the oddity of (123f) arises from conjoining clauses whose verbs — thus events — have no mutual relevance.

The constraints on mutual relevance suggest that clausal conjunction with syntactic parallelism is in essence a **comparative** device, used to contrast the behavior of similar entities (e.g. subjects) that somehow 'belong together' or are 'mutually relevant'. It is expected, however mildly and by whatever cultural norms, that such subjects exhibit similar behavior under similar circumstances. The mutual relevance — or similarity — constraint is the reason why similar behavior is expected.

13.8.3. Gapping

Gapping is a partial syntactic reduction strategy applied to conjoined clauses under the more stringent coherence conditions. It gives rise to closer syntactic integration of the conjoined clauses. In addition to the normal mutual-relevance constraints, the two structures must show close **syntactic parallelism**. Further, one constituent must be identical and at least two others must be different. One type of gapping involves identical verbs, as in:

(124) a. Mary **loved** potatoes and Marvin [Ø] tomatoes.
   b. John **was** a teacher and Mary [Ø] an engineer.
   c. Mary **slept** in bed and Marvin [Ø] on the couch.
   d. Mary **left** on Sunday and Marvin [Ø] on Monday.

The syntactic structure of (124a) may be characterized schematically as:[44]

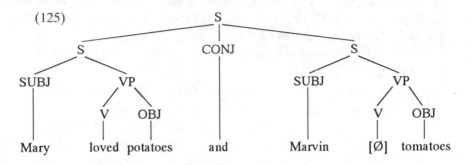

(125)

Gapping may also take place under another condition, of equally strict parallelism, where both the verb and the subject of the two conjoined clauses are identical, but at least two other elements are non-identical. For example:

(126) a.   John gave **flowers** to **Mary** and [Ø] [Ø] **candy** to **Cynthia**.
       b.   John gave **flowers** to **Mary** on **Tuesday**
            and [Ø] [Ø] **candy** to **Cynthia** on **Wednesday**
       c.   Mary went to **the store** every **Tuesday**
            and [Ø] [Ø] to **the club** every **Wednesday**.

The syntactic structure of (126a) may be characterized schematically as:

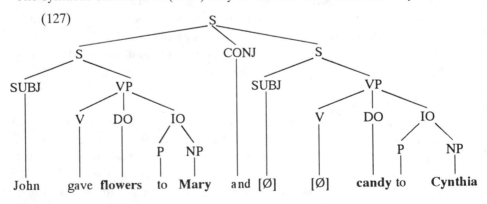

(127)

13.8.4. Verb conjunction

Another type of conjoined structure, with even greater syntactic integration of the two clauses, is obtained when the two clauses share all their components except for the verb. This results in a compressed syntactic structure which may be called **verb conjunction**, whereby to all intent and purpose a single surface clause exists, albeit with two conjoined verbs. This type of reduced structure parallels the NP conjunction described in chapter 6. As an example, consider:

(128) a.   She **admired** [Ø] and [Ø] **respected** him.
     b.   They **assaulted** [Ø] and [Ø] **kicked** her.
     c.   He **courted** [Ø] and [Ø] later **married** his cousin.
     d.   She **came** [Ø] and [Ø] **left** with Joe.

The syntactic structure of (128a) may be given schematically, first as the more semantically-revealing **deep structure** in:

(129)

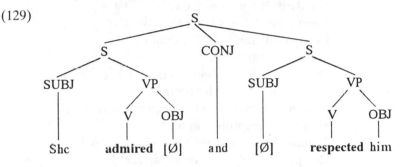

Or, with the appropriate "pruning", as the syntactically more accurate **surface structure** in:

(130)

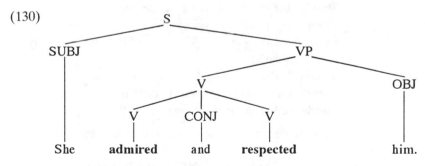

13.8.5. Comparative clauses

Comparative clauses are a type of compressed syntactic structure that in some ways resembles reduced clauses arising from syntactic conjunction. Two rigidly parallel clauses — depicting two parallel states or events — provide the underlying semantic structure of the comparative clause. The two differ from each other in only two constituents:

(a) A **compared NP** occupying one of the main roles in the clause (subject, object, indirect object, adverb);

(b) The **extent** to which the compared NP possesses some quality.

The element whose extent is compared is most commonly an adjective, an adverb or a quantifier. The compared NP is then said to possess the quality in question to a higher or lower extent than another NP in the parallel underlying clause. That second NP serves as the **standard of comparison**. Typical examples are:

(131) a. **Predicate adjective**:
Standard: Bill is **somewhat** tall   ⎫ ⇒
Compared: John is tall**er than that**⎭
Condensed: John is tall**er than** Bill

   b. **Modifying adjective**:
Standard: Sally is a **somewhat good** engineer ⎫ ⇒
Compared: Mary is **better than that**   ⎭
Condensed: Mary is a **better** engineer **than** Sally

   c. **Modifying quantifier (more)**:
Standard: Sue has **some** money   ⎫ ⇒
Compared: Sally has **more than that**⎭
Condensed: Sally has **more** money **than** Sue

   d. **Modifying quantifier (less)**:
Standard: **Few** people came yesterday ⎫ ⇒
Compared: **(Even) fewer** came today ⎭
Condensed: Few**er** people came today **than** yesterday

   e. **Extent adverb**:
Standard: Bill runs fast   ⎫ ⇒
Compared: John runs fast**er than that** ⎭
Condensed: John runs fast**er than** Bill

Syntactically, the comparative construction resembles a simple clause, except at two locations:

(a) The standard-of-comparison NP is attached to the end of the clause as a prepositional phrase with 'than'.

(b) The compared quality is marked, either by the comparative suffix -*er* on an adjective, quantifier or adverb, or by the **comparative quantifier** 'more' or 'less'.

The use of the comparative suffix -er is restricted to short words mostly of Germanic origin. When the element whose extent is compared involves a longer word or a more complex construction, 'more' or 'less' are used. Thus compare:

(132) a. **Adjective**: Mary is **more** intelligent than Bill
         (*intelligent**er**)
      b. **Adverb**: John works **more** diligently than Sue
         (*diligentli**er**)
      c. **Quantifier**: Sylvia has many **more** friends than Joe
         (*mani**er**)

In addition to specifying the extent of the compared quality as either 'more' or 'less', comparative structures can further amplify on the degree of excess one way or another. For example:

(133) a. John is **much** tall**er** than Bill.
      b. Mary has **a zillion more** friends than Sue.
      c. She runs **ten times** faster than he does.

A special type of comparison imparts the meaning of **at least equality**, with the double preposition 'as...as' bracketing the compared quality. For example:

(134) a. John is **as** tall **as** Mary.
      b. Mary has **as** many friends **as** Sue.
      c. Bill worked **as** hard **as** Marvin.

A constituent may also be compared reflexively, to itself at some other time, place or circumstances. For example:

(135) a. John is **taller** now **than** last year.
      b. Mary has **more** friends in Chicago **than** in New York.
      c. Bill works hard**er** when he's happy **than** when he's sad.

In the examples above, the standard of comparison was explicitly incorporated into the comparative clause, and marked with the appropriate preposition ('than'). But the standard of comparison may be also left implicit, or inferred from the anaphoric context of the comparative clause. For example:

(136) a. She seemed somehow sadd**er**.
>   (> than the last time I saw her)
   b. I find this much hard**er** to understand
>   (> than other things I understand better)
   c. He said his house was real big.
>   But you should see his brother's house,
>   It's (**even**) bigg**er**.
>   (> than his house)
   d. So he told me he ran the mile in 4 minutes.
>   So I told him, I said, big deal, I said,
>   I can run it (**even**) fast**er**.
>   (> than 4 minutes)
   e. His dad had little land,
>   but he wound up with (**even**) **less**.
>   (> than his dad)

A special case of implicit standard of comparison involves **superlative clauses**. Here the standard is either set implicitly by some convention, or explicitly by establishing a norm for the relevant class:

(137) **Implicit standard of comparison**:
   a. She worked **the** hard**est**.
>   (> of all there who worked)
   b. He was **the** hard**est** to keep up with.
>   (> of all those I mentioned)
   c. They have **the** most to lose.
>   (> of all those discussed above)

(138) **Explicit standard of comparison**:
   a. John is by far **the worst** painter I've ever known.
   b. He was **the** smart**est** kid in his class.
   c. She had the **most** talent of all of us.
   d. Of all her friends, she tried **the** hard**est**.

The use of the definite article 'the' in superlative clauses is not accidental. It signifies the uniqueness of the compared individual within the comparison class.

Note, finally, that among the short Germanic adjectives that take the comparative suffix -*er* and the superlative -*est*, two — 'good' and 'bad' —

have **suppletive forms** that are used only in comparative and superlative expressions. That is:

(139)

simple	comparative	superlative
tall	tall-er	tall-est
short	short-er	short-est
good	better	best
bad	worse	worst

13.8.6. Pro-verbs in parallel constructions

13.8.6.1. Conjunctions with 'too' and 'either'

There is a special type of clausal conjunction that involves parallel states or events whereby the two subjects are said to have performed the same action, or be of the same state or quality. In such constructions, the verb or the verb phrase are the same. Somewhat akin to pronominalization, the repeating occurrence of the same verb (or VP), in the conjoined clause, is marked by a pro-verb — either 'do' (for verbs) or 'be' (for copular predicates). In addition, either the element 'too' or its negative converse 'either' is added at the end of the conjoined clause. Consider first:

(140) a. **Verbal (affirmative)**:
      John left, and Mary **did too**.
   b. **Verbal (negative)**:
      She didn't talk, and he **didn't either**.
   c. **Copular adjective (affirmative)**:
      Mary is very tall, and John **is too**.
   d. **Copular nominal (negative)**:
      He isn't an engineer, and she **isn't either**.

The element replaced by 'do/be too/either' in such conjunctions is in fact not simply the verb, but rather the entire verb phrase:

(141) a. **Verbal**:
      John **gave three books to his young brother for
      his birthday** and Mary **did too**.
   b. **Copular**:
      Mary **was not the hardest working executive in her
      company** and John **wasn't either**.

When an auxiliary is present in the first clause, the pro-verb used in the conjoined clause is that auxiliary:

(142) a. He **was** working hard, and she **was too**.
     b. She **hasn't** finished yet, and he **hasn't either**.
     c. He **can** run fast, and she **can too**.

A slight variant of the negative plus 'either' involves using the preposed 'neither'. The pre-posing of 'neither' precipitates subject-AUX inversion, as in:

(143) a. He **didn't** work there, and **neither did** she.
     b. Mary **is** not paying attention, and **neither is** John.
     c. She **hasn't** arrived yet, and **neither has** he.
     d. They **will** not budge, and **neither will** I.

13.8.6.2. Conjunctions with 'so' and 'neither'

A similar pro-verb construction involves the comparative adverbials 'so' and 'neither', again associated with subject-AUX inversion. The pro-verb here, whether 'do', 'be' or an auxiliary, again stands for the entire verb phrase. For example:

(144) a. He **was** leaving town, and **so was** she.
     b. He **wasn't** there, and **neither was** she.
     c. She **stopped**, and **so did** he.
     d. She **didn't** stop, and **neither did** he.
     e. He **can** sing, and **so can** she.
     f. He **can't** sing, and **neither can** she.
     g. He **has** seen their mother, and **so has** she.
     h. He **hasn't** seen their mother, and **neither has** she.
     i. She **is** going out, and **so is** he.
     j. She **isn't** going out, and **neither is** he.

13.8.6.3. Conjunctions with 'do so'

The last type of pro-verb conjunction involves the use of 'do so' or its negative counterpart 'do so either'. This construction, however, can only be used with active verbs, excluding the main verb 'be' and clauses with auxiliaries. Thus compare:

(145) **Active verbs**:
     a. John **worked** hard, and Mary **did so too**.
     b. Mary **drank** her milk, and John **did so too**.
     c. He didn't **talk**, and she didn't **do so either**.

(146) **Stative verbs**:
- a. *She **loved** her mother, and he **did so too**.
- b. *He **knows** the answer, and she **does so too**.
- c. *She **is** a chemist, and he **is/does so too**.
- d. *He **has** a big house, and she **does so too**.

(147) **Auxiliaries**:
- a. *She **can** run fast, and he **can/does so too**.
- b. *He **has** arrived, and she **has/does so too**.
- c. *She **wasn't** watching, and he **wasn't/didn't so either**.

13.9. CONCLUSION

The grammar of clause-combining in connected discourse, marking varying degrees of cross-clausal **syntactic dependency**, is nothing but the systematic reflection of the degree to which two events (or states) are **framed jointly** from the perspective of the cognizing or communicating mind. From a purely logical perspective, the two events can be framed separately. But in particular cognitive or communicative contexts, they can also be framed jointly, and to various degrees. And this fact about the cognitive or communicative perspective has syntactic consequences. So that when two events are framed more as a single-if-complex unit of experience, they are also coded syntactically more as a single-if-complex clause.

Inter-clausal coherence spans the range between extremely tight inter-clausal coherence, with many semantic and pragmatic recurrent strands, and extremely loose inter-clausal coherence, whose recurrent strands are few and predominantly pragmatic. In parallel, the grammar codes clauses with tight cross-clausal coherence as highly integrated with their adjacent clause. Clauses with loose cross-clausal coherence, on the other hand, are coded grammatically as more independent of each other, with clear intonational breaks.

At the extreme end of **syntactic integration** one finds clausal subjects and objects (chapter 6), some verb complements (chapter 7), relative clauses (chapter 9) and syntactically-reduced conjunctions of highly parallel states or events (chapter 6; above in this chapter). At the other extreme end, of **syntactic independence,** one finds prototypical finite clauses — chain-initial (or occasionally chain-final) clauses in connected discourse. In addition to the two extremes, the grammar also codes many intermediate degrees of clause integration. Two conspicuous types of such partially-dependent clauses are adverbial clauses and chain-medial conjoined clauses.

The strong correlation between the semantic-pragmatic coherence of adjacent states or events in the flow of experience, on the one hand, and the syntactic integration of adjacent clauses in the flow of discourse, on the other, remains a recurrent theme in the grammar of inter-clausal connectivity. It is also a recurrent theme in the study of grammar as a tool, used to both construe and communicate experience. This instrumental use of grammar makes it possible for us to frame and re-frame, from a variety of perspectives, the ebb and flow of states and events that constitute both our external and internal reality.

NOTES

1) There are grounds for treating verb complements as not having the exact status of objects. This is so because they are not as fully nominalized as true clausal subjects and objects. Thus compare:

His arrival created a commotion. (SUBJ)
They saw **his arrival** from the balcony. (OBJ)
They saw **him arrive**. (COMP)

2) As we noted earlier, these three types of grounding presuppose three mental models, respectively: the episodic model of the current text, a mental model of the current speech situation, and the permanently-stored lexicon. Neuro-psychologists have recognized at least two of the three as both mental capacities and brain structures (Squire, 1987).

3) See discussion in chapters 10, 11.

4) Whether the traditional term "subordinate" as applied here is semantically or grammatically motivated remains to be resolved.

5) The notion of 'frame' here is akin to that of 'schema' or 'script' (Schank and Abelson, 1977; Anderson *et al*, 1983; Walker and Yekovich, 1987).

6) The one-way conditional of logic allows the inference:

$(A > B) > (\text{not-B} > \text{not-A})$

but not:

$*(A > B) > (\text{not-A-} > \text{not-B}).$

7) For some discussion of the history of this type of subjunctive in English, see Bybee (1992) or Fleischman (1989).

8) The Spanish original was:

...Pero le gustaría tanto	si lo **hiciera**-s tu...
but her please/it-COND so-much	if it **do/PAST/SUBJUNC**-2s you/EMPH
'...but she'd be so happy	if you **did** it...'

9) Dwight Bolinger (in personal communication) points out that ADV-clauses such as (20c,d) can also be used to code counterfact conditionals, even when the main clause is not marked with the perfect. That is:

Were I you, I would have nothing to do with it.
(> But I am not you)
Could I understand, I might be able to help.
(> but I can't understand, so I can't help)

10) Thomas Harris, **The Silence of the Lambs** (1988); NY: St. Martin ppbk (p. 356).

11) For participial ADV-clauses, see section 13.3.

12) See discussion of the grammatical aspects of clause finiteness in chapters 6, 7.

13) As noted in chapter 4, the perfect aspect signals an accomplishment or termination of the event. A perfect-marked verb is thus by definition punctual. Further, the perfect also signals anteriority in a temporal sequence. Therefore, a perfect-marked event cannot be simultaneous to another event.

14) In typical verb-final (subject-object-verb) languages, this chaining strategy is predominant or even the only one available. See Givón (1990, ch. 19).

15) From Anon (1828).

16) Some of these clause-types may also be used in other grammatical environments.

17) See chapter 9. That is:
   The cartoon [that is] on p. 67
   The man [who is] sitting at the bar
   The woman [who was] appointed to head the committee

18) From **The Register-Guard**, Eugene, OR, 9-5-91.

19) *Ibid*.

20) This shift in point-of-view is akin to direct-quote contexts, where a more loosely-bound connection was noted between main and complement clause (see chapter 7).

21) Louis L'Amour, **Shalako** (1962).

22) L'Amour's own paragraphing conventions are strange, to say the least, and I have taken the liberty of re-casting the text according to my own sense of thematic continuity.

23) See further discussion of punctuation below. For a detailed study of comma punctuation and the pragmatic links of pre-posed and post-posed ADV-clauses in written English, see Ramsay (1987).

24) From Stockwell *et al* (1973, p. 296).

25) *Ibid*, p. 296.

26) *Ibid*, p. 306.

27) For a large inventory of conjoined structures in a purely syntactic framework, see again Stockwell *et al* (1973, ch. 6), or McCawley (1988, vol. 1, ch. 9)

28) The vast array of more phrasal conjunctions found in English represent the more extreme cases of syntactic integration, presumably under more extreme contexts of event integration. We have surveyed many such extreme cases of event integration, accompanied by their structural concomitant of more extreme clause integration — embedding — in the discussion of sentential subjects and objects (ch. 6), NP conjunction (ch. 6), verbal complements (ch. 7), and relative clauses (ch. 9).

29) Such "action clusters" are also called schemata, frames or scripts. They are highly culture-specific, depending on conventionalized sequences of particular sub-events, often coded by particular lexical verbs. See again Schank and Abelson (1977); Anderson *et al* (1983); Walker and Yekovich (1987).

30) The story here is a bit more complex, since a break in either modality, speech-act or perspective continuity is almost always associated with breaks in many other strands of thematic continuity, certainly a break in action continuity.

31) Conjunctions and punctuation (c) have been discussed directly above. The grammar of tense-aspect-modality (a) was surveyed in chapter 4, and the grammar of referential coherence in chapters 5 and 6.

32) From Anon (1828, p. 119).

33) As noted earlier above, the verb-suffix -*ing* in such chained participial clauses does not mark the durative/progressive aspect, but rather codes sequential events.

34) From L'Amour (1962, pp. 6-7).

35) We noted earlier that post-posed participial clauses tend to be interpreted as durative and simultaneous with the main clause.

36) From L'Amour (1962, p. 11).

37) From L'Amour (1962, p. 7)

38) From L'Amour (1962, p. 1).

39) From L'Amour (1962, p. 5)

40) From L'Amour (1962, p. 1).

41) **The Eugene Register-Guard**, Eugene, OR, 1-10-91. In other types of clause-chaining languages, such a switch is signalled by cataphoric switch-reference verbal morphology in the clause directly-preceding the switch.

42) **The Oregonian**, Portland, OR, 6-25-91.

43) The underlying theme of the discussion is Grice's (1968/1975) logical "maxims" for conversation, which would preclude such tautologies. Since tautologies are not logical fallacies, the rules of logic cannot bar them, although the rules of pragmatics can.

44) For a wealth of further detail on gapping, see Stockwell *et al* (1973, chapter 6); McCawley (1988, vol. 1, ch. 9).

BIBLIOGRAPHY

Anderson, A., S. Garrod and A. Sanford (1983) "The accessibility of pronominal antecedents as a function of episodic shifts in narrative text",
Quarterly J. of Experimental Psychology, 35.A

Anon (1828) *The Harem Omnibus*, Los Angeles: Holloway House Publishing Co. [1967 edition]

Aristotle, *De Partibus Animalium*, in R. McKeon (ed., 1941), *The Basic
Works of Artistotle*, NY: Random House

Aristotle, *De Sophisticis Elenchis*, in R. McKeon (ed., 1941) *The Basic
Works of Aristotle*, NY: Random House

Ashcraft, M.H. (1989) *Human Memory and Cognition*, Glenville, Ill.:
Scott, Foresman & Co.

Austin, J. (1962) *How to Do Things with Words*, Oxford: Clarendon Press

Barthelme, D. (1981) "The Emperor", *The New Yorker*, 1-26-81

Berko, J. (1961) "The child learning of English morphology", in S. Saporta
(ed.) *Psycholinguistics*, NY: Holt, Rinehart and Winston

Bolinger, D. (1967) "Adjectives in English: Attribution and predication",
Lingua, 18.1

Bolinger, D. (1978) "Yes no questions are *not* alternative questions", in H.
Hiz (ed.) *Questions*, Dordrecht: Reidel

Bolinger, D. (1985) "The inherent iconism of intonation" in J. Haiman
(ed.) *Iconicity in Syntax*, TSL #6, Amsterdam: J. Benjamins

Bolinger, D. (1991) "The role of accent in extraposition and focus" (ms)

Bonner, J.T. (1988) *The Evolution of Complexity by Means of Natural
Selection*, Princeton: Princeton University Press

Bowerman, M. (1983) "Starting to talk worse: Clues to language acquisition from children's late speech errors", in S. Strauss (ed.) *U-Shaped
Behavioral Growth*, NY: Academic Press

Bresnan, J. and S. Mchombo (1987) "Topic, pronoun and agreement in
ChiChewa", *Language*, 63.4

Brown, D. (1986) *Grammar and Gender*, New Haven: Yale University Press

Brown, P. and S. Levinson (1978) "Universals in language usage: Politeness phenomena", in E. Goody (ed.) *Questions and Politeness: Strategies in Social Interaction*, Cambridge: Cambridge University Press

Bybee, J. (in press) "The semantic development of past tense modals in English", in J. Bybee and S. Fleischman (eds) *Mood and Modality*, Amsterdam: J. Benjamins (in press)

Bybee, J., W. Pagliuca and R. Perkins (1983) *The Grammaticalization of Tense, Aspect and Modality* (ms)

Carnap, R. (1959) *The Logical Syntax of Language*, Patterson, NJ: Littlefield, Adams & Co.

Chafe, W. (1976) "Givenness, contrastiveness, definiteness, subjects, topics and point of view", in C. Li (ed., 1976)

Chafe, W. (1987) "Linking intonation units in spoken English", in J. Haiman and S. Thompson (eds) *Clause Combining in Grammar and Discourse*, TSL #18, Amsterdam: J. Benjamins

Chafe, W. and J. Nichols (eds, 1986) *Evidentiality: The Linguistic Coding of Epistemology*, Norwood, NJ: Ablex

Chen, P. (1986) "Discourse and particle movement in English", *Studies in Language*, 10.1

Chomsky, N. (1957) *Syntactic Structure*, The Hague: Mouton

Chomsky, N. (1965) *Aspects of the Theory of Syntax*, Cambridge: MIT Press

Chomsky, N. and M. Halle (1968) *The Sound Pattern of English*, NY: Harper and Row

Coates, J. (1983) *The Semantics of Modal Auxiliaries*, London: Croom Helm

Cole, P. and J. Morgan (eds, 1975) *Speech Acts, Syntax and Semantics 3*, NY: Academic Press

Cooreman, A. (1982) "Topicality, ergativity and transitivity in narrative discourse: Evidence from Chamorro", *Studies in Language*, 6.3

Cooper, W. and J.R. Ross (1975) "World order", in *Papers from the Parasession on Functionalism*, University of Chicago, Chicago Linguistics Society

Crouch, J.E. (1978) *Functional Human Anatomy*, 3rd edition, Philadelphia: Lea and Febiger

Davison, A. (1975) "Indirect speech acts and what to do with them", in P. Cole and J. Morgan (eds, 1975)

Dik, S. (1978) *Functional Grammar*, Amsterdam: North Holland

Dixon, R.M.W. (1982) *Where Have All the Adjectives Gone?*, Berlin: Mouton-De Gruyter

Duranti, A. and E. Ochs (1979) "Left dislocation in Italian conversation", in T. Givón (ed., 1979b)

Fleischman, S. (1989) "Temporal distance: A basic linguistic metaphor", *Studies in Language*, 13.1

Foley, W. and R. van Valin (1984) *Functional Syntax and Universal Grammar*, Cambridge: Cambridge University Press

Fox, A. (1983) "Topic continuity in Early Biblical Hebrew", in T. Givón (ed., 1983a)

Fox, B. and S. Thompson (1990) "Information flow and conversation: Relative clauses in English", *Language* 66.2

Fox, R. (1985) "Existential clauses in written English discourse", University of Oregon, Eugene (ms)

Frege, G. (1952) *Philosophical Writing*, London: Blackwell

García, E. (1967) "Auxiliaries and the criterion of simplicity", *Language*, 43.4

Gary, N. (1976) "A discourse analysis of certain root transformations in English", University of California, Los Angeles (ms)

Gernsbacher, M.A. (1990) *Language Comprehension as Structure Building*, Hillsdale, NJ: Erlbaum

Gernsbacher, M.A., D. Hargreaves and M. Beeman (1989) "Building and accessing clausal representations: The advantage of first mention vs. the advantage of clause recency", *J. of Memory and Language*, 28

Givón, T. (1970) "Notes on the semantic structure of English adjectives", *Language*, 46.4

Givón, T. (1979a) *On Understanding Grammar*, NY: Academic Press

Givón, T. (ed. 1979b) *Discourse and Syntax, Syntax and Semantics 12*, NY: Academic Press

Givón, T. (ed., 1983a) *Topic Continuity in Discourse: Quantitative Cross-Language Studies*, TSL #3, Amsterdam: J. Benjamins

Givón, T. (1983b) "Topic continuity in spoken English", in T. Givón (ed., 1983a)

Givón, T. (1984a) *Syntax: A Functional-Typological Introduction*, vol. I, Amsterdam: J. Benjamins

Givón, T. (1984b) "Direct object and dative shifting: Semantic vs. pragmatic case", in F. Plank (ed.) *Objects*, NY: Academic Press

Givón, T. (1985) "Iconicity, isomorphism and non-arbitrary coding in syntax", in J. Haiman (ed., (1985)

Givón, T. (ed. 1985) *Quantified Studies in Discourse*, *Text*, 5.1/2

Givón, T. (1988) "The pragmatics of word-order flexibility: Predictability, importance and attention", in E. Moravcsik *et al* (eds) *Studies in Syntactic Typology*, TSL #17, Amsterdam: J. Benjamins

Givón, T. (1989) *Mind, Code and Context: Essays in Pragmatics*, Hillsdale, NJ: Erlbaum

Givón, T. (1990) *Syntax: A Functional-Typological Introduction*, vol. II, Amsterdam: J. Benjamins

Givón, T. (1991a) "Markedness in grammar: Distributional, communicative and cognitive correlates of syntactic structure", *Studies in Language*, 15.2

Givón, T. (1991b) "Serial verbs and the mental reality of 'event'", in B. Heine and E. Traugott (eds, 1991)

Givón, T. and L. Yang (1991) "The rise of the English GET-passive", in B. Fox and P. Hopper (eds), *Voice: Form and Function*, TSL #27, Amsterdam: J. Benjamins

Goodwin, C. (1981) *Conversational Organization: Interaction Between Speakers and Hearers*, NY: Academic Press

Gordon, D. and G. Lakoff (1971) "Conversational postulates", *CLS #7*, Chicago: Chicago Linguistics Society, University of Chicago

Gould, S.J. (1980) *The Panda's Thumb*, NY: Penguin

Grafton, S. (1982) *A is for Alibi*, NY: Bantam

Green, G. (1975) "How to get people to do things with words: The whimperative question", in P. Cole and J. Morgan (eds, 1975)

Grice, H.P. (1968/1975) "Logic and conversation", in P. Cole and J. Morgan (eds, 1975)

Gruber, J. (1967a) "Topicalization in child language", *Foundations of Language*, 3

Gruber, J. (1967b) *Functions of the Lexicon in Formal Descriptive Grammars*, Santa Monica, CA: Systems Development Corp.

Haberland, H. (1985) "Review of Klaus Heinrich's *Dehlemere Vorlesungen I*", *J. of Pragmatics*, 9

Haiman, J. (1985) *Natural Syntax*, Cambridge: Cambridge University Press

Haiman, J. (ed., 1985) *Iconicity in Syntax*, TSL #6, Amsterdam: J. Benjamins

Haiman, J. (1992) "Grammatical signs of the divided self: A study in language and culture", Macalester College (ms)

Hamburger, C. and S. Crain (1982) "Relative acquisition", in S.A. Kuczaj (ed.) *Language Development: Syntax and Semantics*, Hillsdale, NJ; Erlbaum

Harris, Z. (1956) "Co-occurrence and transformations in linguistic structure", *Language*, 33.3

Hayashi, L. (1989) "Conjunctions and referential continuity", University of Oregon, Eugene (ms)

Heine, B. (1992) "Agent-oriented vs. epistemic modality: Some observations on German modals", paper given at the *Symposium on Mood and Modality*, UNM, Albuquerque, May, 1992 (ms)

Heine, B. and E. Traugott (eds, 1991) *Approaches to Grammaticalization* (2 vols), TSL #19, Amsterdam: J. Benjamins

Heine, B., U. Claudi and F. Hünnemeyer (1991) *Grammaticalization. A conceptual Framework*, Chicago: University of Chicago Press

Herold, R. (1986) "A quantitative study of the alternation between the BE- and GET-passives", paper read at the XVth NWAVE Conference, Stanford University, October 1986 (ms)

Hillerman, T. (1990) *Coyote Waits*, NY: Harper Paperbacks

Hopper, P. (1979) "Aspect and foregrounding in discourse", in T. Givón (ed., 1979b)

Hopper, P. and S. Thompson (1980) "Transitivity in grammar and discourse", *Language*, 56.4

Hopper, P. and S. Thompson (1984) "The discourse basis of lexical categories in universal grammar", *Language*, 60.4

Hyman, L. (1975) "On the change from SOV to SVO: Evidence from Niger-Congo", in C. Li (ed.) *Word Order and Word Order Change*, Austin: University of Texas Press

James, P.D. (1967) *Unnatural Causes*, NY: Warner Books

James, P.D. (1975) *The Black Tower*, NY: Warner Books

Jespersen, O. (1921/1964) *Language: Its Nature, Development and Origin*, NY: Norton

Jespersen, O. (1924) *The Philosophy of Grammar*, NY: Norton [1965 ppbk edition]

Jespersen, O. (1938) *Growth and Structure of the English Language*, Chicago: University of Chicago Press

Keenan, E.L. (1969) *A Logical Base for a Transformational Grammar of English*, PhD dissertation, Philadelphia: University of Pennsylvania (ms)

Keenan, E.L. (1975) "Some universals of passive in relational grammar", *CLS #11*, Chicago: Chicago Linguistics Society, University of Chicago

Kemmer, S. (1988) *The Middle Voice: A Typological and Diachronic Study*, PhD dissertation, Stanford University (ms)

Kemmer, S. (1989) "Reciprocal marking", in D. Payne *et al* (eds) *Papers from the Fourth Pacific Linguistics Conference (PLC-4)*, Eugene, OR: University of Oregon

Kiparsky, P. and C. Kiparsky (1968) "Fact", in M. Bierwisch and K.E. Heidolph (eds) *Progress in Linguistics*, The Hague: Mouton

Lakoff, G. and M. Johnson (1980) *Metaphors We Live By*, Chicago: University of Chicago Press

Lakoff, R. (1971) "Passive resistance", CLS #7, University of Chicago: Chicago Linguistics Society

L'Amour, L. (1962) *Shalako*, NY: Bantam

L'Amour, L. (1965) *Under the Sweetwater Rim*, NY: Bantam

Leonard, E. (1977) *Unknown Man #89*, NY: Avon Books

Leonard, E. (1990) *Get Shorty*, NY: Dell

Levinson, S. (1983) *Pragmatics*, Cambridge: Cambridge University Press

Li, C.N. (ed., 1976) *Subject and Topic*, NY: Academic Press

Lindner, S. (1982) *A Lexico-Semantic Analysis of Verb-Particle Constructions with Up and Out*, PhD dissertation, U.C. at San Diego (ms)

MacDonald, J.D. (1974) *The Dreadful Lemon Sky*, Greenwich, Conn.: Fawcet

Marchand, H. (1965) *The Categories and Types of Present-Day English Word-Formation*, University of Alabama Press

Mayr, E. (1974) "Behavior programs and evolutionary strategies", in E. Mayr (1976) *The Evolution and Diversity of Life*, Cambridge: Harvard University Press

McCawley, J.D. (1988) *The Syntactic Phenomena of English*, 2 vols., Chicago: University of Chicago Press

McKeon, R. (ed., 1941) *The Basic Works of Aristotle*, NY: Random House [22nd edition, 1970].

McMurtry, L. (1963) *Leaving Cheyenne*, NY: Penguin Books

McNeill, D. (1970) *The Acquisition of Language*, NY: Harper & Row

Ochs, E. (1979) "Planned vs. unplanned discourse", in T. Givón (ed., 1979b)

Odlin, T. (1992) "A cross-linguistic comparison of cleft sentences in ESL", paper given at the *Conference on Cognition and Second Language Acquisition*, University of Oregon, Eugene, February, 1992 (ms)

Orwell, G. (1945) *Animal Farm*, NY: Penguin Classics

Palmer, F.R. (1979) *Modality and the English Modals*, London: Longmans

Palmer, F. (1986) *Mood and Modality*, Cambridge: Cambridge University Press

Pearson, T.R. (1985) *A Short History of a Small Place*, NY: Ballantine

Posner, M.I. and C.R.R. Snyder (1974) "Attention and cognitive control", in R.L. Solso (ed.) *Information Processing and Cognition: The Loyola Symposium*, Hillsdale, NJ: Erlbaum

Postal, P. (1974) *On Raising: One Rule of English Grammar and its Theoretical Implications*, Cambridge: MIT Press

Quirk, R., S. Greenbaum, G. Leech and J. Svartvik (1985) *A Comprehensive Grammar of the English Language*, London: Longmans

Ramsay, V. (1987) "The functional distribution of pre-posed and post-posed 'if' and 'when' clauses in written discourse", in R. Tomlin (ed., 1987)

Ransom, E. (1986) *Complementation: Its Meanings and Forms*, TSL #10, Amsterdam: J. Benjamins

Ross, J.R. (1967) *Constraints on Variables in Syntax*, PhD dissertation, Cambridge, Mass.: M.I.T. (ms)

Ross, J.R. (1972) "The category squish: Endstation Hauptwort", *CLS #8*, Chicago: Chicago Linguistics Society

Ross, J.R. (1973) "Nouniness", in D. Fujimura (ed.) *Three Dimensions of Linguistics*, Tokyo: TEC Corp.

Rude, N. (1985) *Studies in Nez Perce Grammar and Discourse*, PhD dissertation, University of Oregon, Eugene (ms)

Russell, B. (1919) *Introduction to Mathematical Philosophy*, London: Allen and Unwin

Sadock, J. (1970) "Whimperatives", in J. Sadock and A. Vanek (eds) *Studies Presented to R.B. Lees*, Edmonton: Linguistic Research

Sadock, J. and A. Zwicky (1985) "Speech act distinctions in syntax", in T. Shopen (ed.) *Language Typology and Syntactic Description*, vol. I, Cambridge: Cambridge University Press

Sapir, E. (1921) *Language*; reprinted 1949, NY: Harcourt, Brace & Co., Harvest books

Schachter, P. (1971) "Focus and relativization", *Language*, 47

Schank, R. and R. Abelson (1977) *Scripts, Goals, Plans and Understanding*, Hillsdale, NJ: Erlbaum

Schneider, W. and R.M. Shiffrin (1977) "Controlled and automatic human information processing, I: Detection, search and attention", *Psychological Review*, 84

Schnitzer, M.L. (1989) *The Pragmatic Basis of Aphasia*, Hillsdale, NJ: Erlbaum

Searle, J. (1970) *Speech Acts*, Cambridge: Cambridge University Press

Searle, J. (1975) "Indirect speech acts", in P. Cole and J. Morgan (eds, 1975)

Squire, L. R. (1987) *Memory and Brain*, Oxford: Oxford University Press

Stockwell, R.P., P. Schachter and B.H. Partee (1973) *The Major Syntactic Structures of English*, NY: Holt, Rinehart and Winston

Strawson, P. (1950) "On referring", *Mind*, 59

Sun, C.F. and T. Givón (1985) "On the so-called OV word order in Mandarin Chinese: A quantified text study and its implications", *Language*, 61.2

Syder, F. and A. Pawley (1974) "The reduction principle in conversation", Auckland, N.Z.: Anthropology Dept., Auckland University (ms)

Thompson, S. (1985) "Grammar and written discourse: Initial vs. final purpose clauses in English", in T. Givón (ed., 1985)

Tomlin, R. (ed., 1987) *Coherence and Grounding in Discourse*, TSL #11, Amsterdam: J. Benjamins

Trout, K. (1974) *Venus on the Half Shell*, NY: Dell

Visser, F. Th. (1973) *An Historical Syntax of the English Language*, part III, 2nd half, *Syntactic Units with Two and With More Verbs*, Leiden: E.J. Brill

Walker, C.H. and F.R. Yekovich (1987) "Activation and use of script-based antecedents in anaphoric reference", *J. of Memory and Language*, 26

Wallace, A.F.C. (1961) *Culture and Personality*, NY: Random House

Wierzbicka, A. (1987) "Boys will be boys", *Language*, 63.1

Wittgenstein, L. (1918) *Tractatus Logico Philosophicus*, tr. by D.F. Pears and B.F. McGuinness, NY: The Humanities Press [1966]

Wittgenstein, L. (1953) *Philosophical Investigations*, tr. by G.E.M. Anscombe, NY: Macmillan

Wright, S. and T. Givón (1987) "The pragmatics of indefinite reference", *Studies in Language*, 11.1

INDEX